CONSCIOUS
LOVING

CONSCIOUS LOVING

The Journey to Co-Commitment

Gay Hendricks, Ph.D.
and
Kathlyn Hendricks, Ph.D.

BANTAM BOOKS
NEW YORK · TORONTO · LONDON · SYDNEY · AUCKLAND

CONSCIOUS LOVING: THE JOURNEY TO CO-COMMITMENT
A Bantam Book / November 1990

Library of Congress Cataloging-in-Publication Data

Hendricks, Gay.
    Conscious loving : the journey to co-commitment /
Gay Hendricks and Kathlyn Hendricks.
        p.   cm.
    ISBN 0-553-05774-X
    1. Co-dependence (Psychology)   I. Hendricks,
Kathlyn.   II. Title.
III. Title: Co-commitment.
RC569.5.C63H46   1990
616.86—dc20   90-40236
                                                        CIP

Published simultaneously in the United States and Canada

Bantam Books are published by Bantam Books, a division of
Bantam Doubleday Dell Publishing Group, Inc. Its trademark,
consisting of the words "Bantam Books" and the portrayal of
a rooster, is Registered in U.S. Patent and Trademark Office and
in other countries. Marca Registrada. Bantam Books, 666 Fifth
Avenue, New York, New York 10103.

PRINTED IN THE UNITED STATES OF AMERICA

BVG   0   9   8   7   6   5   4   3   2   1

We dedicate this book to our amazing children, Amanda and Chris, who have shown us that there is a new and better world of relationships available for the human family.

ACKNOWLEDGMENTS

We are deeply grateful to the thousand or so couples, and the more than twenty thousand clients and workshop participants with whom we have worked over the past two decades. Their courageous struggles toward co-commitment are the proving ground for the ideas in this book.

We are grateful to all the therapists who have taken our professional trainings. They have given us the gift of their compassion, caring and critical feedback. Heartfelt thanks are due to those colleagues who gave us feedback on the manuscript as it evolved.

We offer a bouquet of thanks to Toni Burbank, whose editorial touch is both masterful and exquisitely light.

A particularly deep bow goes to Sandy Dijkstra, dream agent and agent of dreams.

To our parents—Norma Hendricks and Polly and Bob Swift—we give a hug of thanks for everything they are and have done.

We are deeply grateful for John Bradshaw, for his loving spirit and his great contribution to our society's healing.

CONTENTS

PART TWO

FOREWORD

Conscious Loving is a marvelous addition to the nourishing practical wisdom Gay Hendricks has been offering for a long time. I have learned much about self-love and human emotions from Gay. I have learned about intimacy from Kathlyn and Gay. This book is a product of their co-commitment to all of us.

I can't think of anything more important than *conscious* loving. Our culture's severe family problems and massive addictions attest to the unconscious contaminations resulting from our dysfunctional source relationships.

Our models of intimacy are patently out of date. They come from a social era that was survivalistic. When survival is at stake, it is good to have one person in charge. It is also good to be co-dependent and non-feeling.

Our culture is leisure oriented. The old model is totally inadequate for dealing with the new possibilities for love and emotional intimacy which result from the new leisure.

Kathlyn and Gay are offering us a new model. We need it badly. We must help our ailing non-intimate marriages. The marital relationship determines the health of the family to a large degree. In spite of a couple's best intentions, if they use the old model, their relationship is probably going to fail because the old model is based on an imbalance of power. In this book, the Hendricks teach us that intimacy is only possible when there is a balance of power.

Most importantly, they offer us exercises which will help us to achieve this balance of power in our relationships. In fact, the practicality of this book is its greatest asset. The Hendricks offer us a rich array of experiential exercises which can teach us how to love intimately.

I consider Gay and Kathlyn to be my teachers. I encourage you to buy this book and use it to the hilt.

—JOHN BRADSHAW

PROLOGUE

At our wedding many years ago we were blessed to be married by a couple, Mary and Ed Graham, who represented (and still do) the heights of co-commitment to which we aspired. At the pinnacle of the ceremony, they read a poem they had chosen for us; the moment became for us the spiritual epiphany of our lives. It is written by the Jungian analyst, Sheila Moon, and we share it with you as prologue to the journey that we begin together.

LIFE DANCE

What follows, in such time as has not
come, yet waits for me to find it?
What dreams drift in mists
covering what unfamiliar peaks?
What unexpected mime is being readied
for me, and what part will I have?

In any case the tale will be
the Fool's, with his naked joy, his Bride
dancing down the world of time,
somersaulting into wherever they arrive—
awry, askew, rumpled, roses in their hair!
How unthinkable to go with them!
To open fingers, toes, eyes, arms,
for receiving their grace so graceless,
to see their faces clown-white, death-
white, their gaze shining as moonrise!
How unthinkable! But heart
bends to them as toward flowers.
So bend. Perhaps—be mended.

Perhaps—why not?—be thrown by
winds into their wild sweeps of sky
where up and down are words only,
where sea reaches and ragged spume
become living whether or not I
choose it so, where I am pitched
and tossed in a game whose stakes
are higher than I can encompass!

Shout! Rush into all storms
but with honest intent. The Fool
and his Bride are truth,
honest and honestly moonstruck, and
they dance in hurricanes,
in the very eye itself. In peace.
So in some fashion they stand
beyond me in storm. Dancing. Calling.
Blurred and whirling in time
neither before nor after, I must
go, or fall away forever, forever.

PART ONE

ONE

Conscious Loving: The Journey in Brief

For most of us, relationships are a struggle. We each have a strong inner urge toward conscious loving: toward love relationships that are free of mistrust, disharmony, and unspoken words. We want our relationships to be springboards to higher consciousness and enhanced creative expression. Yet within us also lives an urge toward unconscious loving: we are encumbered by the burdens of our past programming. In this book we will present the results of our exploration of relationship issues over the past twenty years. From our work with over one thousand couples we have discovered the key flaws that produce distortion in relationships, and we have developed a precise, step-by-step program for turning your loving into conscious loving. We have also identified the crucial choice points in the evolution of a relationship that enhance or ruin the opportunities for intimacy.

Unconscious loving turns relationships into entanglements which bring out and actually require the destructive habits of each participant. Unconscious loving saps energy and creativity. By knowing the crucial choice points and

3

practicing the skills of conscious loving we describe, a state emerges that we call Co-Commitment. It is a state of well-being which enhances the energy and creativity of each person. In our journey together through this book you will learn the intentions that allow co-commitment to unfold, how to spot and overcome the unconscious patterns that emerge in any close relationship, how to identify feelings and key body sensations, how to tell the microscopic truth, and how to make and keep commitments.

The ideas in this book apply not only to couples, but to any close relationship. They work even if you have an uncooperative partner. They work even if you have no current partner. Many of our clients worked out their major issues while single, then went on to form successful, co-committed relationships. A great deal of powerful change can occur when one person in a relationship breaks free. Don't fall into the trap of waiting to change until your partner is ready. Waiting for others to change is a sign of unconscious loving. Go ahead and make a total commitment to your individual development. However, if your partner is willing to commit to the program, the changes can be rapid indeed.

When we first began to "wake up" we found ourselves mired in many patterns of unconscious loving. Both of us came from dysfunctional families, and in adulthood we had re-created many of their patterns in our own relationships. Unless you are very blessed, you are also trapped in some aspect of dysfunctional relationships. We developed the ideas in this book during our journey to co-commitment. Eventually, an exciting new state unfolded, which we call co-creativity. A co-creative relationship is passionate, productive, and harmonious. We turned the energy that would have been wasted through conflict into creative projects such as writing books, giving seminars and lectures, volunteering for activities, and building a happy family. We found that we had access to much more creativity as a partnership than each of us ever had on our own. Now we have applied the techniques to a substantial number of people in therapy and workshops. We have determined to our satisfaction that, with some intense work on themselves, people can move from co-dependence to co-commitment and co-creativity. Now we want to make the material available to a wider audience.

The Questions that Began Our Search

Our approach to relationship therapy grew out of questions we began asking ourselves many years ago. These are questions that you have no doubt asked yourself, such as: Why are close relationships, which are supposed to be about love, often so painful? What are we doing that causes the pain? What are we overlooking? How can we have more love and less pain? The answers came, not always in the way we expected or in a kindly manner. Sometimes we were so stubborn and resistant to learning that life had to take a sledgehammer approach to teaching us. Ultimately, we got the relationship we wanted, but it was many times better than we ever could have imagined.

Most of us are born into families that are full of conflict or the avoidance of conflict. Both of us came from families in which conflict was always avoided, so we had to learn to acknowledge conflict before we learned to transform it. It is important, however, not to stop there. In close relationships, conflict is not necessary or desirable, although it is what most of us know. In this book you will learn how to resolve conflict effectively and you will find a path that will take you beyond conflict, if you are willing.

The Power of Love

Love is a powerful force. If we do not know how to handle its power, we slip very quickly into its powerfully painful distortions, such as conflict and co-dependence. But know this: It is *resistance* to love that causes the problems. There is nothing wrong with love. Love is a force that focuses its light on the deepest shadowy parts of ourselves. It brings to the surface the parts of ourselves that we most desperately try to keep hidden. When these parts of ourselves emerge, we often retreat, blaming love and those who have loved us. In this book you will learn how to do something radically different, something that will allow you to live in a state of continuous love and positive energy. You will begin where you are, possibly stuck in a troubled relationship or feeling the pain of not having a close relationship, and you will move at your own pace to a place of freedom and real growth.

Part 1 of this book explains all the essential ideas, with examples drawn from our personal experience and that of our clients. (All the examples in this book are drawn from real life. Names and identifying details have been changed to ensure the privacy of the people involved.) The thirty-four activities in part 2 contain the experiential techniques that will make the ideas a reality for you. We want to acknowledge you for beginning this journey with us. Our relationship has been the catalyst for unparalleled growth and creativity in our lives. We hope that you will use your relationships to fulfill undreamed-of potential in yourself. It will help if you commit yourself completely to this process now, at the beginning. The most creative and evolved people we know are those who use every situation as an opportunity to learn about themselves. Openness to learning is a hallmark of evolution. It makes learning and acknowledging even the most soul-shaking facts about yourself easier and more fun. With a strong commitment to inquiring into yourself, the universe does not have to use catastrophes to wake you up.

Unconscious Loving and Co-Dependence

Co-dependence, a term that first appeared in the field of alcoholism treatment, is a particular form of unconscious loving. It originally referred to a pattern that healers noticed time and again when working with addicted persons. Frequently the addicted person was in a relationship that supported the addiction and interfered with the treatment. Often the co-dependent did not drink, but due to deeply flawed interaction patterns, he or she made it possible for the addicted person not to change. However, co-dependence goes far beyond the area of chemical addictions: it can creep into every area of life. We believe that society is on the verge of a breakthrough in which people will begin to notice co-dependent patterns in many of their close relationships.

Co-Dependence Is an Unconscious Agreement

Co-dependence is an agreement between people to stay locked in *unconscious* patterns. Co-commitment is an agreement to become *more conscious*. The dictionary does not yet have a definition for co-dependence, but it does have several meanings for *dependent*. According to *Webster's New World Dictionary*, dependent means (1) hanging down, (2) determined by something else, (3) relying on for support, and (4) subordinate. There you have it: co-dependence occurs when your behavior is determined by someone else's, when others rely on you to maintain their destructive behaviors and addictions, and when you are subordinate to others and thereby not true to your own feelings. The first definition—hanging down—is particularly revealing, because depression inevitably accompanies co-dependence.

When we are co-dependent we do not have relationships, we have entanglements. Relationships can exist only between equals; inequality is a hallmark of co-dependence. The dictionary defines entanglement as a snare and a complication. It is "a net, from which escape is difficult." The dictionary says that two things are entangled when they are enfolded upon each other in such a way that the freedom of each is limited. This is exactly what co-dependence is. It is also an unconscious conspiracy between two or more people to feel bad and to limit each other's potential. The basic contract is: If I allow you to sleepwalk through life, you won't make me wake up either. If I agree not to grow, you won't either. If I don't insist that you change your bad habits, you won't leave me or make me challenge my bad habits. No matter what the deal, it never works. No one has ever been truly happy, awake, and alive in an entanglement.

Co-Dependence Is Inequality

Relationships exist only between equal, whole persons. If two people in a relationship have agreed to be less than whole, their problems are multiplied. For example, when you multiply ½ times ½, you get ¼, less than you had on your own. This is how co-dependence works. Two people come into relationship and limit each other's potential; they end up with less than they had before. The relationship is blamed, often for many years, but it was never a relationship at all. It was an entanglement that began with a tiny moment of unconsciousness and mushroomed into something that brought pain. It is this tiny moment that we will study later in this chapter.

Co-Dependence Is an Addiction to Control and Approval

Co-dependents often do not touch liquor or drugs, but they are addicted, nonetheless, to something much subtler: control and approval. Often these pernicious addictions continue long after any substance addictions have been resolved. One of our co-dependent clients in recovery put the problem very eloquently after a breakthrough session: "Now I feel a center of light and God-consciousness in me, but I've never been able to contact or express it before. Instead, all my thoughts were about how I could manipulate people to give me what I want or how I could get them to like me. I've never had a single pure thought before." This man had made a profound discovery: When you can break through your approval and control programming, there is a natural, organic spiritual essence within you that can be consciously experienced. As long as we try to control ourselves and others, and as long as we strive to get others to like us, that spiritual essence is obscured. When we wake up and start loving ourselves, we claim our divine right.

Control and approval should be treated like any other addiction. As those of you who are in recovery know, stopping the addiction is only the beginning. After you take that last drink, all the problems that the drinking masked rush forward to get your attention. Fortunately, the greater energy that is freed through stopping drinking is at your disposal to handle these problems. Now, we invite you to stop the addiction to controlling other people. We invite you to stop centering your life on seeking approval or avoiding disapproval. Notice how you are controlling and jockeying for approval and drop these patterns first for a minute. Then go without them for a day, then one day at a time thereafter. Others have done it, and you can, too. We want you to make the discovery that there is a completely lovable essence at the center of you that is beyond all your strivings. As you uncover it, you and your loved ones will change as a result.

Often, control and approval are at the very center of relationships. For a dramatic example, consider this interchange between a husband and wife at the beginning of a therapy session:

> THERAPIST: What kinds of feelings have you been experiencing this week?
> WIFE: I've been feeling confused and depressed.
> HUSBAND: No, you haven't.

Here is control in its most spare and stark form. In essence, he is saying to her: "The experience you are having is not the one I want you to be having." Often our attempts to control each other are less obvious. Even the recovery process itself can be corrupted into a control strategy. Another client was given repeated warnings over a five-year period that his wife was going to leave if he didn't stop drinking. Finally she left. Suddenly he turned into a model citizen. He quit drinking and became an active member of AA. After two months he begged her to come back. "Look at how I've changed," he said. "Yes," she replied, "but why didn't you change before I left? I don't trust you now to make any changes just for your own good. It looks to me like you're changing just to get me to come back to you." He went into a rage at this, stormed out, and got drunk that night.

The drive for approval, and to avoid disapproval, dominates the relationships of co-dependents. As one woman put it, "Before I started loving myself and feeling good about me, all my moves were based on trying to get people to like me or to keep them from disliking me. This led me to do a lot of things I didn't want to do. This was a particular problem with men. They would ask me to do something— even have sex—and I would override my own feelings to please them or to keep them from thinking something bad about me. Of course it never worked. I felt so bad afterward that I would find some other way to mess up the relationship. Then they wouldn't like me anyway. I always ended up creating the thing I was afraid would happen." This is exactly what happens in co-dependence: we act from motivations of control and approval instead of from our essence, and we end up creating the opposite of what we really want.

Are You Co-Dependent?

Ask yourself whether you have some of the following issues in your relationships:

• In spite of your "best efforts," people around you do not change their bad habits.
• You have difficulty allowing others to feel their feelings. If someone feels bad, you rush in to make it better, because you think it's your fault. You worry about other people's feelings frequently.
• You have secrets. There are things you have done or not done that you are hiding from another person.
• You do not let yourself feel the full range of your feelings. You are out of touch with one or more core emo-

tions such as anger, fear, or sadness. Anger is a particular problem for you. You find it hard to admit that you're angry, and you have trouble expressing it to other people.

• You criticize or get criticized frequently. You have a strong, nagging internal critic that keeps you feeling bad even in moments when you could be feeling good.

• You try to control other people, to get them to feel and be a certain way, and you spend a lot of energy being controlled or avoiding being controlled by others.

• Your arguments tend to recycle. Conflicts are temporarily ended by one person apologizing and promising to do better.

• In arguments, much energy is spent in trying to find out whose fault it is. Both people struggle to prove that they are right, or to prove the other wrong.

• In arguments, you find yourself pleading victim or agreeing that you were at fault.

• You frequently agree to do things you do not want to do, feel bad about it, but say nothing.

• People seem not to keep their agreements with you.

Do any of these describe you? We are on painfully intimate terms with all these dysfunctional patterns and more; we have done them in our own lives, and we have seen them thousands of times in our work. There are other characteristics of entanglements and co-dependence that we will explore later, but the ones described above will help you decide whether this book can help you.

What Is Co-Commitment?

A co-committed relationship is one in which two or more people support each other in being whole, complete individuals. The commitment is to going all the way, to letting the relationship be the catalyst for the individuals to express their full potential and creativity. In a co-committed relationship between two people, each takes 100 percent responsibility for his or her life and for the results each creates. There are no victims in co-committed relationships. In fact, victimhood is impossible when both people are willing to acknowledge that they are the cause of what happens to them. There is little conflict, because neither person plays the accusatory, victim role. With the energy saved through lessened conflict, both people are free to express more creativity.

Co-Commitment Leads to Co-Creativity

Co-commitment leads to the ultimate reward in close relationships: co-creativity. A co-creative relationship is one in which two people access more of their creativity as a result of their loving interaction. Out of the harmony of a co-committed relationship springs an enhanced energy that enables both partners to make a greater contribution than either one could have made alone. It is rare, and absolutely worth it. We have seen the Taj Mahal and eaten sublime meals in the French countryside, but a co-committed relationship is better than any of these experiences, or any other experience we have had. Although rare, it is easier to attain than you might think. With all this happiness just a breath away, why do relationships go so wrong? To understand, we must look into our very early childhood interactions, which most of us have forgotten.

The Birth of Unconscious Loving in Childhood

As a child you needed to be close to people, primarily to your mother. In closeness with her you hoped to find nurturance of your body, mind, and spirit. People who did not have an early sense of closeness with anyone will suffer for it later. A man in his fifties came in for therapy, expressing that he had never had a close relationship with a woman. In fact, he said, he had not even been touched by a woman in fourteen years. When we asked him about his early contact with his mother, he said that he didn't remember much about it, then quickly went on to another subject. Later, we returned to a closer examination of his first months of life. It turned out that his mother had slipped out of the hospital and disappeared, and he had never seen her again. He was *never even touched by her.* After a few weeks in the hospital, a relative came and took him away, later giving him to another relative to raise.

Relatively few of us have such a dramatic and painful entry into the world of human relationships. However, many of us have had some major or minor traumas that influenced our ability to get close as children.

The Effects of a Childhood Wound

Gay experienced an event at the age of six months that influenced the quality of his relationships until well into his thirties:

"I had an issue that replayed in a number of important relationships with women from the time of my first serious love, at age seventeen, until I uncovered the source of the pattern in my thirties. I would be in a relationship, very happy and secure at first, then I would get an irrational fear of abandonment. I would act this out in several unpleasant ways, often by accusing the other person of wanting to leave me. Sometimes I would leave first, so that the other person would not have a chance to do it to me.

"Although the issue was pointed out to me many times by different people, I steadfastly refused to open up to the possibility that it had anything to do with me or my past. I blamed it on the women: it was their fault, just the way women are! As a therapist, I now find it remarkable that it did not occur to me that it had something to do with my past conditioning. However, it taught me a good lesson: Never underestimate the power of the human unconscious, particularly my own.

"When I finally did explore the source of this issue, the

answer was so obvious that I laughed out loud when I saw it. I had a close connection with my mother for the first six months of my life, then my mother abruptly went to work, due to the death of my father and desperate economic circumstances. I was sent to be raised by my grandmother, changing from breast-feeding to bottle-feeding in one day. Apparently I was so upset about this that I cried for days. The only way my grandmother could quiet me down was by loading my bottle with sugar and vanilla. By the end of my first year I was very fat, and continued to have a weight problem until into my thirties. In fact, I weighed over one hundred pounds more than I do now. When I was upset, I ate. Usually lots of vanilla ice cream.

"As I look at the problem now, I see that I developed an expectation of abandonment in that early situation with my mother. When I would get close to a woman in my adult life, the fear of abandonment would come up, although I was not perceptive enough to pick up that the fear was running me. It would simply start looking like the woman had abandonment on her mind. This caused me to project abandonment onto some women who had absolutely no interest in abandoning me (until I started belaboring the point with them). It also caused me to pick some women who were so dependent and needy that they were extremely unlikely to abandon me. In either case, I generated a great deal of misery for myself and others until I caught on to the pattern. As I began to explore the issue, I opened up to the feelings of abandonment inside myself. When I did that, I no longer seemed to need to act them out in actual relationships. Shortly after I cleared up the issue, I met Kathlyn, and it has never surfaced again."

Co-dependence is fostered when two people unconsciously agree to be the partners in each other's dramas. An unconscious bargain is struck: If you won't make me change my self-destructive patterns, I won't make you change yours. If you will let me project my childhood issues onto you, I'll be the target for yours. The trouble is that co-dependence feels so bad that people start complaining shortly after the dramas get under way. At that point, we start to blame our troubles on the other person.

We All Need Closeness and Space

In a close relationship, we have two distinct needs: closeness and independence. In a co-committed relationship, both these needs are acknowledged and celebrated. You get close, and when it is time, you separate for a while. Then it's time to go for more closeness. A good relationship is a pulsation of closeness and space. Both parts of the pulsation are essential. When issues come up about either one of these needs, you discuss the issues with each other and find creative ways to meet both needs.

In co-dependence, people are out of touch with the issues that arise from both closeness and independence. Here's how it works. Two people get close, and as they do so they awaken whatever issues they have not resolved from past relationships. Let's say that both people have a fear of getting close, based on a past relationship that brought them pain. Perhaps the fear began early in life, in some situation with a parent in which a trauma occurred. They get close in the new relationship, and out of that closeness comes fear, and out of that fear comes the expectation of pain, and out of that expectation they withdraw from each other. Often they blame each other for their pain: "I was feeling okay, then I got close to you, and now I feel bad. Obviously that's your fault."

Their real need is to communicate about these issues, to tell the truth about what they are experiencing, and to take some space to allow themselves to become comfortable again. In a co-committed relationship, that is exactly what would happen. But in co-dependence, the truth is not acknowledged or spoken. Both partners are invested in keeping the other unconscious. If they awakened, the game would be over. So there is considerable emphasis on not seeing the patterns, not telling the truth.

Fundamental Issues Emerge from Getting Close

Here are some common feelings and patterns that pour out of us when we start getting close:

- I'm not worthy.
- I'm still angry and hurt from a past relationship.
- Something is basically wrong with me.
- If I get close I'll get swallowed up and lose myself.

Out of these issues that emerge, we often engage in several typical destructive moves:

- We withdraw and pull back without telling the other person what is going on.
- We manufacture something wrong with the other person or the relationship, to give us an excuse to pull back righteously.
- We numb out, losing touch with our feelings.
- Old tapes begin to play in our minds, memories of past situations and fantasies of the future. These take us out of the present reality.
- We get sick.
- We have an accident.
- We start an argument.

There are others, but these are some of the more common.

Issues Also Arise from Getting Separate

In co-dependence, people have as much trouble becoming independent as they do in getting close. Again, imagine it as a dance. Two people come close, dance together a while, then separate to rest. Both the getting close and the coming apart are essential, because humans are separate beings as well as beings who thrive on union with others. Our individual development is crucial, just as important as the development of our ability to be in relationship. In fact, we probably have as many issues about becoming independent as we do about getting close. Here are some:

- When my partner goes away, I feel abandoned.
- I'm afraid I can't take care of myself.

• I'm afraid of taking risks by myself.

• If my partner really loved me, he/she would want to be with me all the time.

Out of these issues, we engage in the same types of destructive patterns mentioned earlier with regard to getting close. It comes time in the relationship to take some space, to learn something about independence and autonomy, and we sabotage ourselves by getting sick, having an accident, or starting an argument. We then use the argument or the illness as an excuse not to deal with the fear of becoming independent.

Cycles of closeness and space occur frequently. If you are perceptive you will notice them on a daily basis, and surely on a weekly one. In a healthy relationship, both people are always on the alert for their needs for closeness and space and are always in the process of noticing what barriers they are putting in the way of meeting these needs.

The Shock of Awakening

There is a moment when you first "wake up" and begin to notice that you are recycling certain patterns in your relationships with others. At this point you may feel dazed and even discouraged. The moment can be compared to that of opening a closet into which you have been stuffing things for twenty or thirty years. At first you are shocked, then when you turn on the light you get even more upset because you see the extent of the problem. We have seen many people go through this stage, and often they think: "Can't I just go back to sleep again?" No, because that way lies peril. Once you have awakened it is very hard to go under again. But don't despair. It is possible to make the necessary changes with a spirit of learning and fun. Pain is an option, but we do not recommend it. This book describes a loving and gentle path. If you are addicted to the hard path, if you think you have to suffer to learn, you will have to look elsewhere.

The Specific Moment When Unconscious Loving Emerges

We mentioned earlier that there is one thing people do wrong to make their relationships so complicated and unhappy. Let's study that key moment in detail, so that next time it happens you will be able to notice and correct it. For our explanation we will use the example of a close love relationship, although we stress that the same general principles apply to *any* relationship.

Close love relationships often go through several distinct stages:

Romance

This is the stage the songs are written about. It's wonderful, energetic, humming with excitement. It's when everything the other person does is magic, and your cells are a-buzz with the limitless possibility of life. For years your unconscious mind has been assembling expectations about what it would take to make you happy. Finally you have found someone who fits all your pictures. Sure, you may overlook a few flaws, but you're not in a mood to be reasonable. You're high! Your heart is pumping endorphin-charged blood around your body, and your reproductive system is saying, "This is it!" Someone asked at a workshop how long this stage lasts, and we replied, "Anywhere from six minutes to six months." Although we were joking, there is some truth to that estimate. Few people manage to stay in that exalted state for more than six months, because what shortly happens is that romance leads to . . .

The Inevitable

As a result of the closeness you experience in the romance phase, unpleasant parts of your personality will begin to emerge. You learned certain problem feelings and patterns in earlier close relationships, and the closeness you are experiencing now is bringing them to the surface. This is inevitable; you have no choice. Meanwhile, the unpleasant parts of your partner are beginning to emerge. Later a choice point occurs, which will determine the destiny of the relationship. Here are several examples of the personality problems that emerge to color the present.

• *Trust issues*. Usually stemming from the first year of life, trust issues are prevalent in many adult relationships. Is it safe here? Can I trust the other person? Will he leave me, too? Can I trust my feelings, when they've gotten me into trouble so often before?

• *Authority issues*. Usually learned in the second and third years of life, authority issues can color every aspect of existence. Nobody's gonna tell *me* what to do! Let's see, what can I get away with here? This little affair won't hurt anybody, will it?

• *Self-esteem issues*. Nothing can threaten the sense of self-worth like a close relationship. Once we hand over our power to another person, we are at their mercy. At any time, a mere glance can cancel out our self-worth. We ask ourselves: Am I really worthwhile? Does anybody love me for my own sake? Do I deserve to be here? All these questions of self-esteem can be called up by getting close to another person.

• *Long-repressed feelings*. Many times in counseling we have been told something like this: "I never knew that I was an angry person until I got into that relationship." The power of close relationships to bring forth shadowy parts of ourselves can never be underestimated. Of course, they call forth our best, too, but in order to experience this joy for extended periods of time we need to handle the shadow feelings that emerge.

• *Sexual issues*. Will I ever be able to have a satisfying sexual connection with another person? Why can't I ask for what I like sexually? Why do I always want someone else sexually instead of the one I'm with? Sex is the arena in which some of the most compelling human dramas are played out. People have written the most sublime poetry imaginable while flooded with sexual feelings, and they have committed atrocious murders in the grip of strong sexual rage. It takes a close relationship to bring our deepest sexual issues to the surface; without bringing them forward there is no possibility of resolution. Some of the very best relationships we have seen are those in which one or both people had experienced a deep sexual healing. Few things can build a more solid bond.

With the floodgates wide open and our deepest issues pouring out, we are headed for . . .

The Choice Point

In this stage the key choice occurs, which determines whether the relationship will become co-committed or will sink into the mire of co-dependence. We will call the "good" one choice A. Here's where you are: You have gotten close to another person, and now your problem issues are coming to the surface. If you take choice A, you will *inquire into the source of those issues, take full responsibility for them, and tell the full truth about them to your partner.* You will learn to see and love the previously unloved parts of yourself that are emerging. With the liberated energy from seeing and communicating the truth of your patterns and feelings, you will ride to a new, higher level of love and intimacy. That's choice A.

Choice B is *the one thing we do that creates co-dependence.* In choice B, the personality issues emerge, but you keep them hidden. You don't look at them, and you don't tell the truth about them. Instead, you

withhold, withdraw, and project.

• *Withholding* is when you keep inside you things that should be expressed. You swallow your anger. You want something and fail to ask. You have a guilty secret and don't confess.

• *Withdrawal* is when you pull back from contact. You

quit reaching out. You are lonely but you turn down invitations to go out. Someone touches you and you turn away.

• *Projection* is when you attribute to another person something that is actually going on at an unconscious level within yourself. An example of projection: You are sexually attracted to another person but do not tell your partner about it. For some strange reason it starts looking like your partner is sexually attracted to others. If you want to watch choice B at work, turn on a soap opera. We flipped one on at random to get an example of choice B. Within ten minutes, we heard this dialogue:

> MARIA: I'm really furious at Mark for having coffee with Lydia. I just know there's something going on between them.
> VERONICA: Have you talked to him about it?
> MARIA: Of course not! I don't want him to know everything's not okay. Our wedding is only a few days away.
> VERONICA: Do you think Mark suspects anything about Randall and you? (Apparently Maria and Randall had indulged in an impassioned "quickie" in the hospital's laundry room the day before.)
> MARIA: No, and I'll never tell him because it was just one of those things. It meant nothing.

Let's look closely at this situation. Maria was sexually attracted to Randall and acted out her feelings in the laundry room. She withheld this information from her husband-to-be because "it meant nothing." Then, for some reason, it started looking like her future husband was attracted to Lydia. Of course, she withheld her observation from him and did not tell the truth about how she felt. Maybe she's right. Maybe Mark really is attracted to Lydia. It does not matter, because Maria will not see reality until she starts telling the truth and drops her projection.

As an aside, we noticed that most of the commercials were not for soap products at all. The shows were heavily sponsored by pain medications, and I think we can all see why. Much pain is brought about by withholding, with-drawal, and projection.

The Unconscious Deal

Once you have selected choice B, your options become severely limited. One option is that the pain of concealing yourself will become too great for you to remain in the presence of the other person, so you will split up, or at least withdraw emotionally so that you are in effect gone. Another option is to make a deal and continue the relation-ship. Following are some examples of deals people make.

• *Let's both agree not to look into certain areas of our lives.* This is the Ostrich Option, in which both people stick their heads in the sand. Pain is diminished, but so is aware-ness. This option is an agreement to become mutually duller.

• *If you don't change, I won't either.* In this deal the conspiracy is toward mutual stasis. Both parties are afraid of risking change, so they make their relationship a bargain of resisting the forces of growth.

• *Let's focus our attention on alcohol (or food or drugs) instead of on solving our problems.* When unconscious pat-terns start to play themselves out in relationships, it is often tempting to drown out the signals with substances. Our society offers a rich array of ways to blot out reality. Ingenious combinations of fat and sugar line the grocery shelves; tobacco, liquor, and drugs are available for those who want to add velocity to their self-destruction. All of these substances delay the inevitable but never, ever pre-vent it. All they do is give you something else to focus on while your self-development is on hold.

• *If you do all the thinking, I'll do all the feeling.* Our therapy practice is located in an area where there are many high-tech companies. Over the years, we have counseled a number of couples consisting of a superlogical engineer husband and a highly emotional wife. This type of relation-ship is an example of splitting the thinking and feeling functions of two people down the middle. It would not be a bad deal if both people felt all right about it. It is perfectly healthy to put one person in charge of balancing the checkbook and another in charge of reading bedtime stories to the kids, if both people are in agreement. But in many such relationships the partners criticize each other for their respective functions. He criticizes her because she's too emotional; she berates him for being a rigid, unfeeling robot.

The deals allow the relationship to continue, but at a high cost. Both people turn away from the possibility of being whole, they maintain their addictions, and they lose the possibility of co-commitment.

The Payoff

If you have taken choice A, in this stage you move closer to each other. You move to a higher level of intimacy, awaken more, and open the possibility of more creativity. In the first year or two of a close relationship you may go through many cycles of getting close, having old patterns and feelings emerge, handling them, and getting close again. As the relationship matures, the speed of emergence of old patterns tends to decrease, and the people in the relationship spend less time handling issues between them and more time engaged in co-committed projects.

If you take choice B, you will always have cycles. Unconscious material will come up, you will find some way to bury it, and another deal will have to be made. Eventually you will find a comfortable state of mutual somnolence, allowing the relationship to continue but with diminished aliveness. What often happens, though, is that the relationship withers and dies. Most people who come to us for counseling have foundered in a deal. They thought they were saving the relationship by pretending not to notice something they really needed to pay attention to. They buried it only to have it resurface. For example, we worked with a couple who had been having the same basic argument for years. When they came to us they were on the verge of splitting up. They had struck a classic deal. Both of them carried a load of anger from their abusive childhoods. When this anger surfaced in their relationship, they elected not to inquire into the true source of it. Their deal was that he always got to be right, and it was her job to placate him. When they fought, she would apologize and admit to being at fault. The trouble was that this deal would often last only a day or two before the anger resurfaced again.

Eventually, on your third or three-thousandth trip through the relationship maze, you may take choice A and find yourself in . . .

Co-Commitment

In this stage you reap the harvest of the commitment you have made to yourself and each other. Your work on yourself and on the relationship pays off as your mutual creativity begins to flourish. When people are not blocking the truth from themselves and not withholding it from each other, a tremendous weight is lifted from their psyches. This sense of liberation directly affects the creativity of each person. Ideas emerge and are acted upon. Projects that are mutually beneficial are accomplished seemingly without effort. A better quality of friends appears; a social support network grows.

In co-dependence people are chained together, facing the past. They are in thrall to their ancient patterns, and imprisoned by the deals they have made with each other. In co-commitment, people are hand in hand in the present, facing the future. You will discover more about co-commitment—how to make it happen and how to maintain it—in chapter four.

Relationship Traps

However, if co-dependent choices are made and remade over time, relationships sink into predictable patterns and common traps. Here are some examples of patterns our clients bring to us at the beginning of their work on themselves. You will find a complete description of nine common traps in chapter three.

Letting People Get Away with Killing Themselves

Andrew tolerated Ellen's binge eating even though it bothered him. He dealt with his anger and bewilderment by burying it. Over the first few years of their relationship she put on about fifty pounds. This too bothered Andrew, but he never said anything about it. Sometimes, when asked whether her weight gain turned him off, Andrew would joke about liking girls who were pleasingly plump. Finally, one day Andrew exploded when Ellen said she had outgrown her wardrobe. Out poured all of the anger that he had swallowed over the years. Although Ellen was stunned, she found that she preferred hearing the truth to the lies. It made such a difference that she changed her eating habits and lost the weight over the following year. She is convinced that she would have stayed fat if Andrew had continued to withhold his anger.

One common trap, then, is to make it possible for those in relationships with us to get away with maintaining unhealthy patterns of behavior.

Seeking Friends Who Support Our Self-Destruction

A friend of ours finally bottomed out on alcohol some years ago. He woke up in the hospital with no recollection of how he had gotten there. As soon as he became lucid, his wife told him that she was sick of supporting his alcoholism and that the marriage was over. She stalked out, and indeed he never saw her again until divorce court. So, he had lost the main person who let him get away with his self-destructiveness. The problem, though, was that he needed a drink. Out came his phone book, and he began calling his "friends." Several refused him, but finally he found one who would sneak bottles of vodka into the hospital. After several messy experiments he found a combination of liquor and orange juice that his stomach would tolerate. Life went back to normal, until he managed to bottom out worse a year later. Now, with over a decade of sobriety behind him, he is careful to pick relationships that nurture him for being productive rather than destructive.

The Parent Trap

Another common trap is the replay of your parents' dysfunctional relationship patterns in your own close relationships.

For example, let's assume that your father was the strong, silent type who was always being criticized by your mother for not communicating enough. You now find yourself in a relationship where you do not communicate very much and where your partner criticizes you for this quite often. Every week in our therapy practice someone comes in whose whole problem can be summarized by this trap. In fact, one of the most wonderful moments in a therapist's life is the wide-eyed *Eureka!* look of amazement as it dawns on someone that he or she has been playing out a script without knowing it. Finding that you have been on an unconscious trolley track, while all the while thinking you were free, has to be one of the most important realizations of life.

We often create relationships with people whose characters are similar to our parents', even though we may hate these very character aspects. We do this because we experienced our first closeness, attention, love, and food with people who were not perfect. They may have beaten us, but they also fed us and bounced us on their knee now and then. So we take a composite snapshot—Love and Pain—and file it away in our mind. Later, we attract relationships that have this same composite.

A man described the history of his relationships: "I run hot and cold. In one relationship I'll get involved with someone very calm and placid, then she won't be interesting enough. Then I'll fall for someone fiery and angry. Then I won't be able to stand being around her and I'll look for someone calm again. I guess I've done that six or eight times in my life." Upon deeper exploration, he realized that his mother was an exact duplicate of this pattern. She was placid on the outside, but underneath was a deep rage that exploded at him every week or so. Out of these puzzling messages his mind took a composite snapshot and filed it away: Love and Calm and Rage.

Variations of this pattern:

Your parents had an argumentative relationship with much yelling and screaming, so you settle down with a quiet type and never fight. Or, your parents were the silent type so you hook up with someone who is anything but. Or, your mother was always on your back, so you marry a person who would not think of criticizing Charles Manson. Your father was stingy, so you lavish your kids with money.

By acting out of rebellion against your parents' feelings and behavior, you place yourself on another type of trolley track. It can be even more painful than creating the same type of relationship your parents had. Not only are you acting out of a conditioned pattern, but it has an unhealthy dose of hidden anger in it. It is hard to get ahead in relationships when you are secretly trying to get even.

Childhood Trauma, Adult Dysfunction

Sometimes childhood trauma sets the trap into which we step years later in adult relationships:

A woman grew up in a family where her father was always threatening to leave, and finally did. A belief was generated in her mind—"That's the way men are; they always leave"—and this belief set the stage for her later to form a pattern of picking men who would leave her.

A man develops asthma as a child, and when he has a bad attack his mother nurtures him in an extra special way. Later in adult life he gets sick and takes to bed under stress, expecting his wife to make him special treats. She resents this demand, and it escalates into a major source of friction between them.

Addiction to Conflict

Conflict can be powerfully addictive. Some of us are conflict junkies, and that addiction lasts far longer than substance addictions. We may be attached to the drama of fights, even though we may protest mightily that we want serenity. Adrenaline is a powerfully addictive drug, as many studies have shown, and some people seem to get addicted to it so that they feel uncomfortable when things are calm.

In therapy, one person discovered a childhood memory that explained to her satisfaction where the pattern came from. She remembered a scene in which her parents had one of their weekly torrid battles, during which she retreated to her room. A few minutes later all was silent, and she came out to see what had happened. She was actually afraid that someone had been hurt. Instead she heard her parents in the bedroom making wild and passionate love. The memory of the events—Love and Sex and Uproar—became fused in her mind, and only later came to her attention when she found herself creating huge arguments with her husband as an aphrodisiac.

The Agreement to Mess Up

Another trap is the relationship in which one or both people are addicted to messing up.

From our therapy files: A man inherited a large trust fund, then managed to squander it through a series of bad investments that his accountant called "the financial equivalent of the Vietnam War." Down from $750,000 to about $100,000, he entered therapy to find out if there might be some connection between this remarkably bad fortune and his past. It turned out that he had a deep hatred for his father, and also a desire to punish himself for being rich when others were poor. Out of these unconscious patterns he squandered the money to get even. His father, who was obsessed with money, could only be revenged upon by the son through some kind of financial ploy. He found the way: his father never spoke to him again until he lay on his deathbed. The pattern also had repeated itself in his close relationships. He and his wife would get close, then he would find some way to mess up, bringing down her wrath upon him.

Out of self-hatred, we can heap unimaginable punish-

ments on ourselves and those around us. Most bad luck is
not luck at all. It is the direct outgrowth of internalized
feelings of shame, guilt, and self-hate. Out of this feeling of
unworthiness, we mess up in a variety of ways, thus creating opportunities for others to criticize us.

Some of the hardest lessons life has to offer are those
of independence. We have seen people delay learning how
to take care of themselves until they are thrust out forcibly
into the real world very late in life. Many people go from
dependence on parents to dependence on spouse to dependence on children or state with no space for the growth of
their own autonomy. We will have much more to say about
how to develop autonomy in the context of close relationships later in the book.

A variation of this trap is that we may never learn
how to let go into union with others as children, thereby
assuming a stance of pseudo-independence in our adult
relationships. In other words, we stand alone as adults
because we never learned to surrender ourselves fully in
relationships as children. Often our sense of trust can be
damaged through very early pain, such as wounds incurred
during the bonding processes of our first days. Trust can
also be destroyed through betrayals later in life. Once broken, trust is not easily repaired. Many of us take on an
attitude of false independence that is based on the fear of
being close. True independence is not based on fear. It contains within it an ability to be close to others, coupled with
a choice to be free and autonomous. In true independence
we are not driven to stand alone, we choose it.

These traps are pervasive. If you look closely, you will
see them operating everywhere, not just in the realm of
love relationships. These patterns color our dealings with
parents, bosses, friends, teachers, and so on. Many people,
for example, allow their unresolved authority issues with
their parents to color their relationships with the taxman,
the minister, the boss, and the person next door. Even our
relations with the Infinite have the flavor of these patterns.
God will be depicted in the Bible at one point as a raging,

jealous father-figure, and at other points in benign, kindly, all-nurturing terms.

Beginning Your Journey to Co-Commitment

Make a Commitment

First, you need to find out if you are actually willing to make the commitment that will allow co-commitment to unfold. Once you embrace a commitment, you've got it until you consciously decide to change it. Once you commit, you then have to find out if others are willing to play. For example, in our counseling work we have found that the first step is to find out if both people genuinely want to solve the problem. There are many reasons why people come in for therapy, and not all of them are to solve problems. Some people come in simply because their partners have insisted. Others come in to prove to a third party what bad people their partners are. Some want to prove that they were right all along, or that the relationship will never work. The first thing we do is to find out if both people want therapy for their relationship. If so, we work first on getting them both to make a clear commitment to working on the relationship. If we can establish this, then their specific problems can be approached. First make the commitment, we say, and your problems will fall all over themselves trying to be solved. If you don't establish your commitment, nothing you do will solve the problem.

Another reason we focus on commitments in our work is that making a commitment soon brings up the counter-commitments to which your unconscious mind is attached. If you are consciously committed to love and harmony yet engage in frequent uproars, you can readily see that some part of you is committed to uproar. In fact, your commit-

ment to uproar may outweigh your commitment to harmony. People who are committed to staying stuck will
argue that they are really committed to harmony and that
the uproar is someone else's fault. This is a point of view
that divorce lawyers hear all the time. Better to look carefully at what you have, and assume that you have it
because on some level you are committed to it. Acknowledging your hidden commitments is a powerfully liberating
step. And there is no better way to reveal these hidden
countercommitments than to state consciously and publicly
what your positive commitments are.

The Essential Co-Commitments

We have identified several core commitments that are
essential in transforming co-dependence. The word *commit*
comes from a Latin word that means "to bring together."
Think of these commitments as a rapid way to bring your
relationships together on a common high ground. By having all persons agree to these commitments at the outset,
many problems will be prevented.

Co-Commitment 1
**I commit myself to being close, and I commit myself
to clearing up anything in the way of my ability to do so.**

Most of us "sort of" want to be close, but we have so
many negative associations with it that closeness becomes
a cloudy issue. This commitment takes the clouds away and
establishes firmly that you want to be close to your partner
or to other human beings. It also puts you on record as
being willing to work out any of your unconscious glitches
that you use to prevent closeness. This commitment is very
liberating, and we have seen it work wonders with many
couples. At the moment when both people make this commitment, a weight disappears from them and they often
take a deep breath.

Co-Commitment 2
**I commit myself to my own complete development as
an individual.**

Many people are conditioned to think that they have to limit themselves in order to be in relationships. In childhood and adolescence, many of us saw relationships in which people had to be less than they were to make the relationship work. They had to get smaller, to limit their growth. Commitment 2 erases the possibility that you will play this tired old game. Here, you are taking a stand for your own evolution. You are saying that both closeness and individuality are important to you. You are committing yourself to being 100 percent you and 100 percent in relationship with others.

Co-Commitment 3

I commit to revealing myself fully in my relationships, not to concealing myself.

As you will see, the act of withholding any aspect of yourself is fatal to a co-committed relationship. Only by making a conscious decision to reveal all of yourself can you really attain co-commitment. Often, the wounds we have suffered in past relationships give us a strong commitment to hiding. We swallow our feelings and our needs, and do not tell the truth about ourselves to others. Relationships heighten this problem. The only way to deepen and go forward in a close relationship is through becoming transparent. The more you try to hide, the more uncomfortable all parties get. We have worked with many couples for whom this commitment was life-changing. Often couples came in with one person committed to revealing and the other committed to concealing. When both people made a conscious commitment to becoming transparent, real miracles happened in their ability to be close.

Co-Commitment 4

I commit myself to the full empowerment of people around me.

Co-dependence thrives on supporting people for being ineffective and helpless. When you are co-dependent you have a secret investment in people being less than they are, so that you will be able to get away with being less than you are. In co-commitment, you are taking a stand for supporting people in being everything they are. You are for empowerment, for supporting people in opening up to their full abilities. Recall a definition of *power* from mathematics: the multiplication of a quantity by itself, as in raising a number to the second power. When you are for empowerment, you are for assisting people in multiplying their energy by itself. You are not forcing them or enabling them to make them more powerful, you are simply supporting them to make the full use of who they are.

In making this commitment, you are going on record as being in support of your partner's full development. You will not limit that development, you will support it in every way you can. So few of us have had that kind of support that often we are not able to imagine it at first. Giving it to others is a priceless gift.

Co-Commitment 5

I commit to acting from the awareness that I am 100 percent the source of my reality.

Unconscious loving thrives on victimhood. If we do not know that we are the source of what happens to us, if we do not take responsibility for our lives, we are ripe for co-dependence. Co-dependence feeds on projection. When we deny that we are the cause of what happens to us, we tend to project it outside, on partners, bosses, the world itself. Co-dependence is a battle between two people to establish who is the bigger victim. Victimhood is not possible when people are taking 100 percent responsibility for what happens to them. A healthier relationship becomes possible only when both people are willing to base their actions on the knowledge that they are the source of their reality.

Co-Commitment 6

I commit myself to having a good time in my close relationships.

It may seem odd that we would need to make a formal commitment to enjoyment. Yet, when we mention this commitment at lectures and workshops, a wave of nervousness often sweeps over the audience. It's a new idea that relationships can be about having a good time. For millions of years relationships were about survival, and communication was a matter of exchanging grunts. In European culture the idea of romantic love is only a few hundred years old. We have recently raised the stakes of close relationships by requiring that they be about more than survival. Now we are asking that they be about enjoyment. Taking a conscious stand for enjoyment is very important, because many of us have strong beliefs that relationships have to be effortful, painful, and difficult. Committing yourself to enjoyment in your relationships can be one of the most liberating moves you can make, because it opens the possibility of conflict-free relationships.

Three Fundamental Requirements for Co-Committed Relationships

Until we consciously choose to have co-committed relationships, we are stuck with entanglements. We inherit a tendency toward entanglement: it's mainly what we saw around us growing up. We tend to perpetuate entanglements until the moment we wake up and say: "I choose from now on to have co-commitment." Even after you make this commitment you will likely spend a period of time oscillating between the two, but at least your growth will have a positive direction. Think of it as waking up from anesthesia; the transition is hard. But what you *can* do is make a conscious commitment to change in a way that is comfortable and convenient to you and to those around you. You do this by making a silent agreement with the universe that you are willing to learn however you need to, but you prefer gentle lessons. Then you talk to those around you and ask them if they would be willing to have their lessons gently.

There is no requirement that enlightenment be painful, *unless you are trying to avoid pain.* Then the universe has no choice but to teach you through pain. One of the universe's strategies is to put directly before you the things you are trying to avoid. It is possible to grow and learn in a way that is loving to yourself and others. All you do is make a commitment that you want it that way. We have had many of our clients phrase it this way: "I'm willing to see and handle anything I need to be free, and I would like my lessons in a friendly, loving way for me and others around me."

There are three things you must do to bring your commitments into reality.

Fundamental Requirement 1: Feel All Your Feelings

A great deal of energy in close relationships is wasted due to one or more persons trying to keep feelings hidden. Our feelings are central to life—they are made of the raw energy that drives and motivates our existence—and to be cut off from them is to suffer a slow, silent erosion of the spirit. If people made friends with all their feelings, and learned to speak them in friendly ways, there would be few heartaches, and even fewer headaches.

Why do we have so much to learn about feelings? Part of the problem is lack of education and practice. After all, compared to math and science, how many hours of your schooling were devoted to teaching you about your feelings and how to express them? Another reason is that as children we are often talked out of our feelings, instead of given permission to feel them, and sometimes punished outright for having our feelings. If your mind records many instances of "feeling equals pain," you certainly will not want to open up to your feelings very often. Also, many of us find greater safety in the cool certainty of beliefs and concepts than we do in the hot, confusing world of our feelings. For example, it is much easier to escape into the certainty of a belief in a happy life after death than it is to face and deal with the fear of death. In even a small town you can find dozens of institutions selling the certainty of belief, but where do you go if you want to open up and experience reality in the form of your feelings? Imagine yourself going to a church and saying to the minister, "I don't want to believe in anything, but I'd like your help feeling my doubts and fears deeply."

Human beings have a rich variety of deep feelings. Just as there are only a few primary colors, there are only a handful of primary emotions: fear, anger, sadness, joy. But there are infinite mixtures and variations. Opening up to our feelings is a lifetime process; it is essential that we befriend ourselves on the emotional level. It is all the more important because there is a societal conspiracy against it. On TV we are taught that spirit is attained through a soft drink, while serenity is ours through a good cup of coffee. Pain is to be relieved by a pill. We seldom see a commercial that invites us to relieve a headache by opening up to the blocked emotions that were causing it. Yet every week in our office someone comes in with a headache and leaves without it, not by taking a pill but by feeling and speaking the truth about the emotions underneath the pain.

Fundamental Requirement 2: Tell the Microscopic Truth

As you are by now aware, much pain and distortion is created in relationships by not telling the truth. Many times we have asked a client who has just shared a powerful truth whether the relevant other party has been told. Often the person looks at us like we are crazy. Even mentioning the possibility of telling the truth has shock value. The fine art of telling the truth must be developed in order to have co-committed relationships. In fact, the real skill is in telling what we call the microscopic truth. The microscopic truth is when you speak the truth about your internal experience as you are currently perceiving it. For example, "When you said you were going away for the weekend I felt a tight band of constriction in my chest and a bunch of thoughts flew through my mind like 'She's abandoning me' and 'What'll I do all by myself?' " In this case the speaker reported the raw data as it streamed through body and mind. This is telling the microscopic truth, and it has tremendous healing value.

Why human beings do not tell the truth has never been studied in close detail, but in our work several main reasons have emerged. First, many people withhold the truth because they do not want other people to feel bad. You don't tell your spouse about your affair because you don't want to hurt him or her. Look out if you use this reason, though, because it is usually accompanied by the following one: You don't tell the truth because you don't want to feel the consequences of your spouse's bad feelings. If you are not telling the truth because you don't want to hurt the other person, you are also likely protecting yourself from the other's sadness, wrath, or revenge.

Sometimes we do not tell the truth because we have seldom witnessed the truth being spoken. Some people just haven't had the opportunity to learn how to access and communicate the truth. Learning to perceive the truth within ourselves and speak it clearly to others is a delicate skill, certainly as complex as multiplication or long division, but very little time is spent on it in school. It is then left to life itself to teach us about telling the truth—and it does, but not always in a gentle manner.

David, one of our clients, eloquently described the importance of communicating "the little things": "After some experiments with telling only part of the truth, I decided to risk sharing everything. At first I felt silly, talking about all my little reactions and feelings. But I noticed that it *always brought me closer to Diane.* When I would tell the truth, Diane would get something stirred up, then I would get to a deeper level, which would stimulate something deeper in her. It was amazing how much was always under a 'little thing.' I became a believer, because I saw that holding out always created distance and telling the truth always brought us closer."

We encourage you to pay particular attention to those issues that seem not worthy of being talked about. The act of telling the microscopic truth about something seemingly trivial liberates the energy to uncover what is really going on at a deeper level.

Fundamental Requirement 3: Keep Your Agreements

Keeping agreements is a major factor in co-committed relationships. Broken agreements are a breeding ground for co-dependence; learning to make and keep meaningful agreements is required if you are serious about turning this problem around. In co-dependence, people make unconscious agreements and are faithful to them, but they do not make and keep conscious agreements. An example of an unconscious agreement is "I'll let you keep drinking and beating the kids if you promise not to leave me." Co-committed relationships thrive on conscious agreements that are scrupulously kept by both parties.

Your aliveness is decreased when you do not keep your agreements. Your mind stores agreements you have made and records whether you have kept them. When you do not keep an agreement you need to acknowledge the failure and talk about it with the relevant other(s). Your other choice is not to look at or deal with it, and this is a costly choice. If you get in the habit of overlooking agreements you gradually lose aliveness, as well as incurring the anger of people around you. A lawyer acquaintance of ours once served a prison sentence for a white-collar crime he committed. He later said that he talked in depth with several hundred of his fellow prisoners about why they were incarcerated, and not one of them ever mentioned that it was due to breaking the law! Instead they talked of bad luck, being in the wrong place at the wrong time, the failure of society to provide jobs, harsh bosses, ungrateful children, and scolding wives who turned them in. This is an extreme example of what can happen when we fail to make the connection between keeping agreements and maintaining our sense of aliveness.

Another major reason why we do not keep agreements

is that we get the act of making and keeping agreements tangled up with our anger at authority figures. Our minds set it up this way: "Because my boss is such a jerk it's okay to make personal long-distance calls at the company's expense." Or, "It's okay to cheat on my income tax because I'm mad at the government for handing out my money to those welfare bums." Much unhappiness is caused by unresolved authority issues, usually stemming from early childhood, which we then project onto authority figures in our present lives.

Co-commitment is made possible when two people deal with their sense of responsibility and integrity. Being alive to the full range of your feelings, speaking the truth at the deepest level of which you are capable, and learning to keep agreements: all of these actions are required to master a co-committed relationship. When these three requirements are met, the real intimacy begins to unfold.

A co-committed relationship may look like magic, but it really is composed of tiny moments of choice. Choosing to tell the truth. Noticing that you are projecting, and finding the courage to take responsibility. Choosing to feel rather than go numb. Choosing to communicate about a broken agreement. Choosing to support your partner as he or she goes through deep feeling. Ultimately, once these skills are practiced and internalized, the relationship flows effortlessly. Once your nervous system learns to stay at a high level of aliveness and does not need to numb itself by lying, breaking agreements, and hiding feelings, the creativity starts to flow.

Once you embark on the journey of co-committed relationships, you encounter a new set of problems, and you need a new set of navigational tools for finding your way through them. We call this new challenge the Upper Limits Problem, and it is the subject of chapter 5. For now, simply recognize that positive energy is very powerful and creates its own set of issues to be mastered. Chapter 5 will give you the specific techniques for learning to live in a state of continuous positive energy.

Now that you have an understanding of our approach,

let's explore the moment of unconsciousness from which co-dependence springs. You will need a thorough understanding of this moment so that you can see it clearly when it is happening in your life.

TWO

The Moment When Unconscious Loving Begins

A relationship turns into an entanglement in a specific moment of unconsciousness. The moment is always the same, no matter whether the relationship is between spouses, employees, or between you and the gardener. In this moment an event occurs that is so swift and subtle that it often seems never to have happened at all. You must master this moment in order to have relationships that work. We know that we are requesting a giant leap from you. If you can learn a different way of acting in this moment, you are actually jumping years ahead in your growth. It is worth it.

It is important to understand that this moment occurs over and over again until we choose to change. Perhaps you made a series of co-dependent choices a long time ago and are now stuck, but you can remake that choice right now. It is never too late. You are given repeated opportunities to change minute by minute.

The Hidden Influence of the Past

When we get close to another person, it brings to the surface our own unresolved issues from the past—the very things that you would least like to look at. In adult life, the universe puts you in situation after situation in which you have the opportunity to embrace those things you have tried to hide and hide from in the past. For example, suppose one of the formative events of your life was the death of your father when you were a child. Out of that event you stored up a wellspring of grief along with a set of patterns of relating to men that are based on the old grief. Later in life you find that your relationships with men are colored by a dissatisfaction that you cannot put your finger on. What has happened is that the act of getting close to men brings up the unresolved issues from the past. Since nature provides us with trauma, it must also provide us with the organic means of resolving trauma. Nature's therapy process is to put us in situations that resemble past situations in which we have been traumatized. It has to work that way; otherwise, how else would we ever free ourselves from the grip of those issues?

Life has arranged it so that you will get close to people, and by doing so will have the opportunity to clear away the troubled memories of the past. It is set up so that you always have the opportunity to spring free of the past and relate to people in the present as a complete, whole being. Do we always take the opportunity? Of course not. Do we then have the opportunity to recycle the whole thing again? Absolutely.

When you experience the positive energy of closeness with another person, you may find yourself facing issues from early in your life, such as:

- Deep inside, I don't believe I'm worthy.
- Nobody knows how angry I really am.
- I cannot tolerate criticism.

- I don't really trust people.
- I'll never let myself feel hurt again.

Love Brings Our Issues to the Surface

It is because of the closeness and the possibility of love in the relationship that these issues emerge. Many of us blame our relationship problems on a lack of love, but it is actually the love in the relationship that has brought forth the issues. A close relationship is a powerful light force, and like any strong light it casts a large shadow. When you stand in the light of a close relationship, you must learn to deal with the shadow.

Most of us arrive at our adult relationships with a backlog of ancient hurts, fears, and angers. The source of these wounds has often been forgotten, so that it looks like our current relationships are causing us to hurt. In fact, our current relationships are the area in which we have the opportunity to clear up and free ourselves of these patterns from the past. Generalization is one of the most powerful capabilities of the mind. Once you learn to look right and left as you cross a street, you do not have to relearn the skill on every street for the rest of your life. You can generalize from a specific early situation, such as crossing a street in the Bronx, to a later experience of crossing Sunset Boulevard. This very capability of the mind also causes tremendous problems, because you can go from the specific experience of being molested by your father, for example, to the generalized fear of all men. When deeply hurt, your mind and body will overgeneralize, in order to prevent you from hurting that way again.

We lust for closeness, yet are often terrified of it at the same time. Many people reject relationships entirely because they do not know how to handle the issues that come up when they get close. Our clients, often bright, loving people, have told us that they simply don't want to participate in close relationships anymore, out of their fear of being hurt and their lack of knowledge about how to deal with what comes up as they get close. This is tragic, because the whole process of life is to bring us closer to ourselves and to others. If you do not use relationships as a path to your full evolution, you are cheating yourself.

Both Getting Close and Getting Separate Bring Up Issues

The same problem operates in the realm of getting independent. Human beings have deep needs both for closeness and for independence. We need unity with others, and we need space for ourselves. Thwart either of these needs and we create misery beyond belief. Ideally, as children we would learn to feel comfortable both in closeness and on our own. But any number of problems can interfere with the development of this ability. To use an extreme example, if you watch how schizophrenic mothers interact with their babies, you will see how children can be trained very early to resist both closeness and independence. When the child wants to snuggle close, the mother will push it away. When the child wants to squirm away, the mother will pull it close. The natural pulsation of closeness and independence is blocked at such an early age that there is little likelihood the child will recall where its difficulties with closeness and space came from.

The act of getting separate from others brings to the surface the feelings and patterns we have stored away since childhood. Let's say that in childhood you developed a belief that you could never make it on your own. In adult life, leaving for a weekend trip may cause that old belief to emerge. Instead of seeing the weekend trip as an opportunity for space and the nurturance of your independence, it becomes an exercise in fear. Following are some other examples of how we resist independence.

• You get sick just as you are about to leave on a much-needed vacation.
• After much soul-searching, you decide to move out of an abusive relationship. You have an accident just before moving into your own place.

• After a weekend of extended closeness with someone, you both eat a huge meal on Sunday evening and feel miserable all night.

We do not get much choice about the emergence of our old feelings and patterns. We do, however, get a crucial choice about how to handle these situations. To learn how to handle the moment of emergence, let's look in detail at what happens.

The Moment in Detail

You get close to someone. Eventually two things will happen, often simultaneously. On your part, feelings and old patterns emerge. For example, the closeness brings up fear or anger, along with an old pattern of withdrawing into yourself when you are immersed in feelings. All human beings have feelings and patterns; it is how we deal with them that makes us different from one another.

The Shadow Emerges

The other person's feelings and patterns also emerge. Think of you and another person standing in the light of the sun. You have yourselves, and you have the two shadows cast where each of you has blocked the light. There is the relationship between the two of you as real people, and there is the relationship between the two shadows. The shadow is the part of us we do not know about. It is the hidden repository of all our old feelings and patterns. You come into the relationship bringing a shadow with you, as does the other person. If you and the other person do not look into what these shadows contain, your relationship will be between two shadows instead of the two of you as real people.

At the moment of emergence, when the old feelings and

patterns kick into gear, you have only a brief moment to take effective action. If you let it slide, it slides back into the shadow, into co-dependence. Exactly what is this effective action? It is so simple, so powerful, and so profound that there is a centuries-old conspiracy against it. The only effective action is to *see and say the truth*. Does that sound easy? It is, but only once you have the courage to do it a few hundred times. To see and say the truth means that you have to throw over generations of negative conditioning. Today, we do not fully appreciate how dangerous it was to see and say the truth just a short while ago. For example, imagine yourself in eighteenth-century Salem; it's unlikely that you would have been willing to stand up and say, "By the way, folks, there is no such thing as a witch. You're just projecting your own fears onto these poor women." People have been beaten and otherwise abused for simply noticing what was going on in their families and speaking the truth about it. So, we have inherited a tendency to pretend not to see and to swallow the truth.

We Hide

Withholding is a major, core problem. The dictionary says that to withhold is to restrain, to hold back, to conceal. It is a habit learned early, and it fades slowly if at all. Withholding is the act of holding back something that needs to be said. To make this problem crystal clear, we offer the following example.

Ron and Barbara came into counseling with their relationship on its last legs. They had been married for twenty years, and struggling for nearly all of that time. When we tracked down their problems to the source moment, we found that it had started with an instance of withholding. On their first big date, Barbara had felt uncomfortable with Ron's drinking patterns. Specifically, after two drinks Ron was the most charming fellow she had ever met. But as he made his way through his third drink, she saw parts of him begin to emerge that she didn't like. He became slightly paranoid, thinking that a man across the room was flirting with her. He also began talking of all the people who had wronged him, and how he might someday get revenge on them. Barbara was scared of this part of Ron. Had she taken time to explore just why she was afraid of Ron's anger, she would perhaps have noticed that it was the same feeling she had experienced with her father. Her father had been a notorious drunk who manipulated everyone around him through their fear of his rage. He had died behind the wheel, while drunk, when Barbara was in junior high school. Barbara was also disappointed because her expectations were being thwarted. To her, Ron was a prize catch. He was witty, wealthy, and good-looking.

Instead of seeing the truth and saying it, Barbara withheld it. She did not say "I'm scared of your anger. This is just like the way my father used to act. I want you to stop drinking. I won't see you again if you don't." What she did was to replay an old pattern, one that was to run and ruin her life. The pattern was to submerge her own feelings, decide she was being too picky, and think that she could save Ron through the power of her love. This was exactly how she did it with her father, and she blindly did it again in her marriage. It cost her twenty years of hard times, because rather than getting better through the power of her love, Ron got worse. The more she loved him and picked up the pieces caused by his drinking, the more badly he behaved the next time. Finally, his drinking cost him his job. Barbara stepped in, reviving her career so that she could support them both. Even that didn't work, because Ron used his leisure time to have a series of affairs, ultimately having one with Barbara's close friend Paula. In a fit of guilt, Paula told Barbara, who dragged Ron into the therapist's office twenty years too late.

Barbara missed the source moment when her co-dependence began, which was when her closeness to Ron brought up her pattern of withholding feelings and saving men from their self-destructiveness. Her co-dependence was deepened each time she withheld her feelings from Ron. This is the major trouble spot in human relationships. Heal this and you will be free. The most fundamental thing we as humans can do to keep growing is to notice the truth and speak it. Instead, we *withhold, withdraw, and project.*

Withholding Leads to Withdrawal and Projection

Withdrawal and projection are the natural outcomes of withholding. When you withhold, you keep inside yourself things that should be expressed. The very act of hiding these things takes you one step back from the relationship. A result of this withdrawal is that you will begin to project. In other words, you will begin to attribute to other people things that are actually issues of your own. Withdrawal follows withholding so swiftly that often we do not notice the sense of distance at first. Classic exchanges emerge: "What's wrong, honey?" "Oh, nothing." The tendency to hide how we feel is so ingrained that it often lasts long into even the healthiest relationship. In our own relationship, where we have been practicing these principles for well over a decade, we still have to maintain constant vigilance to make sure we do not slip back into hiding our feelings and desires from each other.

Projection comes in several forms. In one major form, we project onto people in our present lives issues that actually belong to people in our pasts.

• We are angry at a mother or father from long ago, but aim the anger at a husband or wife in the here and now.
• We were abused in childhood, but watch suspiciously for it even with people who have no track record of abusing us.
• We were abandoned in childhood, so cling to a present partner to avoid being left again.

Of course, life being as complicated as it is, this form of projection often combines with a second form: when we fail to deal with an issue inside, we begin to see it outside. Louise, who appeared very sweet, frequently asked her husband, Larry, if he was angry. He would usually deny that he was, she would persist (sweetly), and he would eventually explode into anger. "See," Louise would say (sweetly), "I told you you were angry." When we worked on this pattern with them in counseling, we urged Louise to take back the projection. Instead of asking Larry if he was angry, we invited her to look inside herself and say that she was angry. It was not an easy step for her, because she had been hiding her anger under her sweetness most of her life. Eventually she learned to do it, though, and was amazed to find that the act of communicating anger actually brought her closer to Larry.

In therapy a husband and wife were expressing how unhappy they were. The dialogue went something like this:

MARTY: My life was going along all right until I met you.

FRED: So was mine. I had everything I needed.

MARTY: Then things really went downhill after you took that job with Ford. If you'd only gone with GM we wouldn't have moved to that awful tract house where we had such a bad time.

FRED: While you were sitting in that tract house having such a bad time you managed to have that affair with Larry. Meanwhile I was working twelve hours a day at a job I hated.

So it goes. Both of them are obviously unhappy, but the real problem is that both of them are projecting their unhappiness onto the other: if it weren't for you; if it weren't for the tract house; if it weren't for the affair. Once you withhold the healthy expression of your feelings and begin to project, there are endless things and people onto which you may dump anger: your parents, your job, the government, the way the world is, and so on. We have all had so little training in how to take true responsibility for our lives that we tend to slip into projection when the slightest stress occurs.

The Lasso Principle

One of the least understood aspects of relationships is what we call the Lasso Principle. You have probably seen in western movies how a cowboy twirls a rope and lassoes an animal. A similar principle works in relationships. When it is time for us to resolve a particular issue in our lives, we lasso someone to work it out with. We pull in someone who has an interlocking issue that will complement ours. It is vitally important that we see who is doing the lassoing. Otherwise it is very tempting to think other people are doing it to us. For example, a man related the following story.

"I always had problems in my relationships with women. I would get close, they would leave. Then I would find another one, and she would eventually leave. They never seemed to last longer than a year. I thought I just had bad luck, that women were just unreliable. Then one day it occurred to me that I might have something to do with this pattern. But what? I talked about it with a good friend of mine who is a professional problem-solver in a large corporation. He immediately asked me how the situations were similar to my childhood experience. I felt like a complete idiot that I hadn't seen it before, but my childhood was full of being left by women. My mother died of cancer when I was four. Then I went to live with my aunt, who got sick and died within a year. Then I was in and out of other relatives' houses until my father got back on his feet when I was nine. He never resolved my mother's death, so he never remarried or really ever got close to another woman. So, in a way, my whole childhood was about loss. No wonder I made my adult relationships about loss."

This is a classic example of the Lasso Principle. He developed a certain pattern of loss out of childhood traumas. Then he lassoed women and pulled them in to help him replay the pattern. We have seen the Lasso Principle so often that it has given us a healthy respect for the infinite power of the human mind to create its own reality. After all, if this man could manifest several relationships in a row, all of which followed the same pattern, he must have great power to manifest healthier relationships. When people are able to wrest their manifestation power away from their unconscious and bring it up into the conscious mind, they are able to create real miracles. We will have a great deal to say specifically about how to do this in part 2.

Many people go through life thinking their relationships just happen to them. They think of themselves as billiard balls being knocked around by random forces. To understand that you create your relationships out of your unconscious feelings, needs, and patterns is to take a giant step forward in growth. Once you see that you are in charge, you are in charge. Then you can consciously design what you want in your relationships, rather than leaving it to the primitive forces of your unconscious.

The unconscious mind is very powerful but not very smart. For example, it may learn that as a child you got a lot of attention when you had asthma attacks. Thirty years later you are feeling vulnerable and needy, so your unconscious mind creates an asthma attack. Powerful but costly, because it may overlook that you are flying your new airplane when it gives you the attack. The conscious mind, by contrast, is very smart but has little energy. It needs the power of the unconscious to support it. Ideally we have both of these working together: power and intelligence. But this union comes about only through careful inquiry into our feelings, needs, and patterns.

Unconscious Deals

Let's look more closely at what happens once a pattern of withholding, withdrawing, and projecting has been established. In order to keep your relationship together, you have to make deals, usually unconsciously, that limit awareness.

The deals fall into several general categories: Blame, Numbing Out, Power Struggles, and Illness and Accidents.

Blame

One way to keep a bad relationship going is to make somebody wrong. For example, one person in the relationship takes on the role of Bad Guy, while the other gets to wear the Good Guy hat. The classic example of this pattern is the relationship between Long-Suffering Wife and Bad Little Boy Husband. He keeps messing up, and she keeps picking up after him, replete with much suffering. The relationship continues by their both agreeing that he is the Bad Guy. If he ever got better, the relationship would be over, so he must keep messing up.

Another variation of the blame pattern is that both people in the relationship make something or someone else wrong. The partners are united in blame. This can take many forms, but the following are some of the most popular.

• The political establishment is wrong, and our relationship is dedicated to our fight against it.

• Our parents wounded us so much that we are united in our hate against them.

• The environment is such a threat to our health that all our united energies must go into staying healthy.

• We're united in competition against our neighbors, our peers, and the rest of the human race.

As you can see, any of these may have an element of reality, and they would not be harmful unless the people were using the blame as a way of avoiding looking into themselves. Blame keeps the attention focused on externals, preventing the transformation of ourselves that is necessary to reach co-commitment.

Projection is a major subcategory of the blame pattern. Projection begins the moment we forget that we are the source of what is happening in our lives. Projection most often comes in the form of not taking responsibility for the feelings we see in others. Countless times in therapy we have heard one person say to another, "You look angry," or, "You look bored," and upon deeper exploration it turned out that the speaker was the one who was angry or bored. Generally speaking, we tend to see around us those things that we are afraid to confront in ourselves. This is the basis of projection. We will have a great deal more to say about projection and how to heal it in chapter 4.

The Victim Position

A nonverbal blame pattern is fighting for the victim position. Under stress, one or both people in the relationship perceive that they have been victimized. If both people go into the victim position, a fight quickly develops over who is the biggest victim. Most arguments between couples are actually a race to occupy the victim slot. Entanglement begins the moment you step out of an equal relationship with your partner and become an advocate for your victimhood.

Numbing Out

Another deal is when one or both partners numb out. It is not possible to increase aliveness in unconscious loving. In fact, awareness and aliveness must be limited in order to keep the relationship going. One way to do this is to reduce sensation by smoking, drinking, or taking drugs. A less extreme way of going numb is to cut off the flow of feeling from inside yourself. If both partners agree to feel less, or not to feel at all, they can keep their feelings buried so deeply that it becomes impossible to deal with them. Of course, this strategy is not very effective, as buried feelings have a way of coming to the surface, often when they are least expected or desired.

Your Internal Critic

A special form of numbing out occurs when we are being run by our internal critic. By engaging in a dialogue with this inner petty tyrant we lose touch with the reality unfolding around us. We all have editors and critics running around in our heads. These busybodies rehearse what we should say, criticize what we did say, and anticipate how others might respond. This chatter cuts us off from the direct feedback our bodies can provide. It is as if we have a large telephone switchboard with only a few lines plugged in. When we decide to stop listening to ourselves, we close doors that once opened to aliveness and creativity. Repeated denial of our sensations and feelings leads to a sense of flatness, boredom, or literal numbness in some part of the body. We have worked with many people who report no sensation when anyone touches them. In a recent interview we asked a woman how she experienced her husband's repeated drinking bouts and long absences. She said, "I don't feel anything." It took a lot of processing for her to reopen the door to her hurt and anger.

Repeated traumas in childhood can lead to later numbness in relationships. We all had frightening experiences as children where we took the strategy of "playing dead." Kathlyn remembers being eight or nine years old, lying very still in the very middle of her bed. She repeated a litany over and over, "If I'm very still and don't breathe, the monsters on the floor won't get me." Clients we've seen whose early traumas were severe commonly say, "I don't feel anything." Decisions that we made not to show the hurt are interpreted by our bodies directly and powerfully.

In later relationships, the partners of numb people report that they just can't get through. They seem to have no impact. The numb partner may also become very intellectual and logical, taking a position that feelings are useless. One client told us, "I don't tell my wife about my fears because it doesn't do any good. It doesn't lead to anything." But going numb does lead us to something—to stony impassivity rather than to full responsiveness.

Power Struggles

One way to keep a co-dependent relationship alive is through constant power struggle. The game becomes one of conflict instead of exchanging positive energy. Over time, conflict can become a deep and severe addiction. Power struggles end the moment people take responsibility for their feelings and lives, but many people never get the message. In therapy we have seen relationships in which the power struggle began on day one and continued for thirty or forty years. The battle became the focus—who's right, who's wrong, who makes the rules, who has the power to end the relationship—and the relationship stayed alive because of the adrenaline released in the struggle. We have seen many miracles occur when such struggle-addicted couples trade in the adrenaline high of conflict for the smoother joys of self-discovery.

Power struggles are often based on the perception of scarcity. The power struggle is almost never about the content. It's not about the toothpaste or the clothes on the floor. It is usually about not enough love, goodwill, or respect. So each comes out swinging. A close partner knows how to *get you* like nobody else. He or she sees your shadow even better than you do.

Nonverbally, a power struggle can seem like a rope-pulling contest. Both people are entrenched and are furiously or subtly trying to pull the other into their camp. Bodies may look more rigid with unexpressed impulses. These impulses often leak out through small, unconscious gestures. For example, one couple was discussing how to spend their yearly bonus. The woman was clicking her fingernails on the arm of her chair, and the man was chewing on the inside of his lip. We asked them to explore what these gestures might be expressing. The man realized that he was biting back his anger, and the woman saw that she was indirectly expressing her impatience with the length of time it took them to make decisions.

Sex, Money, and Children

In our work with couples, we have found that the three most common power-struggle topics are sex, money, and children, in that order. With sex, the struggles are often about how much. Sometimes the struggle is about with whom. In one memorable instance, a couple fought over whether he had or had not slept with another woman over thirty years ago. Finally, on his sixtieth birthday, he confessed.

Money, of course, provides a nearly inexhaustible topic for power struggles, since almost no one feels they have enough of it. Children, too, can keep us locked in mortal combat for our whole lives. Many couples fight over the style of childrearing, over whose rules will prevail. Others use as their focus who will take care of the kids. One of the most tragic power struggles involves those parents who use children as pawns in their (often drawn-out) breakup. In one of the most awful examples of this we have ever seen, a couple made the following promise to each other: "I will devote every ounce of my energy to making sure the children hate you." And they did. Their power struggle continued for nearly five years after the divorce was final. It took the children many years of therapy to clear out of their lives the effects of their parents' battle.

Illness and Accidents

Sometimes the co-dependent deal involves sickness and/or accidents. For example, we worked with one couple whose relationship was organized around illness. When feelings would arise in the relationship that they did not know how to deal with (chiefly anger), one or the other would get sick. Then the other one would go into a caretaking mode, and the relationship would stay alive through the replay of this old pattern. There was a cost, however: both of them spent a lot of time being sick, because this strategy had to be used four or five times a year. Instead of looking at the feelings and patterns each brought to the relationship, sickness was used as camouflage. In fact, we believe that much if not most illness is a way of camouflaging feelings. Our conviction is strengthened by the many people we've treated who had used an illness strategy but then were able to trade it in on something more positive, such as seeing and saying the truth.

There is a much healthier way to handle the moment when unconscious loving begins; we will discuss the specifics in chapter 4. For now, let's look at one example. We worked with a couple who went, in one session, from heavy projection and withholding to learning a brand-new way of relating.

When Susan and Robert first came in, they were stuck. Susan's projection onto Robert was that he disapproved of her, was overly critical, and never talked to her. Robert's projection was that no matter what he did it was never enough for Susan. In the space of an hour they were able to move from these projections into taking responsibility for how they felt. Susan saw that she had set Robert up to be disapproving and critical. This was the pattern of her relationships with men, beginning with her critical father. In order to be in a relationship with Susan, Robert had to be critical, although in his past he had not been a particularly critical person. Robert's projection had begun, as you might guess, with his highly demanding parents, who were never satisfied with his performance. He transferred this projection to Susan when they married. Soon their two shadows were playing out this old drama, while the real people stood by and grew progressively more uncomfortable.

When we tracked their problems back to the source moment, a beautiful thing happened. They reached over and took each other's hands, looking into each other's eyes. Robert said how scared he had been when they first knew each other. He was afraid that she wouldn't like him and later that she would leave him. He said he sensed from the beginning that she wanted him to play a role in some old drama of hers, but he was too fearful to say anything about it. Susan told Robert, for the first time, how painful it had been to grow up in such a cold and disapproving environment. It was deeply touching to see two people, who had been so stuck, open up and say the deepest truths about how they actually felt inside.

When people drop projection and take responsibility for their feelings, their faces take on an unusual light. Although we have seen this in our practice many times, it never fails to move us. There is always a hushed, electric silence in the room when people are speaking their

deepest truths. The stakes are high, because a good relationship can affect so many people for the better. In the
case of Susan and Robert, there was an immediate payoff.
Within the next week they had the opportunity to practice their new skill. The day after their breakthrough session they got stuck again. Robert was projecting onto
Susan that she was too "illogical." Right in the midst of
it he realized that he was angry about a specific event
and had generalized it, which was exactly his father's
pattern with his mother. Robert immediately expressed
his anger at Susan for making a subtraction error in their
checkbook. He then told her about the pattern his parents
had of not mentioning a specific event, withholding it,
then generalizing it into a character flaw in the other
person. When Robert dropped projection and told the
truth about what was going on inside him, the relationship breathed again. He had caught the moment of emergence and had handled it in a creative way.

The Heart of the Matter

The heart of the matter is that there is nothing the
matter with our hearts. It is not love that is to blame.
But each of us has resistance to the very love we desire.
We also have resistance to the space and independence
we need. So we go back and forth, not letting ourselves
have one or the other. Sometimes it is difficult to accept
that it is our own resistance, rather than other people or
the world, that is responsible for our problems. Try on
the idea, though, because it has powerful consequences.
It means that you are in charge again, and are in a position in which you can do something about how your life
goes.

It boils down to this: Are you willing to have your
relationships be a pathway to fully revealing yourself and
your potential? If your answer is yes, real intimacy can
be yours on a daily basis. Of course, even in the healthiest

co-committed relationship, there will always be glitches that arise as you get closer. If you handle them gracefully and productively as they occur, you will always have the choice to conceal or to reveal yourself? A recent example, from our own marriage, illustrates how material can arise, even after a decade of closeness, that if handled well results in intimacy. Kathlyn: "A man came to the door to offer his services in remortaring much of the stone in our hundred-year-old house. I talked to him and realized that part of our foundation probably needed to be repaired. As I was telling Gay about it he said, 'This is undoubtedly going to cost a lot of money.' I experienced a wave of fear and a flurry of thoughts, such as: I should have known about this, it was my idea to buy an older house, Gay's going to be mad, it's my fault, the house might fall down. Instead of keeping all this secret, I told Gay about the fear and my mind-chatter. He laughed and invited me to inquire into where all that fear had come from. I realized immediately that in childhood I had learned to take personal blame for any mishap in the house. I would rush to clean up the kitchen or the whole house to keep my mother from getting into an uproar. I had simply projected that pattern onto our house and Gay. In fact, as we talked about it I saw other situations in which I had replayed that same pattern."

Once you have decided to take responsibility for the quality of your relationships, you need several specific tools. First, you need a map of the territory. You also need ways of spotting and dealing with what comes up on your journey. You need to open up to experience positive energy and to speak the truth about who and how you are. Out of our own relationship, and out of our work with couples over the past two decades, we have found a way that works and have refined the process so that we can teach it to others fairly quickly. The ideas presented here and the activities in part 2 have all been tested in that most rigorous of laboratories: the real world of close relationships.

THREE

The Nine Traps of Unconscious Loving

When you first wake up, you may find that your current relationship is based primarily on your unconscious needs, structured around old patterns usually learned in childhood. We call these common relationship patterns the Co-Dependent Traps, and we would like you to look closely at them. Only by seeing the trap clearly can you find your way out of it.

As you read about these common patterns, do your best not to become discouraged. Sometimes people feel that they are hopelessly mired in these traps. When you finally realize that you have been acting out a pattern, you always have the option of feeling hopeless. But there is little payoff for feeling that way. Hopelessness comes out of having no set of steps along which to proceed. In the program described in this book you have a very specific set of steps that will take you out of co-dependence and into co-commitment. Rather than feeling hopeless and discouraged, simply acknowledge that you are acting out an old pattern, and begin to take steps to remedy it. We've found that it's possible to view the whole process as fun and interesting instead of as a chore.

Trap 1

In my relationships I let people get away with destructive behavior.

This pattern is perhaps the most pervasive trap. People in relationships with you carry out self-destructive patterns. They drink too much, smoke, or overeat. Out of your unconscious need to be loved, you support your loved ones while they hurt themselves. You pick up the pieces for them, cleaning up their messes behind them. You fail to take a stand for their health and well-being, usually by failing to make them accountable and responsible for their behavior. Instead, you participate unconsciously in their self-destruction. Consider the following real-life example.

Linda married Frank on the rebound from a destructive relationship in which she was emotionally and physically abused. Frank was grossly overweight—he weighed 300 pounds. Frank tried to lose weight repeatedly during the first few years of the relationship. Each time he lost a few pounds and began to feel good about himself, Linda would suddenly decide that she wanted to dine out at a fancy restaurant. She would badger Frank into taking her, and of course he wasn't able to resist the temptation. His diet would go out the window and he would gain his weight back. Another pattern: Frank would start to lose weight; Linda would bring home a big box of chocolates or ice cream, two of his can't-resist favorites. Linda was clearly sabotaging Frank's attempts to master his eating problems. They made a commitment to find out why they kept replaying this pattern. They began by reading self-help and eating-disorder books. The following is what they discovered.

Linda had a backlog of submerged anger from two past situations. She was still furious with her ex-husband for his abusiveness to her. Plus, when she was at puberty, her very overweight father had died. Both she and her mother had a great deal of anger at him for eating himself to death and for leaving them. Unconsciously Linda was sabotaging Frank's weight-loss attempts in order to replay that old childhood script. She was participating in Frank's killing himself as a way of expressing her anger at her father and her ex-husband.

On Frank's side of the pattern, his mother had allowed him to overeat from the time he was an infant. Frank was a latch-key child, and there were always gourmet goodies around the house in the afternoons. He would assuage his loneliness with a box of butter cookies or a heaping bowl of ice cream. As an adult, he had simply traded in his mother for Linda, who was happy to replay the pattern with him. She was outwardly concerned about his weight but secretly conspired in his self-destruction.

This sort of thing is quite common, although it may not be as glaringly obvious as in the example of Frank and Linda. Millions of people unconsciously participate in and support the destructive behavior of those whom they love. A more subtle version of this pattern is the relationship in which two people do not support each other's expression of their full potential. They let each other get away with being less than their best. There is no agreement between them that the relationship is going to be the catalyst for growth. There may be no overt self-destructiveness such as drinking, drugging, or overeating, but the pattern is basically the same. It is a conspiracy of mediocrity.

Trap 2

I form relationships with people who let me get away with destructive patterns.

This trap is the flip side of Trap 1. Do you pick close relationships in which people support you for your bad habits? Or do you go out of your way to surround yourself with people who demand the best of you? Many people have awakened to find themselves surrounded by "friends" or family who support their worst aspects. An example: Danny, at age twenty-three, was having a hard time leaving adolescence behind. Teenagers are notorious for avoiding responsibility. They perceive themselves as victims of a universe that does not understand them. They are loath to take responsibility for their lives, preferring instead to heap blame on parents, teachers, or anyone else who permits it. Danny was still of this frame of mind. His basic statement to the world was: "I didn't ask to be here, I don't want to be here, and it's all your fault." This did not make him attractive to employers, several of whom fired him, only to become more evidence of an unfair universe. How did he get away with this attitude? Who picked up the slack for him? Daddy.

His father was a wheeler-dealer in his early forties whose deals were always just this side of illegal. In fact, many of Danny's attitudes were also held by his father. But one day a crisis occurred that forced both of them to look at their behavior. Danny borrowed Dad's Porsche without his knowledge. In fact, Danny had been forbidden to go near the car after he had bent one of its fenders a few months before. Danny, after a few beers with his friends, was speeding in the Porsche when he hit a mother and child crossing the street. The woman and her son both had broken limbs, and, perhaps more to the point, the husband and father was a lawyer. Danny spent time in jail for driving under the influence, and his father had several properties attached, causing him to go bankrupt. They were both forced to go into therapy as part of their rehabilitation. Even with abundant evidence that their behaviors and attitudes were not bringing them prosperity and happiness, they were both still very attached to their victim position. According to them, they had gotten the wrong judge, their lawyer was no good, and the laws were stacked against them. With a great deal of patient work, their therapist was gradually able to help them see that there was no payoff to the victim position. They saw that their whole relationship, and indeed their whole lives, had been organized around taking little or no responsibility. They supported each other's victim point of view and maintained the relationship because it let them get away with their destructive behavior. Fortunately, they eventually saw the light, and both Danny and his father turned their lives around. Danny joined the navy and has now worked his way up to noncommissioned officer; his father made a real midlife about-face and became a seminary student.

The difference between a comedy and a tragedy is very clear. In theater, movies, and TV, the hero or heroine must solve a problem or deal with a character flaw. If the hero wakes up in time and gets the message, a happy ending results. But if the hero stays attached to the old pattern and sleeps through the universe's wake-up call, tragedy is the result.

Trap 3

I am in a relationship that resembles my parents' relationship.

One of the most common forms of unconscious loving occurs when you copy your parents' style of interacting. As the sage Yogi Berra once observed, "You can see a lot by watching." Your parents' relationship forms a template for your own. Some of us react to what we have seen by duplicating it later. Others, as you will see in Trap 5, rebel against what they have seen and create the opposite. Eric, for example, grew up in a family with an alcoholic mother and a workaholic father. At times his mother would shower the children with affection; a few hours later, after a few drinks, she would be raging around the house, threatening them literally with death and dismemberment. His father was seldom home, and when he was he assumed a passive, long-suffering attitude toward his wife's outbursts. His father confided to Eric one night that they had slept separately for years, and that he had felt trapped in the marriage for most of their time together.

Ingrid, Eric's wife, had an entirely different upbringing. There was no liquor in the house, but there was certainly an abundance of co-dependent patterns. Ingrid's mother had given up her career when she married and had nurtured a long-smoldering resentment against Ingrid's not-quite-successful father throughout their stormy marriage. Mother withheld sex, often refering to it as "the disgusting act." Ingrid's father acted out his frustration with inappropriate sexual behavior toward his daughter. For example, he sometimes would storm into the bathroom while Ingrid was taking a shower and would hit her for some unclear infraction.

Ingrid and Eric began their power struggles shortly after marriage, each complaining vigorously about the other. Ingrid argued that she had given up her studies to move across the country to join Eric in his new job, where he worked sixty to eighty hours a week and was "never at home." "And when he is here," Ingrid said with a shudder, "all he wants is sex, sex, sex." Eric exploded, "What do you mean? We haven't had sex in three weeks. All you do is nag, and when I want to be close you push me away." When it was pointed out to them that they were playing out a replica of their respective parents' relationships, they were stunned. As it slowly dawned on them that they were on a trolley track that had been laid down in childhood, they began to feel better. Soon, it became clear that 90 percent of their complaints with each other had more to do with the past than the present. They still had a lot of work to do to overcome these old patterns, but at least they had some idea of the right direction.

One of the most important steps in adult life is to begin to notice where and how your behavior is programmed. You will never be completely happy until you are a free agent, and this requires that you see and transcend your childhood conditioning. For most people, these awarenesses begin in their twenties and mount in intensity throughout their thirties. Some people avoid looking at these issues by diverting their attention to work, addictions, and diversions of various sorts. Many of us put off dealing with our negative childhood programming until well into our forties and fifties. These issues come politely knocking at our door in our twenties, then rap louder in our thirties. If you delay looking at your programming until your forties, you are likely to have the message delivered with sledgehammer blows.

One man we worked with blindly followed in his father's footsteps, becoming a junior partner in the law firm and working steadily in his father's shadow. At thirty-nine a massive heart attack put him on the sidelines for several months, and he wisely took the opportunity to look carefully at his life. He realized that he had never wanted to be a lawyer. He recalled a conversation with his father in which he confessed that he really wanted to work with his hands. His father, whose own father had worn himself out working the family farm, said with derision, "You'll never make a living with your hands, son. You've got brains and you're going to use them." So he put aside his dreams of being a sculptor and took up the law. In addition, he went along with a semiarranged marriage to the daughter of one of his father's other law partners, and became even more deeply mired in a life he had not chosen. His heart attack occurred the day after he had talked to a friend about the possibility of separating from his wife. Fortunately, with a great deal of work on himself he was able to reconstruct a life that fit him. He became the lawyer for a consortium of art galleries, allowing him to work with the art world while using his business skills. He and his wife acknowledged the passionless nature of their relationship and separated amicably once their two children were in college.

This trap is so pervasive that we would like to illustrate it with another example. Ellie told us that she was "not able to delineate my father and my husband." Ellie was an engineer, as was her father. As a child, Ellie had seen only his stoic and unexpressive side. Her mother, who had a drinking problem, felt isolated and victimized by her husband's lack of attention and of emotional expression. She made up for it by being very loud with her emotional expressions, often in public. In Ellie's relationship with her husband, they reversed the roles. Her husband would stay out late drinking and smoking cigars (which Ellie loathed). Ellie would respond by stoic acceptance and burying her feelings. Her mother had engaged in several affairs, which eventually led to her parents' divorce. Ellie's husband also had affairs, about which Ellie knew but said nothing.

In Ellie's work on herself, she had to open up to her feelings of sadness and anger, and also deal with her mother's feelings, which Ellie had taken on inside herself. Often when you begin to deal with your inner feelings you find that some of the most troublesome of them are those that you borrowed, adopted, or assumed from other people. As a sensitive child, being around parents, grandparents, and others means that you can "soak up" their feelings and mesh them with your own. While some people feel frustrated at having to deal with other people's feelings, you can feel glad that many of the things you have been troubled by are not solely yours. You can learn to distinguish your own feelings from those of others. In fact, learning to do so is one of the most important skills you can acquire as an adult.

Trap 4

I form relationships with people whose personalities and behavior resemble that of one or both of my parents.

As children, we felt our first closeness, nurturance, and love with people who often had deep flaws in their character and behavior. We may despise those flaws, but many times we re-create them by having adult relationships with people who have the very same flaws. For example, Mark's father was a real charmer who could sell anything to anybody when he was sober. Mark adored his father, who was witty and a good storyteller. He thought of his mother as being nervous and uptight (she was always busy keeping the family together and cleaning up Father's messes). She was very bitter, often saying to Mark, "You're going to end up just like *him.*"

As an adult, several times Mark found himself in work situations in which his boss had created grandiose plans but could not be relied on to see them through. Mark had lost contracts and had even been in a legal battle while trying to rescue one of these "fathers" from self-destruction. Mark was replaying an old pattern, in which his father was the hero against an unfair system. He overlooked the character flaw in his bosses because it was the same one he overlooked, out of love, in his father. It cost, and it hurt, and many of Mark's friends told him how stupid he was to back these losers. In spite of these cues from the universe, Mark did not get the message until he nearly went to prison because of one of his bosses' shady dealings.

Trap 5

Out of reaction to parental relationships, I create relationships that are the opposite of my parents'.

For every person who duplicates his or her parents' relationship, another person takes the path of opposition by rebelling against what was experienced in childhood. It is a different trolley track, but a track just the same. In fact, this one can take you to an even more painful destination than simply playing out the same relationship as your parents had. By taking a rebellious stance, you are reacting instead of acting. In addition, you are basing your life on anger—a costly and dissatisfying foundation.

Until she woke up in her thirties, Mary had based all her significant adult relationships on making sure that they were the exact opposite of her parents' relationship. She had basically raised herself. Her parents were young and irresponsible when she was born, and she learned early that neither her mother nor her father could be relied on. She recalled that her parents often came into her room at night to complain about their problems. She listened and even gave them advice, although she was secretly furious with them for not taking care of her. Having seen her parents' immaturity, she decided to grow up quickly and was essentially an adult by the time she was ten. In her school pictures she looked severe and drawn, with lips pursed and a slight scowl on her face. In school she became an outstanding high achiever, but by her senior year she had developed ulcers. Fortunately, she had a very understanding doctor who got her to talk about her life instead of covering up her symptoms with medication. Out of their conversations grew an awareness of how she was living her life in reaction and opposition to her parents.

Righteous indignation, which H. L. Mencken called "envy with a halo," is another form of living out of opposition. You make yourself right and others wrong. Your life becomes one of endless opposition to the faulty behavior of others. One of the most striking images of the late 1980s was of the righteous Jimmy Swaggart, disguised in his wig, cruising the streets of the depraved city against which he railed, looking for the pornography against which he preached. Whether we set ourselves up as the problem, or pit ourselves against others who are the problem, living in opposition robs us of energy that could be used to reach our full potential.

Living out of opposition can be very hard in another way. If you are living out of rebellion you have a greater

likelihood of running afoul of authority figures such as principals, judges, and police. Your life becomes occupied with
being a problem rather than being productive. This path is
hard, because once you and the world define you as a problem, your whole life can become occupied with trying to
handle this problem. In conversations with hard-core
addicts (such as longtime heroin users), we have repeatedly
heard it said that their addiction simplified their lives, by
giving them one big problem to focus upon. Rather than
having to deal with the myriad problems of having a job,
supporting a family, dealing with feelings, and the other
complications of a busy and productive life, they found it
much more attractive to refine their problems down to getting a fix. Perhaps this is why so many people turn to addictions as a way of handling life. As one recovering alcoholic
put it: "When I was a drunk, my life was simple. I was
either drinking, drunk, or passed out. I didn't have to spend
time in those troublesome intermediary states like being
awake and alive! Now, even though I feel infinitely better
and more productive after five years of sobriety, I sometimes yearn for that simple life. I avoided responsibility,
feelings, other people's feelings, and all the things I now
have to deal with."

Trap 6
**Out of childhood trauma a pattern is generated, and I play
out that pattern repeatedly in my relationships.**

Helping people see how they are replaying childhood
dramas is the very stuff of therapy. The following are some
examples from our casebooks.

Ron came in furious about a situation with his friend
and lover, Paula. He had been feeling very close to her for
a record length of time without creating any upsets. Then
the bomb dropped. At a seminar connected with her work,
she had developed a friendship with another man. They had
a number of close conversations about significant events
in their lives. Although nothing sexual had occurred, Ron
became obsessed with Paula's potential sexual involvement
with the other man, even though Paula considered this fan-
tasy ridiculous. With some gentle prodding, Ron shifted

from his victim position ("Why is the universe doing this to me?") and began to look into what it might be about. By opening up to his feelings of anger and fear, he accessed a childhood event that relieved him immensely. When he was three years old, he was used to sleeping with his mother. One day his father came back from the war after an eighteen-month absence, and that was the end of sleeping with his mother. He screamed for three days, then developed asthma. When he would stop breathing and turn blue he always got his mother's attention. His asthma became a major issue in the family. His father argued that it was all in Ron's head, while his mother took him to doctor after doctor trying to find a medical solution. In other words, Ron became a problem.

When Ron saw what he was doing, he had a rare moment of insight. He saw that he was playing out this same childhood drama in his relationship with Paula. Her friendship with the other man did not look like friendship to Ron: it was loss and betrayal and somebody else getting to sleep with his mother. He had even felt his chest tighten with constricted breathing ever since Paula had initiated the relationship with the other man. This fact amazed Ron, because he had not had an asthma episode in ten years. When he made this connection, his chest instantly relaxed and he breathed freely. He left with the intent to talk to Paula and thank her for bringing all this into his awareness through her new relationship.

To look into your recurring patterns, to find out where they came from, is one of the primary healing activities of adult life. By going to the source, you have a better opportunity to deprogram yourself so that you can get off the old track and into a life of your choosing. Sometimes the old pattern starts very early. For example, there was a large-scale study of children born to mothers who had been starved for a specific period of time during their pregnancies. (The starvation was due to a Nazi food embargo to parts of Holland during World War II.) Researchers were interested in whether the mothers' hunger would have psychological and physical effects on the children. It did. Children born to these mothers had a much higher incidence of obesity as children and adults. In another, related study, children were studied who had lost their fathers. One group of mothers had been widowed during pregnancy, while another group had been widowed shortly after the child's birth. The children who had lost their fathers while still in utero turned out to have a much higher incidence of physical and emotional difficulties.

For an insight into the early nature of relationship patterns, consider the example of Ann, a top executive who began looking into a recurrent pattern. She felt she was "too emotional," and upon deeper inquiry she said that in relationships she always felt she was taking up too much space. As she opened up to the source of this feeling she had a *Eureka!* moment in which she realized that it all started in the womb with her twin brother. In a rare medical condition, she had been conceived a month later than he, from a different egg. In addition, she was an Rh-negative baby. When she was born, she was whisked away for blood transfusions. She did not see her brother or mother for ten days. In adult life she replayed this pattern primarily with male bosses and co-workers. She always felt she was bothering them with her requests and plans. She allowed them to interrupt her at meetings and to override her decisions. Out of the fear that she was taking up too much space, she withheld her feelings and needs in these situations. She noticed that she compulsively kept an eye on her boss, looking up from work often to check if he was still there, afraid that he might disappear. As she worked with the issue it seemed to her that it all stemmed from her early relationship with her twin brother. She felt that the twin relationship was so intense that all her life she had been looking for that type of closeness. But with the early closeness had come deep fears that she was taking up too much space, that her needs might kill her twin brother. By taking all of her parents' attention, money, and energy because of her blood condition, she felt she had deprived her brother of a good life. Obviously these are not rational, conscious thoughts but rather the skewed view of a hurt and confused child. This view showed up in adult life with

her pattern of relating to men, from whom she had difficulty separating her brother.

As she opened up to the early source of these issues,
she was offered a better job, one in which none of the old
issues cropped up. Her social life also took a turn for the
better after she separated from her twin/boss. She was able
to see men for who they were, rather than confusing them
with her unresolved thoughts and feelings about her
brother.

Many troubled relationship patterns stem from childhood events. But others seem to come from earlier
moments, such as the events around birth, our time inside
our mothers, or even the time of conception itself. Although
it cannot be proved that these early events are formative
and influential, it is wise to accept all possibilities, for in
that way we open the greatest space for healing ourselves
on all levels.

Trap 7

**I participate in continual conflict in my relationships,
or I avoid conflict at all costs.**

Sometimes co-dependence is based on addiction to conflict. If one or both persons are conflict addicts, there is no
space for intimacy and co-commitment to unfold. Conflict
addicts spend their time and energy preparing for, engaging in, and recovering from uproar. The opposite is also
part of this pattern: you avoid conflict by sidestepping it,
minimizing it, or refusing to consider negative feelings. The
seeker and the avoider of conflict often have the same background. Many people are exposed to conflict as they grow
up. Some people take a snapshot of all the uproar and make
an unconscious decision that this is just how relationships
are. They go on to create continuous uproar in their adult
relationships. Others experience conflict and make the
opposite decision: Not me—I'll never have this kind of
uproar in my life. Following are two extreme examples of
relationships in which there was significant conflict addiction of both the seeking and the avoiding variety. Your
background may not have been quite this dramatic, but

you may recognize elements of yourself in each of these women.

Barbara's father was killed in a bloody industrial accident, and from then on her childhood took on a nightmarish quality of constant conflict. Her mother held a series of waitressing jobs, sometimes in bars, where the children were often brought to the back room for their one daily meal. She had a series of "stepfathers" who were alternately abusive and supportive. She saw that men were often loving and wonderful out in public, then violent at home. Her mother, who had never been strong, became erratic and irrational in her treatment of her children. As her mother descended into madness and eventual death, Barbara saw a steady stream of eccentric behavior. Some days her mother would make the children participate in bizarre cleaning rituals, while other days her mother would stay in bed all day and refuse to cook or get the children ready for school.

When she came in for counseling, Barbara was not aware that her early conditioning was causing her to repeat her early pattern of chaos, disharmony, and loss. Now in her second marriage, she was still in constant battle with her first husband. There were long-standing battles over custody and alimony, coupled with weekly skirmishes about visitation. Plus, her current husband threatened divorce about once a week, frequently hit her when angry, and taught his three children, who lived with them, to ignore her requests. It was an utter mess. The wake-up event had occurred one day when Barbara came home to find all the locks changed and her belongings arranged neatly on the front lawn. After howling *"Victim!"* for a week or two, Barbara finally decided to look at her role in perpetuating this endless cycle of uproar in her life.

She saw that she had formed an image of how life ought to be—fraught with grief and conflict—out of the horrible events of her childhood. She recognized that she had no tolerance for things going well. If her life looked like it was running smoothly for more than a day or two, she would do something to mess it up. If she didn't, somebody else would oblige. But she was able to grasp how staying in the victim role was not serving her. She decided to claim full responsibility for having created conflict, which then entitled her to take full responsibility for changing her life. Taking responsibility shifted everything. She stopped putting up with uproar among her children, got a lawyer to handle things with her ex-husband, and went into counseling with her present husband. It took her over a year to get her life working smoothly, but saved her decades of future misery.

In contrast, Sharon took a different path as an adult. Her family background was similar to Barbara's, but her reaction to it was completely the reverse. She said that her mother and father screamed all the time. Father and older brother would get into fistfights at the dinner table on the average of once a week, while her mother was in the habit of coming after people with whatever kitchen utensil was at hand. Sharon said that she spent her nights "frozen in fear." She always planned her escape route at night, and slept with a Swiss army knife under the covers. She was the only one of the children who subsequently escaped the dominion of the family. She left as soon as she could and went to live on the other side of the country.

Later she took an excellent job as, of all things, a corporate troubleshooter. Her job was to smooth over difficult situations, and she proved highly skilled at it. Her strategy with her family and her past was to pretend that it had never existed. But the past has a way of catching up. Sharon was so terrified of conflict that she refused to discuss meaningful issues of any kind with her husband. She was particularly adamant about not having children, and it was this issue that finally drove them into conflict. When conflict erupted, Sharon was paralyzed and entered counseling to find out why. The past came forth, and with a great deal of work she saw how she had reacted to her childhood uproar by refusing to engage in any sort of conflict as an adult. Another wake-up event happened at about the same time: her mother had a stroke. Sharon had to go home and deal with her family. She was thrust into the fire, and she realized that she would have to deal with her feelings or go crazy. So she courageously opened up to her whole range of feelings, told the truth as scrupulously as she could, and learned to deal with the people she had sealed out of her awareness decades before.

Conflict addiction is established like any other addiction. Suppose that as a child you sat down at four o'clock every afternoon and had a chocolate bar. You wouldn't be surprised to find that as an adult you got the urge for a chocolate bar at four o'clock. Conflict is at least as addicting, because it involves adrenaline, one of the most powerful drugs known to science. Recent studies suggest that conflict addicts and others, such as those prone to thrill seeking, actually become dependent on tiny self-administered shots of adrenaline. They do not feel good unless they create drama in their lives to get their fix of the "drama drug."

Overcoming this addiction requires that you accustom yourself to longer periods of serenity and feeling good. While this may seem an easy task, it is not. Later in the book you will find specific ways to learn to tolerate more positive energy.

Trap 8
With the possibility of success at hand, I mess up.

When first hearing this pattern described, many people think, "How stupid!" Then they realize how often they have done it themselves. (This pattern is a version of the Upper Limits Problem, which we will address later.) Here's how it works. Due to some circumstance in life you develop an allergy to success. When you get close to it you find some way to avoid it. Allergy to success can come about in several ways. The most straightforward background event is that you saw this pattern around you in childhood. One or more members of your family had a pattern of messing up when success was a possibility, and you filed this program away in your mind as the way it should be done. A variation of this pattern occurs when people mess up to get even with somebody. Let's say that as a child you had a negative view of your successful father. You filed away an unconscious program of "I don't want to be anything like *him*." In addition, you know that if you do not do well in your life, it will offend him more than just about anything else. Later in life, long after you have forgotten this thought, you mess up every time you get close to success.

Another variation occurs among those who have such a severe lack of self-confidence that they mess up to keep from having to go through the pain of a larger failure. One client of ours came into therapy because she'd had it pointed out to her that on three separate occasions she had gotten in trouble at work just before her annual salary review. She would do fine all year, then mess up just before the opportunity for advancement came her way. A more extreme example is a man we know who was about to take a high-level position directing a city's youth programs when he was arrested for child molesting. It turned out that the whole thing was a terrible case of mistaken identity, but rather than dismissing it as a mistake, the man inquired into why this had happened to him. Out of this inquiry he recalled an incident in his childhood. His mother, with her dying breath, had told him that she wished she had never given birth to him and that he would never amount to anything. Although intellectually he knew that she was just dumping anger on him for the bitterness of her own life, his inner being registered the shock of this message with a lifelong mess-up program. When he was under consideration for the Honor Society, he was suspected of cheating on a test and was dropped as a candidate. When he had an athletic scholarship almost in his pocket, he got caught drinking and was rejected. Then, the wake-up event of his life occurred with the child-molestation charge in his late twenties. Finally, he began to suspect that this was a pattern, not just a case of bad luck. Having the courage to look into this pattern allowed him to get free of it at last, so that he did not repeat it in a bigger way in his thirties.

For many couples, having affairs is a way to get even and mess up at the same time. From our case notes, here are some of the reasons people give for their affairs:

- He's never home.
- She doesn't understand me.

- He never listens to my feelings.
- She let herself get fat.
- He's always tired or consumed by work.

All these are expressions of stored anger. When anger goes unspoken for long, the conditions are ripe for getting even. Sometimes two or more motivations are at work. For example, a man with whom we worked discovered that he had begun his affair to get even and to avoid closeness with his wife. He was angry at her for a number of things, which he had withheld, and he had also tasted a few days of intense closeness with her after she had told him she was pregnant. This closeness was apparently too much for him to handle, for within days he sought out another relationship. Of course he was caught, which generated uproar at home and destroyed the possibility of closeness.

If you have decided that you cannot win in a particular situation, then you may try to avoid the pain of losing. You can do this by getting sick, having an accident, creating an upset, or by messing up in one of dozens of other ways. These strategies take the focus off of your pain and put it "out there." For example, you may have agreed to give a speech, then felt afraid of doing it. It is much more socially acceptable to get sick than it is to say, "I'm afraid to do this and I don't want to." If you come down with a sore throat the day of the speech, you can shift the blame to the offending microbes.

Trap 9

Because I have never learned true independence, I create relationships in which I perpetuate dependence.

True independence is a rare thing. Many people think of independence as being able to stand alone successfully, but true independence is something else entirely. It is the ability to stand alone *and* have close relationships. It is not hard at all to withdraw to a cave or a monastery to be independent. True independence requires that you be able to relate closely to others while maintaining your sense of self. This is much harder. One of the central fears of life is that we will get so close to others that we will be swallowed up. Learning to be fully you at the same time as you are fully in union is the capstone of a healthy life.

We have seen many people whose co-dependence literally involved dependency. For example, one of our clients grew up in a family with a very dominant Old World father and a submissive mother. She recalled that her mother was seldom seen out of the kitchen and her father was seldom seen in it. At sixteen she began dating a man five years her senior, the son of one of her father's employees. At eighteen her father "helped" her decide to get married. There was a meeting in the living room, at which her father, in a formal speech, handed her over to her husband-to-be. At twenty-five she had a wake-up event that changed her life. Her husband casually mentioned that he had been seeing another woman, and then slapped her around when she became upset about it. As she later recalled, "He actually seemed surprised that I would have any objection to it." As a result of this event, she examined her life and saw that she had lived it all in other people's shadows. She had no idea how to be herself, have her own feelings, think for herself, or in any other way be independent. She saw that even her ability to be close, which seemed her only skill, was destructive because it came out of submission. With a great deal of work she was able to build an independent life that allowed her to be in union with men as equals.

As you look into your close relationships, are you avoiding learning the lessons of independence? Are you learning to be completely yourself while also learning to be completely in union with others? If not, you may be in this trap. If you are avoiding independence, you could be setting yourself up for some of life's harshest lessons. Some of the most unhappy people with whom we have worked are those who resisted or delayed learning how to be their own persons until long past the proper time. If you live your life through other people, you create a deep dependency that can backfire in a major way if they move away. When separation comes, you have no sense of self to sustain you. Facing life as an empty shell can be deeply troubling; we have seen many co-dependents try to do this for the first time in their fifties and sixties. If you think the description of this trap fits you, it will be particularly helpful for you to work through the activities in part 2.

These nine traps are the major ones we have seen repeatedly in our practice. No doubt there are other traps, and dozens of variations of the ones we have described. But these are the major ways people sleepwalk through life, and if you see yourself reflected in any of these patterns: *Wake up!* It's time to get conscious about how you want your relationships to be. Don't let your old patterns run the show. You'll never be happy in the dim dreamworld of unconscious entanglements.

The waking-up process involves seven specific steps to transform any relationship from unconscious to conscious loving. In the next chapter we describe these steps in detail.

FOUR

The Seven Steps to Co-Commitment

These steps will allow you to make a smooth and comfortable transition to a new way of being. We are highly in favor of people growing in ways that are comfortable and loving to themselves. Growth can be painful or it can be comfortable, depending on your intentions. We have found that the best way to make a comfortable transition is through following the seven steps, preferably in order. If people skip over one of the key steps, they often have to go back later and pick it up remedially. When you get to the activities in part 2 you will notice that they are laid out in the same order as the seven steps in this chapter. We *highly* recommend that you work through the experiential activities in addition to learning the seven steps. To learn life-changing material is much more than an intellectual exercise: it involves your mind, body, emotions, and ultimately your spirit. Only by practicing the activities can you really integrate the material at all levels of yourself. This material is the work of a lifetime. Give yourself plenty of permission to learn, make mistakes, correct, and relearn: in short, be easy with yourself as you work with these new ideas.

We will begin with the specific commitments that set the process in motion. As we discussed briefly in chapter 1, there are six specific commitments that can make the attainment of co-commitment much easier. If you and your partner begin your transformation process by agreeing to these six intentions, the whole process will unfold much more smoothly.

Step One: Commitment

A co-committed relationship rests on several intentions that are agreed on by both persons. It takes two to play this game. If one person wants to have co-commitment and the other does not, co-commitment is not possible. If you are the only one who wants to play, you can certainly be healthier and happier by working through these steps on your own, but it is only when both people agree to play that the real intimacy becomes possible. If you are willing to make the following commitments but your partner is not, it is highly likely that you are in a co-dependent relationship. Beware, because it may indicate that you are doing more than your share of the work in keeping the relationship going. If this is the case, you need to examine why you have set up your life this way.

Commitment 1

I commit myself to full closeness, and to clearing up anything within me that stands in the way.

With this commitment you take a stand for closeness. Both of you agree that this is what your relationship is about. You also commit yourself to working out all the little things and the big things that people put in the way of being close to each other. We desperately want union with other people, but often we are also deathly afraid of it because of the pain it has brought in times past.

When two people agree that they desire closeness, and particularly when they state that they are willing to clear up their barriers to it, the intimacy begins. This conscious commitment is necessary because, until you make it, you are often in the grip of countercommitments that get in the way. For example, many people have an unconscious commitment to ignoring or hiding their barriers to intimacy rather clearing them up. Others have never really considered why they are in relationships at all. They have never gone public with their intention of being close to others.

Here is an example of how making Commitment 1 saved a marriage. John and Rhonda came in for counseling feeling very stuck. As we worked with them it became clear that neither of them had taken the stand of committing to closeness. In addition, neither was willing to work through their barriers to intimacy. John had a pattern of getting close to Rhonda, then finding some way to alienate her. We asked him to track instances of what Rhonda called his "obnoxiousness." Over two weeks he had engaged in six different "obnoxious" actions. One of the major examples was that he had overlooked agreements he had made with her. He might agree to take their son to soccer practice at 4 p.m., but not arrive until 4:30. He discovered that all six of his "obnoxiousnesses" came right after being close and tender with Rhonda. Rhonda's pattern was to get sick as a way of fleeing intimacy. Throughout their relationship Rhonda had had a great number of minor health problems: sniffles, skin eruptions, lower-back aches. These problems drove John nuts, as they reminded him of his hypochondriacal mother. While John was tracking his obnoxious behavior, we asked Rhonda to track her illnesses. She too found that most of them occurred just after a period of intimacy. Their unconscious conspiracy, then, was to limit closeness by engaging in their particular brand of programmed behavior.

We asked them if they would make a commitment to each other to be close, and to clear up any barriers to being so. They both exploded in a flurry of justification. "Of course I'm interested in closeness," John said. "I'm here, aren't I?" We pointed out that many people come to counseling to reinforce very problematic intentions. One person comes to get better, while another comes to get even. We asked them both to look at their counterintentions that got in the way of their conscious intention to be close. With some detective work, it became clear that both of them were deeply afraid of being close for fear of being hurt as they had been in past relationships. After venting some of these old hurts, they were able consciously to commit themselves to Commitment 1. By putting themselves squarely on the line in agreeing that closeness was their goal, a shift occurred that took much of the struggle out of their relationship.

For example, it had never occurred to Rhonda that her frequent headaches were a way of stopping herself from getting close to John. She took them very seriously, dowsing herself with painkillers and various nostrums. When she saw how she had been using her headaches, the game was up. Within a short period of time she was virtually free of headaches.

Commitment 2

I commit myself to my own complete development as an individual.

In Commitment 1 you take a stand for being close. Here you take a stand for separateness. You cannot have ultimate closeness without being fully able to be separate. In other words, the more fully developed you are as an individual, the more you are able to give and receive love in a relationship. In child development, we first must be able to be close. That is where the nurturance is. Later we must develop the skills of autonomy. Many of us have never had the opportunity to commit ourselves consciously to our own growth. In addition, many of us saw relationships in our past in which people had to compromise their individual development in order to maintain the relationship. They had to get smaller to squeeze themselves into an ill-fitting box. By taking the stand in Commitment 2, you both are going on record as agreeing that individual development and closeness to the other person is important.

In a co-committed relationship, space is as important as closeness. It must be all right for both people to have space and time for themselves. Only through taking space for ourselves can we integrate the learnings in a close relationship. This does not mean you need to go away for a week at a time to rest up (though sometimes that, too, may be a good idea). Taking space may be as simple as a solitary walk or a daily meditation time. In co-dependence, taking space almost always brings up fear. In co-commitment, taking space usually results in a fresh burst of creative ideas. By taking space and time for themselves, partners in a co-committed relationship renew their individual connections with the universe. Through coming apart and coming together again, the dance of the relationship is renewed and kept lively.

A commitment to individual development is crucial, because a co-committed relationship emerges only when both people are willing to be 100 percent themselves as individuals. If either person is being less than 100 percent, the ground is ripe for power struggles. Each person will be trying to find places to hide from responsibility in the relationship, the places where the other person is at fault. When you are being less than 100 percent, you will tend to want to diminish the other person to match your level. Once you enter the arena of power struggles, there is only one way out: both people must claim 100 percent ownership of the problem. We will explain how to do this later in the chapter.

Commitment 3

I commit to revealing myself fully in the relationship, not to concealing myself.

A major event in our lives occurs when we shift our intentions from concealing to revealing. Most of us learned to hide our true selves in order to survive growing up. It is not surprising that we take this practice into our later relationships. It costs, because a close relationship thrives on transparency. Being fully transparent heals the shadow. If your energy is tied up in concealing who you are and how you are, there is little energy left over to fuel creativity.

For example, Marge and Randy appeared to be committed to revealing themselves. Marge acknowledged to us (but not to Randy) that she was having an affair, but she would not budge when we asked her to talk to Randy about it. She spoke freely about her feelings of anger and sadness, but when it came down to revealing this major secret, she balked. She persisted in holding the point of view that Randy could not handle the truth. She actually chose to end the relationship with Randy rather than share the truth with him. They split, with him never knowing exactly why. Later, after six months apart, Marge finally saw the light. She saw that her whole life had been organized around hiding who she really was. She saw that the pattern came from hiding the truth of her emerging sexual development from her abusive father. She was afraid that if she was open about herself at a deep level, her survival would be threatened. So she worked up the courage to tell the truth to Randy, who was at first very angry, then ultimately forgiving. He said he preferred knowing the truth, even though it hurt, to stumbling around in the dark. They got back together and worked out a relationship based on a shared commitment to becoming fully transparent.

Commitment 4

I commit myself to the full empowerment of people around me.

In co-dependence you enable other people to be ineffective. In co-commitment you enable them to be powerful. With this commitment you take a stand to allow others to assume their full power. Imagine how much two people can accomplish when their commitment is to each other's full growth! Contrast this with how little can be accomplished when both people are committed to restraining the other. Yet, how many of us have actually made a commitment to the full empowerment of those around us? Robin and Michael, in the following example, took this step and changed their lives by doing so.

They woke up one day to the awareness that much of their creative energy was being drained by power struggles. Robin felt that Mike was a wimp and invested a great deal of time and attention in trying to improve him. Michael, an accountant, spent a lot of his energy in devising elaborate explanations for his behavior and in criticizing Robin for her sloppy housework. On a given day they could be expected to argue about who was taking care of the kids, who had cleaned the bathroom last, and who was going to make dinner. They had turned the ideal of equality in relationship into a way to beat each other up emotionally.

In therapy, we confronted them with whether they were really committed to empowering each other. They said they were, but with deeper exploration they uncovered an ambivalence to supporting each other's full growth. Robin revealed an old program that was influencing her relationship with Michael. She had been a mistake, an "afterthought," born long after her three brothers. She grew up feeling her parents' hidden resentment of her, convinced that she was treated unfairly as compared to her brothers. She saw that she was always on guard with Michael to make sure she was treated fairly, meanwhile requiring him to treat her unfairly to fit her old pictures and give her a good excuse to dump her anger on him. Michael's attitude toward the marriage was that it was a distracting burden, and when he looked closely at this attitude he saw that it was an instant replay of his father's attitude toward his mother. He was busily projecting it onto Robin, with the predictable results. While their surface commitment was to supporting each other, their hidden countercommitments were chipping away at each other's developing sense of self. When they saw how they were sabotaging themselves they began to work on Commitment 4. They made a list of specific ways they could support each other in material, emotional, and spiritual ways. Michael took charge of the children for a year while Robin completed her teaching credentials. She made an agreement not to use her credit card as a weapon against him; a weekly budget meeting was arranged to clear expenditures. With a great deal of careful work they were able to get clear on what each wanted, and how they might support each other to get there.

Commitment 5

I commit myself to acting from the awareness that I am 100 percent the source of my reality.

Many of the problems in relationships are caused by both partners fighting to claim the victim position. The moment you fail to claim 100 percent creation of your life, you step into a trap. Unconscious loving feeds on victimhood, which can exist only when people are not taking responsibility for what is happening to them. When two people are willing to be the source of their reality, real intimacy becomes possible. There is no energy wasted over whose problem it is, who's right and who's wrong, whose fault it is, or other power struggles.

We have worked with many couples in which there actually appeared to be a victim and a villain. Take the example of abusive relationships. If a husband beats up his wife every week, is she not a real victim? Yes, she is, but this confirmation will never solve the problem. She will never move toward greater health until she claims 100 percent responsibility for having created her marriage that way. What moves the relationship forward toward resolution is the asking of key questions, such as: Why have I set up my life so that I am a victim of abuse? Is there a pattern here that I'm not seeing? Am I willing to risk being alone to end the abuse? There is absolutely no healthy payoff for claiming victimhood. Never. Ever. The most effective way to get out of an abusive relationship is to acknowledge your role in perpetuating it, then get out. When you persist in being a victim you settle for being right instead of being a winner. Being right is definitely a booby prize, never a substitute for a satisfying life. So, while there are cases in which someone is clearly a victim, nobody ever got free and happy by viewing it that way.

Consider the following example of a couple who started out deeply entrenched in victimhood, to the point where their relationship was on the line, but were able to turn it around by embracing Commitment 5. On the surface it appeared that Jack was the victim and Ginny was the perpetrator. Jack was so furious and full of righteousness about Ginny's transgression that he had managed to convince her that she was the bad guy in their drama. But now she was tired of the role and was beginning to perceive herself as the victim of Jack's repeated insults. The situation was that Ginny had taken an overnight trip to a conference with her boss, during which they had engaged in a heavy petting session in her room. Their attraction had been building for some time and finally boiled over. They mutually decided not to go into a full-fledged sexual affair, and when they returned Ginny told Jack of the incident. Six weeks of what Ginny called "mental flogging" later, they came in for counseling.

In the realm of close relationships things are not always as they seem. If we had looked only at their superficial actions, we could have said that Jack was right and Ginny was wrong and that was that. But with further exploration, another story unfolded. When we inquired into Jack's past, we found that his previous wife had done something very similar, as had a woman to whom he had been engaged in college. A pattern emerged, and when we tracked it down to its source, we found that it had actually begun in childhood, when Jack's mother deserted the family to go off with another man. Jack's father had never fully recovered from the loss and had passed down to Jack a long string of beliefs about life, such as, "Just when you think you can trust somebody they'll let you down." Jack, out of his own unresolved grief about his loss of his mother, was more than fertile ground for these beliefs to take root. All his adult relationships were about loss of trust and loss itself.

When you are replaying a pattern it is very hard to see it. In this situation, Jack could not see that he had any role in setting up these situations. It actually looked like it was always the woman's fault. In fact, he got mad at us for bringing up the possibility that he had something to do with it (therapists are accustomed to this reaction—the truth will set you free but at first it's likely to set you off). After a session or two of verbal arm-wrestling, Jack finally was able to take responsibility as a co-creator of this situation. We asked Jack and Ginny if they were willing to base their relationship on a commitment to both of them being 100 percent responsible for what happened to them. At the moment they made the commitment, a visible shift took place: they actually stood up straighter and looked more alive. Arguing about who's the biggest victim is an energy drain in any relationship; for Jack and Ginny, it had almost cost them their marriage. Embracing Commitment 5 is a long, often slow learning process. It took Jack and Ginny a solid year of working on themselves before they were able to make this commitment a continuous, living reality in their household, but over that year their relationship grew tremendously. Every Christmas they send us a card that says: "We remember!"

Commitment 6

I commit myself to having a good time in my close relationships.

In the process of growing up, many of us embrace a view of relationships that causes pain later on: we think that relationships are about suffering. We believe that if the relationship is not a struggle we must not be doing it right. As a child, how many people did you see around you who were in a state of joy in their relationships? What about right now? We feel strongly that a formal commitment to having a good time is necessary to move into a state of co-commitment. We do not know the entire meaning of life, but we are very sure it is not to have a bad time. Why not take a conscious stand for joy in your close relationships? You make the rules for your relationships, so try having them be about joy. If you find that you prefer suffering, you can always go back.

When we observe troubled relationships, we often see that the people are strongly committed but that the commitments are unhealthy. The commitments are to things such as:

• Power struggles (who's right, whose problem is it, who's having the worst time)
   • Taking care of each other
   • Cleaning up the other's messes
   • Providing three meals a day
   • Getting ahead financially

There is absolutely nothing wrong with getting ahead financially or providing three meals a day, but without joy what's the point? When both people make a conscious commitment to having a good time, it doesn't matter what kinds of activities are engaged in. Getting ahead financially is much more rewarding if you are doing it out of joy rather than suffering.

The Russian mystic Gurdjieff said that addiction to suffering was the one he had the hardest time getting his students to give up. Long after they had kicked alcohol or cigarettes they still displayed a deep unwillingness to let go of the need to make life hard. This is a time in evolution when we have the opportunity to have a natural, organic good time. We stress natural and organic because many people associate having a good time with artificial stimulants and depressants. That's cheating, and it costs. The real trick is to adjust your deepest intentions so that you can have a good time while going about the basic processes of life and love. Commitment 6 can be a crucial move toward enjoyment for you and your loved ones.

Goal setting takes on greater importance after you have embraced the six major co-commitments. Part of the process of having successful relationships is harmonizing your personal goals with the goals of those around you. However, many of us have never consciously figured out what our goals are, nor have we found out what people around us want. When you practice the thirty-four activities in part 2 you will find that the activities involving goal setting cause great leaps forward in your relationships. When you know what you want, when you find out what others want, and when you harmonize the two, you are greatly propelled toward reaching those goals.

Step Two: Learning to Love Yourself

A co-committed relationship can exist only between two whole people. One hallmark of wholeness is the ability to love yourself. In the realm of love, a paradox exists: you can effectively love others only when you can love yourself. If you cannot love yourself, you will try to fill the void of your own lack of self-love with the love of others. You will tend to demand from others what you cannot give yourself. This demand places an unfair burden on those around you. It makes you a bottomless pit; no matter how much love they give, it is never enough. The same problem exists if you try to give love to other people who do not love themselves. You will turn yourself inside out loving them, but it will not help. We all must learn to give ourselves the love we want. Then other people can love us and it will feel satisfying because it is not filling a void. It becomes love dancing with itself.

Why do we not love ourselves? There are several prominent reasons, the first being that until recently it was thought to be sinful to appreciate your self. If you were not actively obsessing on your weaker points and berating yourself for your imperfections, you were simply not taking advantage of the opportunity. Now, however, we define self-hate as neurotic, part of the problem, but it was not long ago that it was considered the royal road to self-improvement: if you applied enough self-loathing you might motivate yourself to do better.

Our childhood experiences of love often play a role in later ability, and inability, to love ourselves. Ideally, we would be loved and wanted from conception on through childhood, and this external love would gradually become our internalized sense of love and respect for ourselves. Unfortunately, according to one survey, over 60 percent of us are unplanned and over 45 percent are unwanted from the moment of conception. Of course, many parents who conceive unplanned and unwanted children love them anyway. But others do not. Developing a sense of self-love is difficult enough, but it is even harder if we grew up in an atmosphere where our very existence was not appreciated.

For many of us, love was conditional. It depended on how we looked, or how we threw the ball, or how we danced the ballet. Expectations were high, and we often failed to meet them. Later, this conditional love becomes internalized and we apply it to ourselves. We set impossibly high goals and feel bad most of the time because we have not met them. Love becomes a reward, something we give ourselves only if we have done well. True self-love is not conditional. It is there whether we are being good or bad, strong or weak, performing up to par or falling on our faces. In order to love ourselves we need to learn to separate our selves from our actions. If we wait to love ourselves until we have performed well, we are using love like a dolphin trainer uses a sardine. Plus, there will always be aspects of our actions that are unlikable. Learning to love yourself does not mean that you give up working to change negative aspects of your behavior. It means that you make a distinction between your self and your actions. Love your self deeply and uncritically. Continuously monitor your acts to see if they are bringing positive consequences to you and those around you.

True self-love is not conceit. Conceit is trying to prove to yourself and the world that you are all right, after you have become mired in self-hate. True self-love is an ongoing celebration of who you are no matter how well you perform. It is an ability to greet the dark parts of yourself with the same gracious embrace as you greet the light. Love draws no distinctions. It *is*. Love exists outside the normal constraints of time and space. That is why love can heal something in a second that has been bothering you for a decade. If you are angry or afraid, for example, and have never loved yourself for feeling that way, one moment of loving yourself for having those feelings can set you free. Not long ago we worked with a man who said he had not cried in many years. He talked about his hardness and rigidity, and how it had kept him from experiencing love. We asked him where he felt most rigid in his body. He tapped his chest. Kathlyn placed her hand on his chest. "Have you ever just loved yourself for being hard?" she asked. He shook his head. "Then let's do it together," she said. He burst into tears and continued to cry for twenty minutes while we invited him to feel his sadness and to breathe with it.

The beauty of love is that you can grow it yourself. You

do not need to wait until it is put there by someone else. In fact, if you wait around for someone else to love you, you could be in for a long wait. Each of us must take responsibility for sourcing love. We need to find our own way to meet and greet all parts of ourselves with love. You will find in part 2 specific ways to start the process of loving yourself, but never forget that *you* must produce for yourself each moment of love.

It is helpful to set the goal of learning to love yourself as you begin the process of transforming your relationships. Along the way to co-commitment you will have the opportunity to see and feel many aspects of yourself that you may not have known existed. You will be more comfortable if you can greet those parts of yourself with love. If you are willing to see all of life as an expanding series of opportunities to grow in love toward yourself and others, you will have a much smoother journey.

People often have the most difficulty learning to love their feelings. From working with people over the past twenty years, we rank the basic feelings from easiest to hardest to love as follows: sadness, fear, sexuality, anger. Sadness and fear, while troublesome to many people, are relatively easy to love compared to anger and sexual feelings. Often people try to get rid of their anger and other feelings by being angry at them. Obviously this strategy has a major flaw. Ultimately, the only way to come to terms with your feelings is to love them. The act of loving your feelings smooths them out. The technique for doing this is very simple but takes much practice to master. When you experience any feeling, notice the sensations of where you feel it in your body. Is anger a tightness in your neck? Is fear a racy feeling in your chest? Is sadness a dull heaviness in your chest? Notice these as they occur, and love them directly, just as you would love someone or something that is very dear to you.

Our feelings toward our parents cause much unhappiness. It is very hard to let ourselves feel the full range of our feelings toward parents. How can you let yourself be angry at, or sexually attracted to, the people who raised you? But often these taboo feelings are the ones that are keeping you stuck. Your energy is going into hiding those feelings. You will need to do much work on yourself in order to allow yourself to feel those long-put-away emotions that you have in response to your parents.

Learn to Love Your Body

Many people have negative feelings about their bodies. Some of us will love just about anything but our thighs, or our arms, or our eyes. The advertising industry has figured this out to perfection and feeds upon it by selling us something for nearly every square inch. There is certainly nothing wrong with using cosmetics or cosmetic procedures to improve your looks, but if you use these external tools as a substitute for self-love, look out. It is vitally important for mental and physical health that we learn to feel and to love all our feelings, including those about our bodies. If we simply cover up our self-hatred with more cosmetics we are wasting money and digging ourselves a deeper hole from which we must eventually climb.

Step Three: Learning to Feel

Learning to distinguish your feelings from the other swirling masses of information in your body is certainly one of the major steps toward psychological maturity. It is also essential in moving toward creative relationships. Learning to feel your feelings is a radical act, and by doing so you will be overturning centuries of conspiracy against feeling. The poet and seer William Blake two hundred years ago told us that in his time, "Love—sweet love!—were thought a crime." It has only been in the past thirty years that there has been a widespread movement toward psychological health, which has included learning to be in touch with feelings. Although learning to feel your feelings can make you healthier in every possible way, we do not recommend that you do it for this reason. You should learn to feel your feelings with no expectation of reward. If you are committed to being more alive, you will want to know who you are and how you feel. Just for its own sake. Not because it will make you a better spouse or lover or will further your career. Some things are done because they have a payoff, and other things are done simply to nurture the spark of awareness that we each are given. There are grand payoffs to opening up to your feelings, but the only one that is ultimately important is not really a payoff at all: to be more alive.

There is a delicate balance between repressing your feelings and letting them overflow. It is in this narrow zone that psychological health resides. If you shut your feelings out of your awareness you deaden yourself. If you let your feelings spill over inappropriately, you risk social censure and worse. It is now considered necessary to bring our feelings out of the shadows and into the light. Hidden feelings have been implicated in nearly every human ill, from headache to cancer and heart disease. In our therapy practice we have come to see that the act of hiding feelings is perhaps the most crippling component of relationship difficulty. But it is just as important to learn when and where to express your feelings in ways that will be well received.

Give Yourself Time

Learning to feel your feelings is such a delicate art that we recommend giving yourself a lifetime to master it. Befriend your feelings as you would befriend a shy pigeon in the park. If you want to feed the bird, hold out the food in your hand and be patient. Don't run madly after the animal, throwing handfuls of food at it and cursing at it. Many people try to get in touch with their feelings with an urgency that scares away these shy parts of ourselves. There are other barriers to overcome. There is an active conspiracy against your knowing your true feelings. If you can be kept in the dark about how you truly feel you can be manipulated to buy or to believe virtually anything. Just watch TV for one day and you will see in action the machinery of turning feelings into purchases. Feeling lonely? Eat our brand of chocolate. Feeling pain? Here, munch on our brand of pain reliever: "Four out of five doctors recommend it." You are not likely to hear a kindly doctor-actor come on and say: "Feeling pain? Look at the emotions that you are blocking that are causing the pain. Feel them and notice that your pain is likely to go away. If it doesn't, try one of our pain relievers as a last resort. But whatever you do, don't get in the habit of taking pills instead of looking into the real reasons why you are hurting."

Learn the Core Feelings

One barrier that you will encounter early on is the difficulty in knowing what the fundamental feelings are. In our work we have found that there are only a few core feelings. These are sadness, fear, anger, joy, excitement, and sexual feelings. Other common feelings, such as guilt, boredom, anxiety, and depression are actually mixtures of the basic feelings or responses to one of the core feelings. For example, the Gestalt therapist Fritz Perls said that anxiety is "excitement without the breath." When people remember to breathe into their fear, their anxiety often turns into excitement. We often tell our clients that fear is frozen fun. People often get the most afraid just before they are about to step out into the creative unknown, into a new possibility. Fear mobilizes your body for action, but if you do not take action the energy curdles in your body.

Depression is often the outcome of long-repressed anger. Guilt is a mixture of anger and fear. Boredom is a sleepy feeling that comes from keeping your true feelings repressed. All of these feelings can be felt and loved. Love is deeper than any of the core feelings. It can embrace all feelings. Even self-hate can be loved. We can say this with certainty because every week we sit with people while they work their way down through the surface feelings of boredom and depression to contact their deep, core feelings of rage and fear. But they do not stop there. If they persist, they find love at the bottom of everything. That is why we say that any feeling, fully felt, leads to love. A courageous woman, age twenty-seven, illustrated this principle for us. Her symptoms were overwhelming sleepiness and boredom, both of which were interfering with her work. She had recently gone to work for a new boss, who seemed to trigger the feelings. She explored the specific sensations of the boredom and sleepiness and found that the underlying emotions were anger and fear. "Who does your boss remind you of?" we asked. "My brother!" she screamed. As the catharsis unfolded, she relived her sexual abuse at the hands of her brother. Over the next few sessions she contacted all the old, deep rage, powerlessness, and fear of being twelve years old again. But she did not stop there. As she opened up to her deepest feelings, she found a new love for herself and for all of her feelings. She had not been able to love herself because she was stuck in the surface feelings of boredom and sleepiness. And then more emerged: she began to feel spontaneous waves of forgiveness for her brother. We encouraged her to share her rage and fear and forgiveness with her brother by letter and phone, and she followed through on it. Her courage forced him to look at the way he had treated all the women in his life. He experienced growth in this area, and our client developed a new and healthy relationship with him.

Separate Your Feelings from Your Parents' Feelings

Another barrier to feeling your feelings is distinguishing between your feelings and those of your parents. As children we often take on the feelings of parents and other significant people around us. This problem may even start in utero. For example, in ultrasound films, fetuses have a startle reaction when their mothers take a puff off a cigarette. They also have a startle reaction when their mothers *think* of having a cigarette. This fact has alarming implications. What if we are registering Mother's emotional changes from the very beginning? Unless we learn to distinguish our feelings from others', we are condemned to a life of experiencing other people's emotions. Your feelings are responses to experience. You have the experience of being attacked by a gorilla, and your response is fear and flight. However, your sensitive body can register someone else's feelings—*their* responses to *their* experience. In our therapy practice we have collected hundreds of examples of feelings that troubled our clients that turned out not to be the result of their personal experience at all. It was actually Mother or Father's sadness or anger or fear they were experiencing. It is important to recognize and open up to the full range of feelings, whether or not they were sourced by your personal experience. The feelings are yours now—you have taken them on indirectly. If you feel it, it's yours. But finding out that you have been troubled by someone else's feelings can be extremely liberating, and we have often seen great weights lift off people when they made this connection.

Be with Your Feelings

Possibly the most important skill you can learn about your feelings is to be with them. Think about it for a moment: we learn to do just about everything else but be with our feelings. We learn not to feel them at all, or to express them inappropriately, or to eat or smoke or drink to get rid of them, but we have no training in simply being with them. When you are feeling sad, how many friends do you have who will say: "Let yourself feel that sadness fully. Just be with it for a little while." If you have friends like that, hang on to them, because they are giving you a rare gift. Many people come to us with problems that clear up just by our giving them permission to feel their feelings.

Give Yourself Permission to Feel

For example, a man came in just before the holidays feeling very depressed. In talking with him it became clear that he was doing everything but feeling his feelings. He was rushing around doing things for the family, going to and throwing parties—in short, the whole holiday scene. In his busy-ness he was trying to escape some old feelings that were coming up. In an earlier marriage he had been left by his wife just before the holidays, and his father had died shortly thereafter. He had rushed into the holidays and then into another relationship without ever being with his loss and grief until it reached an organic completion. "Why do I have to deal with these feelings from the past?" he asked. "I'm happy in the relationship I'm in now—so how come I'm so depressed?" The past has a way of cropping up when you think you have successfully shut it out. We encouraged him to let himself be with those feelings he was trying to avoid. Sadness poured out of him, and finally he was able to contact anger beneath the sadness. It was letting himself feel the anger that cleared out his depression. He had been sitting on his anger for years, having never expressed it to anyone since those grief-stricken holidays five years before. Every holiday season he felt sad but never knew why and never did anything about it. Finally, his body would not let him get away with it anymore and went into depression.

Learn That You Can Feel Without Acting on Your Feelings

Learning that you can feel your feelings without having to act on them is extremely important, particularly in regard to anger and sexual feelings. For example, many of us think that if we let ourselves feel our sexual feelings we are required to act on them. This causes us to repress much sexual feeling that we could let ourselves enjoy. Human beings are here because of several million years of sexy ancestors. If you start to have sexual feelings, you don't have to act them out if you don't want to, or if it would be inappropriate to do so. You can be with the feelings until they pass, as they always will if you let yourself feel them. The same is true for anger. We have heard many clients say that they cannot open to their anger because if they did, they would kill someone. It is important that these clients learn to feel their anger and to find creative, healthy ways to express it.

Locate Your Feelings in Your Body

Probably the best way to deal with your feelings is to locate them in your body. Feeling your emotions as body sensations takes much of the scariness out of them. Feelings are always located somewhere: a tightness in the throat, a quivery sensation in the solar plexus, a heaviness in the shoulders. But until you pinpoint the feeling as a body sensation it can seem monstrous, bigger than you are. In fact, the first key move in releasing yourself from the grip of a feeling is to locate it in time and space. We often have our clients translate their vague complaints into clear and specific descriptions of their feelings. A man came in talking of depression. Within a few minutes he was able to describe it as "a weighty, burdened feeling, like a yoke on my shoulders." This type of description is extremely helpful. Depression is a concept, while "a weighty, burdened feeling" is the way he actually experiences it. By going beyond the level of concepts and finding out how you actually experience your feelings, you are in a much better position to free yourself from their grip. In this man's case, his next step was to open up to what the burden was that he had been carrying. If he had remained only at the concept level, without tuning in to how his body was experiencing the depression, he might not have moved so fast to relieve it. So often breakthroughs come right after people have let themselves feel and sense their emotions in their bodies. It is as if the universe has arranged it so that we cannot move forward before we let ourselves be where we are.

Let Yourself and Others Go Through Complete Energy Cycles

In relationships, one of the most important skills to master is the art of letting yourself and those around you experience their feelings to completion. Feelings have cycles, just as other phenomena of nature. Like a thunderstorm, which has its prelude, its peak, and its postpassion calm, feelings come through us and go. If we hold our feelings lightly, they pass on through with little ado. But many of us learn a habit of interrupting ourselves and others in midcycle. Interfering with feeling-cycles throws the energy system out of kilter, leading to a pervasive sense of disquiet. In working with couples, we have frequently been struck by how seldom people are able to let each other experience their feelings to completion. She will begin to cry; he will say "Please don't cry." He will open up to his fear; she will rush in to make it all better. Perhaps the intentions are well meaning, but the results are unfortunate. By preventing others from feeling their feelings to completion, we cheat them out of a profound human experience. We all need to know that it is okay to be all of who we are; this requires that we be willing to open up to the true intensity of our feelings.

The truly helpful person will assist others to feel all of their feelings all of the way. When our partners are sad we will not say, "Don't cry," but, "Let yourself feel as sad as you are." When our partners are scared we will encourage them to contact their fear deeply and stay with it until it dissolves. Just as we can let ourselves feel our own feelings to completion, we can support others in letting their feelings run their organic course. You will be surprised that when you allow yourself to feel a given feeling, it usually does not last long. Repress it, or interrupt yourself in the middle of it, and it will usually last much longer.

Figure Out What You Want

Another category of human experience is our *wants*. Learning to know what you actually want is an important part of moving toward co-commitment. Beneath all our feelings, and certainly beneath all our complaints, are things that we want. There is as much of a conspiracy against figuring out what we want as there is against knowing how we feel. People who know what they want are not easily manipulated, and, as we have pointed out, many of society's institutions have a strong interest in manipulating you. Several thousand times we have asked adults in therapy to think about what they want in a given situation. Although it was almost always something quite simple that they wanted, in at least two-thirds of the occasions the person had considerable difficulty figuring it out. A breakthrough often occurs just by asking ourselves what we want, regardless of how long it takes to come up with an answer. Don't give up if you come up dry the first few, or few dozen, times you ask yourself what you want. In counseling people, we often start by inviting them to ask themselves about extremely basic wants: Would you like a drink of water? Do you want to sit on the chair or on the couch? Do you want to stretch? Once the person says, "Yes, I want a drink of water," we can explore how he or she found that out.

The reason why we have so much trouble knowing what we want became clear to us one day when we were having lunch in Berkeley. A mother was having lunch at the table next to us with her twin boys, age four or five. The twins were eating hamburgers. One ate half of his and said that he was full and did not want any more. The other finished all of his and said he wanted another one. There is a simple solution to this problem: give the other half of the burger to the other kid! But no, too easy. Mom said furiously to the full child, "You're going to eat every bite of that hamburger or you're never going to get another one as long as you live!" To the child who had finished his she said, "You're a pig." This event is a microcosm of how we lose touch with what we want.

Two of our therapy clients had been at odds for over a week. The conflict had begun on a Friday night, over what kind of restaurant to go to for dinner. There were two stages to the conflict, and both of them illustrate key problems in figuring out what we want. John said, "I don't care where we eat. Where would you like to eat?" Margaret said, "I don't know. Wherever you'd like." Part of their co-dependence was to go along with whatever the other one wanted.

This habit is dangerous, because all of us have wants, and we need to know how to access them. At any rate, the habit broke down in this situation, because neither one of them wanted to figure out what he or she wanted. The first stage of the argument broke out at this point, with each of them criticizing the other for not taking the lead in deciding on a restaurant. Finally this part of the conflict ran out of steam, and both agreed to think of a restaurant. Margaret chose Chinese, while John wanted Italian. Margaret, exercising one of her co-dependent strategies, quickly said that Italian was all right with her. Her programming was to submerge what she wanted in favor of John's wants. This time John objected, though. He called her on her pattern of going along with his wants, and soon they were off and running again. After a while they both decided to stick with their original wants. In a huff, they stormed out and ate at separate restaurants, alone. Not only did they not enjoy their meals, but the fight was still in progress over a week later. In their counseling session we asked them to come up with two creative solutions to the situation that were new in terms of their prior experience. With a bit of coaching, they hit upon these solutions. First, they could have decided to go to separate restaurants in a friendly and mutually supportive way. In other words, they could have done what they did anyway, but without conflict. The second solution was, we thought, brilliant. They could have gone to a Chinese restaurant for one course and to an Italian for the second. Neither of these solutions came forth in the heat of the argument, because their unconscious agreement was that wants were a source of conflict in their relationship.

In the early stages of our own relationship we had to deal with this issue on numerous occasions. It seemed to take us about a year to get the message that it was safe to open up to and express our wants with each other.

GAY: My pattern was to make all the decisions in all situations. When I met Kathlyn I had been successful for quite a few years and was used to always being the boss. However, I was beginning

to wake up to wanting an absolutely equal relationship with a woman, and I knew that the "I'm
the boss" program had to be replaced.

KATHLYN: Gay's pattern interacted perfectly
with mine (don't they always!), because my program was to always go along with what the man
wanted, but to collect resentment about it. I also
got away with not having to do the work of figuring
out what I actually wanted. I had grown up with
a powerful father and two extremely bright brothers, so my programming definitely did not include
acting independently of what men wanted.

GAY: When Kathlyn and I got together, I wrestled with this issue a lot. Sometimes I would find
myself automatically making all the decisions
about what we would do, where we would go, what
movies or restaurants to go to. Then I would catch
myself and ask Kathlyn, "What do *you* want?"

KATHLYN: And I would blank out. I had no idea
what I wanted. I would stall around and try to
manipulate Gay into saying what he wanted. But
frequently he would ask me again. At first I was
confused, even mad sometimes. After all, it's his
job to figure out what I want! After a while,
though, I understood that he was genuinely interested in knowing what I wanted. After about a year
and a lot of practice I began to be able to access
what I wanted fairly easily, although I can still slip
back into my old pattern now and then.

It is vitally important that you learn how to know what
you want. If you look deeply into any conflict area in your
life, you will find that there is something you want that
you probably have not expressed. Why we do not say what
we want is another issue, to be covered in Step Five. For
now, suffice it to say that we have often been punished for
expressing our wants, and we have been brainwashed to
want what people tell us to want. There is little or no training given anywhere in life on how to tune in to what *you*
actually want.

Step Four: Claiming Creativity

All the seven steps are key movements toward co-commitment, but this one is a sine qua non. If you took this step and none of the others, you would be able to have co-committed relationships. But without this step you could do all the others and still never make it to co-commitment. Claiming creativity is the act of taking 100 percent responsibility for creating things the way they are. Claiming creativity is when you switch from being a victim to being the source of what is happening to you. Claiming creativity is when you drop a power struggle with someone and take full responsibility for the problem, *regardless of whether the other person takes responsibility for it.* Co-dependence ends the moment you interrupt an argument and say: "I'm willing to own how I have created this situation in my life." Co-commitment begins the moment the other person says: "I'm also willing to find out how *I* have created it." Co-dependence is two people fighting over who is responsible. Co-commitment is two people agreeing that each is 100 percent responsible. Many people do not realize that in a relationship between two people there is 200 percent responsibility to be divided between them. When two people fight over the division of 100 percent responsibility, a power struggle is inevitable. A 50–50 division will not do it; 100–100 will.

We have never met a happy person who had not learned this step well. Every couple we know who has moved to co-commitment has learned this step, often after great struggle. It seems so simple: You create what happens to you. But otherwise-intelligent people often mount a titanic struggle against getting the message. They take on a belligerent tone and say: "What about the Jews? Did they create the Nazis? What about abused children? Do they create Daddy coming home drunk and beating them up?" "Of course not," we say, "but are you willing to be responsible for your life regardless of what the Nazis did? Are you going to keep avoiding responsibility for *your* life because of

Nazis and abused children?" Life is full of random events. The abused two-year-old does not create Daddy getting drunk and does not cause Daddy to perpetrate the abuse. But later in life, this same child absolutely must stop using the events of the past as a way of avoiding responsibility for his present life. We have to take responsibility *now*, and not get caught up in whether we were responsible back then.

Holding on to the victim position is one of the most seductive traps life has to offer. It seems so real! The moment you slip into victim you actually begin to see the world that way. And in the victim position you attract friends who are fellow victims. A network is born, each member of which supports the others for their victimhood. In a relationship, what is required is for both people to look into how they have mutually created any troublesome situation. To look for fault is to slip into victimhood. It is a heroic move to stay out of victimhood, because the tendency to feel sorry for ourselves is deeply ingrained. To claim creativity means that you are courageous enough to overthrow a lifetime of conditioning. It is much easier to point the finger away from rather than toward yourself. In addition, many of us have grown up equating responsibility with blame. Assuming responsibility becomes associated with making ourselves wrong. To avoid the pain of being wrong, we project blame back outside ourselves.

Projection

Projection is the act of denying that you are creating the experience you are having. Instead of acknowledging that you are the source, you get caught up in who "did it" to you. By the end of our first year in practice, we were amazed by the amount of projection that occurs in relationships. We developed the view that projection is the major cause of relationship conflict. This view has been strengthened by twenty years of work with people: Look into any struggle and you will find projection. And the people who most resist taking responsibility are those who are the most obvious and persistent in creating the same patterns over and over! We worked with one man who had been left by a number of women because of his threats and abusiveness. He came in pleading victim: "These women! You just can't trust 'em." When we invited him to take responsibility for this pattern, he became furious and roared, "You're making it sound like *I'm* some kind of angry person." It was impossible not to laugh.

Projection comes in several forms. The most common is seeing in someone else a feeling that is actually going on in you. You fail to acknowledge an upsurge in general sexual feeling in yourself, then suddenly notice that your partner has a wandering eye. You fail to make moves toward freedom, then become obsessed with how much your partner limits your freedom. Another form of projection is to attribute to an external source something that is actually an internal process. "He made me furious," we may say, when in reality "I'm furious" is the truth of the matter. Even if you can get two dozen friends to agree that he really did "make" you furious, what is the payoff? Happiness is projected onto external sources, as the advertising industry figured out a long time ago. A friend of ours put it well: "I thought I would be happy if I lost twenty pounds and had a better job. So I lost twenty pounds and got my dream job. Guess what—I still wasn't happy."

The Way Out of Projection

There is only one way out of projection. Co-commitment begins when each person claims 100 percent responsibility for creating everything that goes on in the relationship. The negative and the positive are both claimed by both people. In an argument the question becomes: How am I creating this conflict, and how can I give and receive more positive energy? The question is not: Why is he or she doing this to me?, or: Why isn't he or she more fun?

At this point you might be asking: Is everything projection? Aren't some things real? Isn't it sometimes really only one person's fault? In fact, sometimes one person can be running an old, unconscious program while the other person is relatively clear. If the second person stays clear and does not become entangled in the other's game, the issue usually resolves itself quickly. But what often happens is that both people get entangled in the issue. In any case, it never does any good to think that you are not involved. If you are involved, admit it. You might as well start claiming creation as soon as possible, thereby avoiding the potential of an ugly power struggle. If you want to have competition in your co-committed relationship, why not compete about who can take responsibility fastest?

Co-Dependents Take Too Much Responsibility, and the Wrong Kind

Co-dependents often fall into the trap of taking more than their share of responsibility. Instead of taking 100 percent and demanding that others take 100 percent, co-dependents often take 200 percent. While this may look well-meaning to the untrained eye, it is actually a major disservice to those in relationship with the co-dependent. The co-dependent takes responsibility from a position of victimhood. It is not clean, true responsibility, because it is in the service of disempowering others. Instead of demanding that others be 100 percent responsible, the co-dependent says: "You're not capable of being fully human, so I'll do your share for you." Taking too much responsibility is as much of a co-dependent pattern as taking too little.

We worked with a woman who exemplified this pattern to the maximum. She had made a considerable fortune by starting several businesses, so she had plenty of money to finance her unconscious loving. Taking too much responsibility permeated her life, from her personal relationships to her business associates. She complained bitterly and often about how irresponsible her husband and grown children were, but she gave each of them a very generous monthly allowance. She supported both of her parents. Her father had a drinking problem that resulted in numerous indiscretions; her solution was to increase his allowance and bail him out each time. Dismantling her network of co-dependence took the better part of two years of conscientious work on her part. Eventually she got everyone on their own or supported at a reasonable level.

The following example shows how a couple got into a classic power struggle, based entirely on projection, and then got out of it by claiming creation. Jonathan was having a midlife crisis but had not seen it as such. He was unaware that other men around age forty get a sudden urge to buy a motorcycle, go out with teenage girls, and run off to Tahiti. He was bored with his job and full of sexual feelings for other women. His crisis was inspired partly by his unwillingness to confront death, a key psychological issue that people often face around forty. He projected it all on his wife, who was also going through a vulnerable time. She was trying to decide whether to take the risk of going back to school after being at home while the children were growing up. To Jonathan, Sara looked boring, sexually uninteresting, and concerned primarily with the repair of appliances and bathroom fixtures. To Sara, Jonathan looked like her oppressor, the guy who had enslaved her at home for twenty years. She was projecting onto him her fear of going back to school. The more they entrenched themselves in their projections, the deeper their alienation became. Finally they made the courageous move of coming in for counseling. When invited to take 100 percent responsibility for creating the struggle, they were nonplussed. No, Sara argued, it actually *is* his fault! No, Jonathan argued with equal passion, it really *is* her fault. They had been in projection so long that they could not even begin to see it.

Several sessions later they had a breakthrough moment. Jonathan saw that he was bored with his own life and had fallen into victimhood. From that position it looked like Sara was the cause of his boredom. Sara owned her fear of going out into the world and dropped her projection of Jonathan-as-oppressor. They became willing to support each other for going deeper into their respective feelings, finding out how they had come to feel that way. Jonathan realized that he was deeply afraid of dying, because he had not really risked living to his true potential. Sara saw that her fear of stepping out into the world was part of a lifelong pattern of being afraid in new situations. Once they stopped projecting and began taking responsibility, the intimacy came back into their relationship. Sexual feeling was rekindled and they became excited about communicating with each other again. They had a lot of work to do on themselves, but the process became fun.

Responsibility Has Risk and Power

Claiming creation is the hardest step for most people to take. Even in healthy people there are often subtle, hidden pockets of victimhood tucked away in areas of their personalities. These areas are revealed under the stress of relationship difficulty. To take responsibility again requires a real step of courage and faith. We wonder: "If I take responsibility for this issue will the other person jump on me and say, 'Ha—I knew it was your fault all along. Now you've admitted it.'" Acknowledging responsibility *is* a risk, because responsibility carries power. Power belongs to the people who take responsibility; it flows to those who claim creation. There is no power in victimhood. In relationships, when one person claims creation there is a radical power shift. If the other person will also take responsibility, the power balances out at 100 percent each. But if the other person won't claim creation, the resulting imbalance can be volatile. It is our experience that this volatility is healthy—it shakes up things in the relationship that ought to be shaken. But you should know that claiming creation is an action with true power. Be prepared for life to look very different once you get out of the trunk and into the driver's seat.

Step Five: Learning to Tell the Microscopic Truth

Telling the truth helps catapult you into co-commitment. Once you are there, it keeps the relationship running smoothly. If you do not tell the truth, you have an entanglement, not a relationship. We all have our reasons for not telling the truth, but they all add up to the same result: co-dependence. Following are some of the reasons people in relationships gave us for lying to each other. See if you have used any of these in your life.

- He gets mad at me when I tell him the truth.
- She just wouldn't understand.
- I simply don't know how to tell the truth—I get confused.
- I've been lying so long I don't know what the truth is anymore.
- I get a kick out of lying. It's a turn-on to get away with it.

Withholding the truth is a form of lying. It leaves us in a state of suspension. The arrested communication often takes the relationship off center. Physically, the act of withholding can show up in several ways. See if any of the following nonverbal symptoms are familiar.

- Tight throat
- Clenched jaw
- Headaches at the temples or back of the neck
- Held or shallow breath
- Tension areas between the shoulder blades or in the forearms
- Fluttering sensations in the stomach
- Evasive eye contact

We have a lot to learn about telling the truth. Why?

Picture yourself saying, in a very matter-of-fact voice, the following things to your mother or father:

- I'm a deeply sexual being.
- I have a lot of sadness and anger in me.
- Sometimes I hurt a lot.

Could you have done that at age thirteen? Could you do it now? If so, you are lucky and have a rare relationship. We use this example because most of us learn to lie in our relationships with our parents. We learn early on that certain things, if said, cause us great inconvenience. We get censured, laughed at, or beaten up. We take a mental snapshot: Truth = Pain. Pretty soon it doesn't even consciously occur to us to tell the whole truth. If you escaped childhood with an easy ability to tell the truth, you are blessed and in the minority. Most of us carry into our adult relationships a reluctance to telling the whole truth. It takes a great deal of loving work on ourselves to become free and easy with the truth.

People who were not punished for telling the truth in childhood may still have trouble in this area. They simply do not know themselves deeply enough to tell the truth at a meaningful level. They cannot say "I'm scared" because they don't know their feelings well enough to be sure about them. These people do not have to overcome a reluctance, but they do need a lot of practice in distinguishing what is true from what is not, so that they can communicate the truth in a meaningful way.

How can you know what is true? Our definition: the truth is that which absolutely cannot be argued about. For example, take the statement "John is a jerk." It is clearly not true, because at least John would probably argue about it. In any case, it *could* be argued about and therefore is not true. If you say, "I'm angry at John," that is much more likely to be true. Even closer to the truth: "I'm scared of that part of me that John represents." It would be hard to argue about it because only you could possibly know whether you are angry or scared. If what you say gets an argument response, use this as a signal that you need to go to a deeper level of your truth. In a close relationship, the truth is most likely to be *a clear statement of feeling, of body sensation, or of what you actually did.* Following are some examples.

- I'm scared.
- I'm hurt.
- My shoulders are feeling tight as you talk.
- I have a pain in my chest right now.
- When you told me about the other woman, I felt a wave of nausea and I'm still feeling it.
- I talked to my ex-wife today.

If you draw a response like, "Well, you shouldn't have talked to her!" use this as a cue to go to a deeper level of truth: "I'm feeling guilty that I talked to my ex-wife today," or, "I'm afraid that you're going to be mad at me for talking to my ex-wife today." In any case, you do not have to be concerned about your partner's reaction. Your responsibility is to tell the microscopic truth for its own sake, not to please your partner. Use others' reactions as feedback on how closely you are homing in on the truth. We repeat: The closer you get to the microscopic truth, the less likely it is to cause or perpetuate argument.

Draw a clear and sharp distinction between truth and judgment. Judgment is:

- You're a real bastard.
- You're so stupid.
- You were too harsh on Jimmy today.
- If you would only change, I would feel better.

All these statements are arguable. None is true. Remember, that which absolutely cannot be argued about is the truth.

Draw a distinction also between the intention simply to communicate the truth and additional intentions that ride along as hidden baggage, such as:

- Justifying a position: "I had so much to do today, I just forgot to pick up the laundry."

• Blaming: "It wouldn't have happened if I'd had a little help around here."
• Being a victim: "It's all right, I'll finish the dishes."
• Seeking approval: "I'd like to wear this dress, but I think it makes me look fat. What do you think?"

Disguised intentions are often accompanied by nonverbal cues, such as sighing, looking down, shrugging shoulders, tapping fingers, or pursing lips. If you say something and do not get the response you want, look at your underlying intention. Telling the truth *just* to communicate your internal experience is the only intention that is freeing. For example, if Max comes home and says, "Honey! I got the raise today!" with the intention to prove he's a success, he may be vaguely disappointed when Karen says, "Good, we were expecting it to help with John's tuition." The truth may be, "You know, when I got the raise today, I felt sad, and that surprised me. When I thought about it, I realized that I keep trying to prove I'm good enough. Dad would always just grunt when I brought home a good report card or made varsity."

Betty delayed mentioning to her fiancé, Allan, a telephone conversation she'd had with a former boyfriend. It was just a short conversation and she didn't think it was important. However, she did find herself thinking about telling Allan when she was with him that evening. It kept popping into her mind to mention, but she avoided the thought and it finally went away. Allan even asked her if anything was wrong, and she replied, "No, I'm just tired." Later in the evening she noticed that her throat was dry and she had the beginnings of a headache. She also noticed that she was not feeling particularly close to Allan. She finally realized that she was afraid to tell Allan because he might get angry. So, she overcame her fear and told Allan, who actually did get angry. He accused her of still having sexual feelings for the other man. The situation devolved into a power struggle, with many counteraccusations.

In counseling, we coached them on how to tell the truth to each other. When they slipped into projection or judgment, we asked them to get down to statements that absolutely could not be argued about. Using this criterion, they began communicating the truth:

- I'm sad I didn't tell you earlier.
- I'm afraid you'll leave me.
- I'm more vulnerable with you than I've ever been before in my life, and this brings up more fear that something will go wrong.
- I have an expectation that if I tell you the truth you'll push me away. As I say that, I have a memory of my father pushing me away.

Communications like these end power struggles. These statements are the very stuff of which a co-committed relationship is made: two people being real with each other and taking full responsibility for their feelings. We have seen hundreds of couples who, after ten minutes of this type of truth-telling, pulled their relationships back from the brink of breakup. The truth is always moving, though not always initially palatable.

When people learn to tell the *microscopic* truth, their growth is greatly enhanced. In this context, *microscopic* refers to the deepest and most subtle truth you can see and feel. The microscopic truth is never external; it always refers to truths inside yourself. Following are some examples of microscopic truth from recent sessions.

- I feel a pressure in my upper chest, as if I had just run into a bar.
- I just heard a critical voice in my head saying, "You ought to move more."
- When I moved away from you I saw an image of a large cloud behind my head that I seemed to expand into.
- I feel a big weight on me.
- I feel like something's poking me in the back. As I say that, I feel a lot of energy in my heels, as if I'm digging my heels in. I feel like I'm trying to get away. I can hear my mother's voice telling me how stubborn I am. I feel like I can't go at my own pace.

Notice that each of these statements is simply report-
ing what *is*. None of the statements contains judgments
or criticisms of the speaker or anyone else. When simple,
profound truths like these are spoken, the words have a
luminosity. For example, as the woman who was speaking
the truth of the last statement above, the rest of the therapy
group fell into a hushed, trancelike state.

Here are some statements that are *not* the microscopic
truth.

- When you said that, it made me feel awful.
- You ought to be ashamed of yourself.
- You want hear the truth?—*I'll* tell you the truth. You
are the most self-centered human being in the history of
the human race.

Each of these statements could be turned into the
microscopic truth if the speaker is courageous enough to
open up to a deeper, more personal level.

- I'm feeling nauseated as we speak. (Notice the difference between this statement and the direct cause-and-effect
relationship implied in "When you said that, it made me
feel awful.")

Be very suspicious when you hear yourself making
definite cause-and-effect statements. The people who are
the most sure about who or what is causing their problems
are often the most likely to be projecting. An example: We
worked with a man who came in on an emergency basis
because he was in pain because his girlfriend had left him.
His initial statements were full of the language of victimhood: "Why is she doing this to me? What have I done to
deserve this? She's ruining my life and taking away all my
dreams." First, of course, we supported him while he felt
his pain. Then we had him take a clear look at why this
was happening to him. It emerged that she had left after
about a year of telling him that she was going to leave if
he didn't stop drinking. Finally she left, and only then did
he stop drinking. In his mind he had turned himself into

the victim and her into the perpetrator. He thought that surely she ought to come running back, now that he had quit drinking. But we did not stop there. Upon further exploration it emerged that this pattern had occurred *six times* in past relationships! His pattern had been set in motion when he was in college, when his first true love left him for a professor. To keep from feeling this pain he had started drinking, and twenty years later he was still repeating the pattern. His initial point of view—"She's doing this to me!"—turned out to be exactly the opposite of reality. The truth: he had brought her into his life to play out the perpetrator role in his old drama. She had complied, out of her own background and programming, but it really had nothing to do with her. She had been simply a willing participant in his pattern. This moment of awakening, when we first realize the possibility that we are simply playing roles in each other's drama, has to be one of the most chilling in human life. It is humbling, much different from the righteousness with which we often proclaim our victimhood.

The microscopic truth is never righteous. It is always a clear, specific statement of what is happening inside right here and now. Even growth-oriented people with much communication experience find it a challenge. For example, in a recent group we conducted, made up largely of therapists, we asked that everyone practice telling the microscopic truth. Following are some of the things that came up as we were coaching them on how to do it.

- Speaking in vague generalities: "I guess I feel kinda tight."
- Getting confused: "I don't know what I feel."
- Getting righteous: "That's not just my feeling—that's how my husband actually *is*!"
- Interpreting and psychologizing: "I feel hurt because I never seem to get the love I need from Charlie."
- Justifying: "You'd feel this way too if you had been through what I've been through."

You will have the opportunity to practice telling the

microscopic truth when you do the activities in part 2. Likely you will find it a challenge, but if you do the activities you will get a feeling in your body that you may never have experienced before. Telling the truth brings about a state of lightness and energy in your body that few other things can engender. Hiding the truth blocks energy at a very fundamental, cellular level. When you tell the truth, particularly at the microscopic level, it liberates energy that has been trapped. If this sounds mysterious, you can render it less so by telling the microscopic truth. Once you have tasted the clear, high feeling that is the payoff for telling the truth, you may be hooked, as we have become, on the experience.

One of the hallmarks of an evolved person is the ability to tell the truth with no fear of punishment or expectation of reward. Due to our conditioning, many of us have a deep fear of telling the truth. Conversely, we may want a guaranteed positive payoff if we are going to go to the trouble. In the co-committed relationship, the truth is told for its own sake, for the ongoing purpose of celebrating awareness and life itself.

Of course, you always need to be conscious of timing when telling the truth. Be mindful of your own state of willingness and the receptiveness of others to hear you. If your husband is a great football fan, you may not want to interrupt his viewing of the Super Bowl to tell him about your affair with his best friend. Be aware, however, of the distinction between being conscious of timing and concealing the truth out of fear. We have worked with many people who put off telling the truth for years because they "couldn't find the right time."

Step Six: Keeping Your Agreements

Keeping agreements is essential to co-committed relationships. If you and your partner cannot keep agreements with each other, the cost will be very high. Broken agreements have played a role in the problems of almost all of the troubled couples we have counseled. Always, aliveness is diminished when agreements are not kept.

Each broken agreement leaches energy from within us and from the relationship itself. Energy in a relationship depends on fairly delicate communication. Break an agreement and you drop a brick on this fragile structure you have built. In close relationships it does not matter whether the agreement is big or little: break one and it lessens aliveness. Following are some examples from our recent cases.

• A man agrees to tell his wife whenever he has contact with his former girlfriend. The agreement has been made because she has noticed that he acts peculiarly after he has seen the girlfriend. Nevertheless, he still sees her now and then. When confronted, he at first denies it, then confesses. A month is spent sorting out the various hassles.

• A couple agrees on certain chores that each will do around the house each week. Both repeatedly "forget," causing many arguments.

• After repeated episodes of cold dinners and an angry family, a man agrees to call if he is going to be late from work. After spending an (expensive) hour of therapy reaching this agreement, he breaks it the next day.

• A woman agrees to be monogamous. A period of calm ensues, then she finds herself in bed with a co-worker. She later says that she does not even really like the man, but she felt it was something she "just had to do."

What could be going on here? We were at first mystified by the amount of wasted energy in relationships around the issue of broken agreements, then we realized that many people are so terrified of closeness and the radical aliveness of a co-committed relationship that they will do virtually anything to mess it up. When given the choice between drama and actual closeness, many of us choose drama. If your commitment to uproar is greater than your commitment to intimacy and co-commitment, you will find a way to stop the aliveness in your relationship. There is hardly a better way to create uproar than to "forget" to do something you have agreed to do.

For many people, breaking agreements is a way of communicating hidden anger. If you hold on to anger at someone, your unconscious mind will cause you to forget to keep your agreements with that person. For example, Barry had a reputation for showing up late for meetings with colleagues, his wife, and others. When confronted with this behavior, he frequently reacted with anger and justification. Finally, he saw that he seldom arrived late if the activity was something he wanted to do. It became clear that he had a habit of making agreements he did not want to make, feeling angry about it, stifling the anger, then breaking the agreement as a way of discharging the anger. Then he could righteously defend his position, taking the attention away from the fact that he had broken the agreement.

A mark of evolution is how you react when confronted with having broken an agreement. The more evolved you are, the more quickly you will simply acknowledge it. At more primitive stages of evolution you will tend to justify, change the subject, get angry, or use some other ploy. They never work, because only when you acknowledge a broken agreement can you begin to find out why you broke it. The person who is committed to aliveness will always be scrupulous about keeping agreements.

What happens when you absolutely cannot keep an agreement? For example, you agree to be at a meeting at 2:00, but you show up at 2:20 because you got caught in traffic. What do you do? Tell the microscopic truth! For example: "I'm late. I got caught in traffic. I feel angry and frustrated and also scared that you might be mad at me." There is a lot of truth packed into these three sentences. Can you communicate this kind of truth to those around you? Learning to keep agreements is mainly a matter of courage and practice: courage to get started and practice for the next thirty or forty years. The reward in increased aliveness will be evident in your body and in the heightened creativity of your relationships.

Step Seven: Learning to Live in a State of Continuous Positive Energy

Steps One through Six will put you into co-commitment. Step Seven will allow you to rest comfortably there.

Due to the way energy pulsates throughout the universe, much of life has a pulsatory quality. For example, animals go through a pulsation of activity and sleep each day. The pulsations of the heart and lungs are a continuous reminder that life is pulsation. Human beings have another pulsation that is unique to us but is absolutely *unnecessary*. This pulsation is to feel good, then to bring yourself down in some way. How does this pulsation come about?

Early in life many of us get an association between positive energy and pain. It can happen in many ways. Here is an example involving Gay's daughter. "We were riding our bikes back from an outing to the swimming pool when Amanda was six. It had been a fun father-daughter afternoon, and both of us were feeling happy and close. Amanda was also proud of her ability to take such a long ride with me. On our way home Amanda started singing a song that she had just learned in first grade. Showing off for me, she was singing at the top of her lungs when she took her eyes off the road and hit a pothole and fell off her bike. She only had a few scrapes and bruises, but I think her tears were mainly because she had been so happy one moment and so unceremoniously dumped the very next." Another mental snapshot was created: Happiness is followed by pain.

Childhood is full of events like the following.

• We are trying out something new and we hurt ourselves doing it.
• We are playing "doctor" and get caught, with much subsequent uproar.
• We are playing happily when suddenly we get punished for something we did yesterday.
• We are excited about some upcoming event and some

authority figure says, "Don't count your chickens before they hatch."

We build up a program in our minds that says: Don't let yourself feel too good. If you feel good, something bad is likely to happen. Better keep the brakes on, even while your foot is on the accelerator.

Consciously, our parents' intention was for us to be happy and not to be disappointed. But their unconscious intention was for us not to feel too good about ourselves. Too much positive energy can upset the delicately balanced structure of many families. Parents and other authority figures have a vested interest in the status quo; they have learned to live at a modest level of positive energy, and we must match that energy.

Later in life we develop a pulsation based on these early experiences. The pulsation is: feel good, feel bad, feel good, feel bad. Out of that early association between positive energy and pain, we develop a program that causes us to bring ourselves down after we have felt good. Depending on the severity of this program's grip on us, we may bring ourselves down after feeling good for a few seconds, a few minutes, or a few days. An excellent example of how this works came up in our therapy practice not long ago. A woman in her late forties was working on her anger and sadness over her recent divorce. She had been feeling victimized by the event, but after letting herself feel those feelings she found a deeper awareness awakening. She was actually enjoying the independence and freedom of not having to answer to anybody. She had gone directly from parents' house to husband's house at eighteen, without ever tasting life on her own. She said: "My friends have all told me that I should feel awful about being alone, and I do a lot of times, but I actually love it, too. I wrote the first poem the other day that I have written since I was a teenager. Something is beginning to come back that has been gone a long time." We asked her to pause and let herself experience that good feeling. She was able to do so for less than ten seconds. A cloud suddenly came over her face. "What just happened in your mind to cause you to stop feeling good?" we asked. "I just heard my mother's voice telling me not to count on feeling good." We asked her exactly what her mother's voice had said. "She actually said, 'Just wait—start feeling good and the bottom will drop out.'" This is a clear example of the kinds of messages we use to keep ourselves from feeling good. A little bit of positive energy creeps in—ten seconds' worth—and we immediately rush in to slap it down.

We have been with people as they sobbed or raged for an hour, but we have seldom seen anyone stay in bliss for longer than a few minutes. Starting in childhood, most of us seem to put a lid on our positive energy in order to stay at the humdrum level of existence necessary to function in the workaday world. It costs us, because we cheat ourselves out of a tremendously heightened range of positive experience. We often ask clients to bring in pictures of themselves at different stages of life. It is often saddening to see how the light disappears from their faces as they learn to live in the world. The preschool picture is often happy and bright, but by high school the person wears an impenetrable mask. By adulthood the face in the picture often looks like that of a robot.

A great deal of careful work is needed to resurrect the ability to live in a state of positive energy. We all know how to feel bad, and we all know how to feel neutral. What we need to learn is how to feel good. Society tells us that we will feel good if we smoke the right cigarette, eat the right chocolate bar, or sip the right liquor. These are costly lies. Feeling good is a natural right, and you can do it all the time, with no artificial stimulants, if you follow a few basic instructions. In a co-committed relationship the central task is to learn to stay in positive energy for longer and longer periods of time, with the ultimate goal of living continuously in a state of positive energy. There are specific skills you can learn for doing just that. They are important, perhaps crucial, for the full development of ourselves. These skills are the subject of the next chapter.

FIVE

The Only Problem You Need to Solve in a Co-Committed Relationship

See if you recognize this pattern: You are feeling close to your partner, happy and having fun. Suddenly out of nowhere you are embroiled in a fight. Where did it come from? Why did it happen right then?

See if you have experienced a related pattern: You are at home alone, feeling happy and comfortable. Suddenly your mind is full of worry thoughts, everything from the condition of the world to the condition of your carpets. Why right now, when you were feeling so good?

The culprit is the Upper Limits Problem.

We are programmed that we cannot feel good for very long without invoking some negative experience to bring us down. Our programming tells us we must have fun/have a crash, get close/get sick, be close/start a fight. We have an old association between feeling good and pain, so that when we feel good for a little while we find some way to create pain. Most of us cannot be close to others for very long without creating a problem to limit the positive energy. Similarly, we cannot be close and loving with ourselves for more than a few seconds before we find ourselves in pain.

The Upper Limits Problem is the phrase we use to describe this unique human tendency. It is the only problem you have to solve, because in a co-committed relationship you trade in all your former problems for this one: **how to let yourself expand continuously into more positive energy.** When you get close to someone, the positive energy is multiplied beyond what each of you has attained on your own. Due to our past conditioning, we all have a limit on how much positive energy we can tolerate. Go past this limit and an alarm goes off in your unconscious mind. If you do not rest at this point, allowing yourself time to integrate the energy, your unconscious mind will find a way to stop the flow of positive energy. Its strategies can be very primitive: arguments, illness, accidents. It is far better to become adept at noticing when your limit has been exceeded, so that you can consciously find a way to integrate the energy rather than leave the task to your unconscious. It is also to your advantage to find ways of raising the limit daily so that you can tolerate more and more positive energy.

Human beings have been suffering and struggling for millions of years; we are highly skilled at handling negative energy. We believe that at this time in evolution our species is actually creating new channels in ourselves for experiencing positive energy. How to feel good naturally, without chemical assistance, is a new task in evolution. You have come this far in the book with us, so we assume you have made a commitment to positive energy. Now you need to learn how to open additional positive-energy channels.

The Upper Limits Problem is crucial for those in recovery from addictions. The specific effect of any addiction is to limit positive energy. Even cocaine, which is considered a stimulant, is really a depressant in the sense that it blocks your positive energy. It takes your attention off of things you should be paying attention to. Many cocaine addicts with whom we have worked say that they take the drug because it makes them feel up, happy, and confident. In fact, however, the drug actually depresses them, by taking their attention away from looking into why they are not organically up, happy, and confident. The addictive depressants, such as alcohol, obviously function in the same way, but more directly.

A marijuana addict with whom we worked offers a vivid example of how any substance addiction contributes to the Upper Limits Problem. He smoked daily from ages seventeen to thirty, and he made a handsome living from cultivating the herb. When he stopped smoking, all the psychological issues that are appropriate for adolescents to face rushed in on him, twelve years later than normal. Even his body was affected: his beard began to grow, and his voice dropped half an octave. In essence, he postponed adulthood for twelve years. Think of your personal growth as being like climbing a mountain. Some of us, when the climb gets difficult, simply stop and rest. That's the smart choice, but not necessarily the popular one. Others of us handle the pain and pressure by blotting it out with alcohol, while others artificially stoke their energy stores with various kinds of stimulants.

Any addiction—food, drugs, liquor, sex, shopping—always masks deeper, fundamental problems in a relationship. Many of the couples in recovery with whom we work discover several layers of Upper Limits Problems. As their time of sobriety lengthens, they see that they used their addiction as an Upper Limit, but also that they have other problems that serve the same function. For recovering alcoholics, the addiction to liquor is often an attempt to blot out troublesome worry thoughts. The worry thoughts do not go away when they quit drinking; in fact, they often increase for a while. As one recovering alcoholic put it, "I drank to get away from my mind, to escape my anxiety and worry. Drinking then became a bigger problem, which allowed me to focus on it rather than on what I was worried about in the first place. When I quit drinking, all the worry thoughts came back in spades. Then I saw that my worrying was a way I had developed to block my positive feelings toward myself and the people around me. I had never realized why I worried. I thought that was just what you were supposed to do. I saw that I worried to stay in control. If I figured out all the possibilities, I could control myself and everybody around me. My big lightning bolt of learning was that all my worrying and controlling was actually about keeping myself from feeling good. Why? Because I'm worthless and don't deserve it." This man's statement is an eloquent example of a problem that nearly all of us share. We cannot deal with our feelings, so we retreat into our minds. Then we cannot deal with our minds, so we retreat further into an addiction. At the bottom of it all is that we don't think we deserve to naturally feel good about ourselves.

Let's begin by understanding the alternative to the positive/negative pulsation of have fun/crash, get close/have a fight, and so on. Pulsation is here to stay—that's how the universe works—but it does not have to be a positive/negative pulsation. You can install a better program in your mind and body, one that consists of positive/rest, positive/rest, positive/rest. In relationships the program goes like this: get close/rest at the new level, get close/rest at the new level. Instead of bringing yourself down through an argument, an illness, or an accident, you let yourself rest at the new level until it is completely integrated. To accomplish this, you will have to become extremely vigilant in noticing how you bring yourself down. To help you see how you stop your flow of positive energy, we offer examples of some of the more popular ways in which people in relationships bring themselves down.

Deflecting Positive Energy

Many people learn to keep their positive energy down by avoiding it altogether. Deflection is one of the most common means of avoiding positive energy. At a dinner party we witnessed a guest trying to give the hostess a compliment while she tried every means to duck it.

GUEST: The roast is absolutely delicious.
HOSTESS: It's overdone by a mile.
GUEST: Well, I really like it. It's just the way my mother used to cook them.
HOSTESS: This butcher shop isn't half as good as the one I used to go to.

It went on like this for a while, but each time a simple thank-you would have sufficed. When you try to give positive energy to someone who has a habit of deflecting it, you are wasting your time and draining your energy. Don't be surprised if you feel tired and dissatisfied afterward. Deflecting positive energy is a form of narcissism. Notice that the hostess above did not respond to what the guest was saying; she dwelled entirely on her point of view. Perhaps few of your own deflections are so blatant. But if you observe yourself closely you may find subtle ways in which you turn aside positive energy even on an hourly basis.

We have also seen people ignore positive energy as if it had never been there. For example, a man in therapy with his wife complained that she always criticized him and never bolstered his self-esteem. She replied, "There are lots of things I really like about you." He continued talking as if he had not heard her. We challenged him about this and he appeared in fact not to have registered what she had said. His defenses were up so thoroughly that the information did not get through. We played the tape back for him (we were videotaping the session) and showed him the relevant moment. He was surprised that he had not even heard what she had said.

Many opportunities for the exchange of positive energy are lost when people are caught up in their mental processes. A John Lennon song said something to that effect: Life is what is going on all around us while we're busy making other plans. A colleague of ours was once in a group in which a famous trance channeler was speaking profound spiritual truths. The channeler was talking about the necessity of loving ourselves and one another. After the talk, a person in the group said, "Great, let's do it. Let's hold hands around the circle and silently exchange love." At this the channeler became highly agitated and angry, saying that it would be dangerous actually to do what she had been talking about. She began babbling incoherently. The meeting broke up in an uproar, far removed from the lofty words of a few minutes before.

Another form of deflection of positive energy is to stay attached to the past. If you are caught up in a past event you are by definition avoiding the possibilities of the present. A friend of ours went home for the holidays and returned with the following report: "I got to see so clearly how I learned to reject positive energy. There we all were, all four kids, and we had traveled thousands of miles just to give love and attention to Mom. And she did everything possible to reject it. She talked about how wonderful holidays were when she was a child and how bad they are now, she criticized us for things we did twenty and thirty years ago, she criticized my long-dead father for giving her a ring that was too small back in the 1950s, and a bunch of other things that were undoubtedly true but poorly timed. It seemed like every time we would all sit down together she would say or do something that would block the possibility of anything loving or kind happening. It was like a cartoon version of someone rejecting love."

Worry Thoughts

People have a keenly refined ability to worry. Odds are that if you peeked into someone's mind at random, you would find that they were worrying about something. What is interesting to note is that we often worry the most just when we have begun to feel good. We get caught up in the drama of our worries, and our good feelings go out the window. You can watch this process in your mind. Next time you feel really good, notice the thoughts that start creeping in. Many people have told us that within seconds after beginning to feel good their minds start to buzz with

worrisome words and pictures. Worrying may be here to
stay, but we can avoid the mistake of taking these thoughts
seriously. It is the process that is important, not the content. In other words, what we need to notice is when and
where we worry, not necessarily what we worry about.
Nowadays, the information explosion has brought us an
expanding number of things to worry about. If you are so
disposed, you can worry about pollution, nuclear winter,
the greenhouse effect, and the destruction of the rain for-
ests, in addition to the traditional worries such as kids,
mortgages, health, and the vagaries of your major appliances. Some people may think: "Well, I *should* worry about
those things." They get righteous about worrying. They
somehow think that if they worry enough, some productive
action may emerge. In fact, no one has ever drawn a corre-
lation between worrying and effective action. Usually the
opposite is true: worry prevents effective action. Nuclear
winter and your health are best acted upon, not worried
about. In particular, notice if you use worrying about large
or small problems as a way of blocking positive energy.

You may recall the scene in *Annie Hall* where Woody
Allen is running around the bedroom obsessing about the
conspiracy theory of John F. Kennedy's murder. His wife
confronts him on this, accusing him of using this issue as
a way of avoiding getting close. He stops and thinks for a
moment. "You're right," he says. Would that we were
always so congenial about spotting and dropping defenses
to intimacy.

In relationships the same process unfolds. Two people
get close, and positive energy begins to build. Someone's
Upper Limits button is pushed, and a worry is launched
into the atmosphere: "Gee, honey, did you remember to fix
the upstairs toilet?" *Pop!* goes the positive energy balloon.
Once the energy is deflated it is not easy to build it back
up again.

Many people use criticism to slow the flow of positive
energy. When they are beginning to feel good, they think:
"Why did I do that? Shouldn't I have . . .? If only I weren't
so . . . I wish I were like . . ." In relationships, they may use
similar critical behavior to limit the positive energy that is

being exchanged. In our therapy practice we saw a classic example of using criticism to stop good feeling. Wife, after a problem was resolved, moved toward Husband to embrace him. They had hugged for about three seconds when he sniffed and said, "Your hair smells funny." *Pop!* went the balloon. Soon they were embroiled in another hassle. When it was brought to his attention what he had done, he roundly denied that his Upper Limits button had been pushed. "Nope," he said, "I just thought it was my duty to let her know that her hair smelled funny." But his wife thought: "That's what you always do. I get close to you and you pick that time to tell me something that's wrong with me!" We had them try again. They embraced, and we asked them not to say anything but just to feel whatever they felt inside themselves. Ten seconds into the embrace he burst into tears. He cried for a little while, then he said that if he let himself be close to people he was afraid he would be hurt. More than a few seconds of closeness triggered sadness in him, so he found a way to push his wife away. It was easier for him to deal with her anger than to confront his own sadness.

Arguments

The most prevalent, predictable, and rapid way to stop positive energy in close relationships is to have an argument. Here's the way we often hear it in our office: "We had been feeling really close and then out of nowhere we were in a huge fight. Then it took weeks to get over it." The reason more people do not recognize what they are doing is that they confuse content with process. It is seductive to get caught up in the content of an argument. Your adversary in the argument is usually skilled at finding the one thing that will hook you.

Once you are embroiled in the content it is not easy to pay attention to the process. But the process must be noticed. In working on your relationship issues it is vital to be aware of when and where you argue, not what you argue about. Often the content simply serves as a vehicle—

it has no intrinsic meaning. Noticing the process of your arguments is one of the most liberating steps you can take in clearing them up. This is why good therapy is sometimes like good detective work. A couple will come in, totally enmeshed in the content of their argument. Their concerns will be things like who is right, who is wrong, who said what, who did what. Once you are in this game there is no way out. The detective work may reveal that the argument started in bed three nights ago when John asked Sally to make love. Further investigation reveals that they had felt close for a week, and needed to take some space from that closeness. Neither had taken the initiative of asking for space and time off, so their unconscious minds had found a way of making sure they took space. The content of the argument was so juicy and seductive that they did not see the process.

Going Unconscious

You are in essence unconscious when your unconscious mind is running its old programs. You are on automatic pilot, out of touch with your conscious intentions, fully in the grip of an old pattern. Growing up is really about waking up: coming up out of the slumber of your past programming and learning how to get what you really want in the present. Some people react to being awakened with all the grace of a bear jostled out of hibernation.

A dramatic example of going unconscious was brought to us by a successful couple in their midthirties. Their complaints about each other were vague, but they knew they had felt stuck for at least a month. When we tracked down the stuck feeling to when and where it had begun, it turned out that the stuckness had followed a period of intense closeness. In fact, the closeness had been initiated by both of them committing themselves totally to the relationship. A few days of bliss had followed, then they had both gone unconscious. It appeared that their commitment, and the ensuing closeness, had tripped their Upper Limits switches, causing them to go on automatic pilot.

We invited them to tune in to how they were feeling right now. They felt drained, low on energy. As they spoke, she actually yawned. We asked her to follow the yawn, to make it bigger and to open up to the feeling underneath it. She did so, and looked for a moment as if she would pass out. "My jaws are so tense," she said. We invited her to stretch her jaws. Without warning she started screaming; the scream seemed to have been liberated from the stretching of her tight jaws. She then went into a full-blown catharsis of anger and fear. When the emotional release had subsided, she told us that she had relived a terrible memory from age twelve. She was being given nitrous oxide by her dentist and became afraid as the anesthetic took hold. She felt that the drug was releasing her sexual feelings and that she would go crazy if she surrendered to them. She perceived that her dentist was angrily saying, "Open wide! Open wide!" and that if she did she would die. She began hallucinating about her relatives who had been killed in the gas chambers of Nazi Germany.

The awareness that emerged was far more incredible than the most imaginative fiction. Her partner's requests for deeper intimacy had triggered this ancient fear of losing control of herself, and only by being tired and sleepy and stuck could she keep this fear out of her awareness. She realized that if she even took a deep breath the fear would be stirred up. So she breathed very shallowly, and the oxygen starvation kept the feelings at bay but added to her exhaustion. His drama fit hers perfectly. His childhood pattern was to want closeness with his mother, who usually withdrew from him. In his present relationship he asked for more closeness and got it, then found his partner yawning and being exhausted when they were together. Their closeness caused these interlocking programs to roll, and the result was a month of unconsciousness.

This example is extreme, partly because it involved the actual unconsciousness of anesthesia. But every day, in subtle ways, we go unconscious, in thrall to old programs. These patterns from the past take us out of the present, sabotaging our conscious intentions. The only way out is to wake up, to notice how and when we are going on automatic. By noticing the process of going unconscious, it is possible to stay awake and open to positive energy for longer periods of time.

Indulging in addictions is a common way of going unconscious. Many people bring their energy down through overeating or eating foods that are toxic to their bodies. In the process of transforming our own eating habits, we had ourselves tested to find out which foods were and were not strengthening to our bodies. To our surprise, it turned out that the foods to which we were most addicted were also the ones to which we were most allergic. The addictive foods had a weakening effect on our energy systems. By overeating certain foods—ice cream and chocolate were two—we were actually lowering our energy.

Concealing Feelings

When an Upper Limit is approached, your unconscious mind may try to protect you by shutting off feeling. The resulting deadness brings the energy back down to familiar levels. The cost is that you are less alive, both inside yourself and in your relationship. Without access to your feelings, you are broadcasting words but no music. Feelings are the lifeblood of relationship, and they must be nurtured for the relationship to thrive.

For example, Terri found herself inexplicably angry in periods of closeness with Bob. Out of the blue she would start having angry thoughts about things he had done or not done. Had she opened up to those feelings she would have found that they were entirely related to her relationship with her runaway father twenty years before. But she took another path; instead of opening up to the anger, she censured it and drove it out of her mind, telling herself that it was inappropriate. Think of feelings as a wake-up call, like a ringing telephone. If you put a pillow over your head you may shut out the ringing, but you do not make it go away. When you have a pillow over your head, it can obstruct your view of life completely. This was basically what Terri did. Repressing the anger, and particularly not looking at the old issue to which it was connected, caused her to lose energy. She soon noticed that she was dreading making love with Bob. Sex had always been a strong point in their relationship, and when it began to wane she knew something was wrong. We invited her to look at when the actual deadness had started. She traced it to concealing the anger and forcing it out of her mind instead of inquiring into it. She sorted out the issue by dealing with her anger at her father in therapy, instead of aiming at Bob. By waking up and answering the phone, it quit ringing and she got back her intimacy.

Lies and Broken Agreements

As we said in the preceding chapter, two of the crucial steps in attaining intimacy and co-commitment are to tell the truth and to keep agreements. As you might expect, these are also two of the most common ways in which people bring themselves down when their Upper Limits have been reached. Lying and breaking agreements distort the flow of energy between people. Any distortion in the system sets up a rattle that takes time, energy, and attention to work out. This energy could have been used in moving forward toward the mutual goals of the people involved.

This problem affects any organization, not just close love relationships. In any purposeful gathering of people, from churches to corporations, it is possible to calculate the ratio of rattle to progress. Think of what could be accomplished when there is little or no rattle! When energy does not have to be wasted cleaning up the messes caused by concealing the truth and breaking agreements, much more productivity is possible.

Notice the process of lies and broken agreements, not just the content. While the content may have significance, the process is always more important. The broken agreement may have been that you did not pick up the milk at the store—by all accounts a trivial incident. But the process may have a great deal of meaning. It could have followed a period of good feeling in your relationship, when your

Upper Limit had been exceeded. You need to ask yourself: When did I break the agreement or conceal the truth? Was it just after a period of closeness? How and where did I tell the lie? Did it have the result of bringing the relationship down to a more modest level of positive energy?

Observe Results

The best way to see the workings of your unconscious is to look at the results you create. You can see your unconscious in your dreams and in slips of the tongue, but these are often symbolic and roundabout. It is easier just to look at what you create, because the results never lie. This is particularly true in relationships.

For example, you and your lover have a weekend of intense closeness, then both get colds on Sunday night. "We certainly didn't mean to get sick," you may say. But wait. Just observe the results. You felt good, then you got sick. Another example: Husband agrees to take out the trash every Thursday. When he forgets, Wife gets mad, and an uproar ensues that flattens a positive mood they had been enjoying. "I certainly didn't mean to forget," he says. But wait. Just observe the results: the positive mood was destroyed. It is crucial that we get accustomed to observing the results we create, rather than righteously pretending that the results were just coincidences.

It is wisest to assume that whatever you created was what some part of you wanted to create. Naturally, people do not like to look at life this way. When negative or painful results have been created, it takes real courage to say, "Yes—a part of me obviously wanted it that way." In a co-committed relationship both people must agree: "What we wanted was what we got." From this position of responsibility and creativity, real intimacy is possible.

Pay Close Attention to Your Body and its Sensations

Your body is your best friend in helping you transform your co-dependent patterns. Co-dependency shows up in the body in a variety of forms. If you can learn to be aware of the meaning of different body sensations, you can move toward co-commitment more efficiently. In co-commitment your body language is clear and congruent. Breathing is full and nourishing, eye contact is straightforward, and muscles are free of excess tension. The Upper Limits Problem shows up dramatically in the body. Positive energy is all about expansion. When your positive-energy limit has been exceeded, you contract into negativity.

Unconscious loving is a contraction; we become less than we actually are. This contraction shows up in the body. The moment we slip out of co-creation and into co-dependence the breath loses vitality, the muscles tighten, the posture slumps, the eyes glance away. In this regard we are like big, complicated versions of the one-celled organisms you can observe through a microscope. For example, consider the amoeba. Left to their own devices, amoebas will float around, expanding and contracting. That's their lifestyle: expanding and contracting. But watch what happens when a scientist takes a tiny, sharp tool and pokes an amoeba with it. If the poke is not severe, the creature will stay contracted for a while, then pop back into expanding and contracting again. Poke too hard, or too often, though, and the amoeba stays contracted. If the stresses of our relationships have been great enough to cause a deep contraction, we may not be able to pop back into expanding and contracting again without help. Our bodies register the current state of our expansion and contraction.

Body tension is a common problem. Along with restricted breathing, tension is our most immediate way of concealing feelings. In fact, the unconscious can co-opt our bodies rather easily in the service of hiding feelings. Illness and accidents are other body-involved processes that often are used as ways of dealing with feelings. By holding the peripheral muscles of the body in a state of chronic tightness, we block the flow of information that we could be getting from deeper inside ourselves. The muscle system is like a jacket around our organs. If the jacket is buttoned too tightly we cannot feel what is closer to the core. One renowned internist, Edmund Jacobson, said that if he could make only one intervention with all his patients it would be to teach them how to relax their muscles. He found that chronic tension played a role in the vast majority of ills that people brought to him.

The Co-Committed Alternative to the Upper Limits Problem

We have experimented with dozens of ways to handle the Upper Limits Problem creatively. What emerged are the following things you can do to keep the positive energy flowing continuously. Some of these ideas are described in chapter 4, so we will mention them only briefly here. You will also find specific experiential activities in the Co-Commitment Program that turn these ideas into step-by-step instructions.

Making Space, Taking Space

To allow a co-committed relationship to grow and flourish, you must take space for yourself and make space for your partner. It must be absolutely all right for you to take time off from closeness to allow yourself to integrate and to prepare for moving to the next higher level of intimacy. You also need to let it be all right for your partner to take space for the same reasons. Think of it as resting from a particularly energetic jitterbug before going back onto the dance floor.

For example, one couple had been using arguments as their main unconscious strategy for limiting positive energy. After working on this pattern for several weeks they were able to see the process of how they were using arguments to prevent closeness or to stop it after being close. They found a better alternative through learning to take space. They saw that they were running a Friday/Sunday pattern. They would often fight on Friday evenings, preventing closeness over the weekend. Or they would fight Sunday nights, ruining the good feelings they had enjoyed. Their solution was creative and eliminated the problem.

What they did was to take a little space by themselves before getting together on Friday nights. Rather than rush home from work to be together, they took an hour apart to rest, meditate, and clear themselves of the energy of the workplace. Then when they saw each other they were ready for intimacy.

The Sunday-night strategy was similar. They gave themselves an hour or two of space late Sunday afternoon. He generally went for a walk while she took a nap. Then, rested and ready for intimacy again, they had dinner together. We have worked with couples to adopt many such variations of taking space, and it always seems to work miracles in people's ability to stay in a state of positive energy. You would not think of working all day without sleeping at night. Neither would you think of eating a big meal without giving yourself time to digest before eating another one. Intimacy works the same way. You need those times of solitude in order to integrate the powerful energy of closeness. By resting between each energetic dance, you are ready next time to take the floor at a new and higher level.

With practice you can learn to take space before you create problems. For example, Bev and Ed uncovered an Upper Limits pattern that had been causing problems for weeks. Married less than six months, they had been feeling exquisitely close to each other for two weeks. Then one day Bev noticed a subtle sense of "off-ness" in her body before going to work. At work, she got overwhelmed in a number of problems she had to solve and forgot about the sensation. She had just missed the first little cue that it was time to take some space. In midmorning she talked to Ed at work and felt some distance from him—cue 2. That night she and Ed had a five-minute spat involving the purchase of the wrong kind of bacon: cue 3. The next morning the following conversation took place in the front yard when Bev came out to talk to Ed, who was shoveling snow.

BEV: You know, Ed, you don't really have to shovel the driveway.

ED: Oh, it's fine. I'm actually kind of enjoying the exercise.

BEV: Well, I just want you to know that it's not really necessary.

ED (slightly irritated now): Do you want me not to shovel the snow for some reason?

BEV (backing off): Oh, no, I just want you to know that it's . . .

An uproar soon was in progress. Neither got much sleep that night, and the next day they felt tired and bewildered at how they had managed to destroy the closeness they had felt for so long.

In working through the issue, they had several key realizations. Bev saw that her body had given her the first cues that it was time to take some space. She missed that cue and had to go through two more levels before getting the message. It took a full-scale argument to do the job. When they reviewed the incident in the front yard, they discovered that they had not told the truth. Bev realized that she had covered up her real feelings about shoveling. It was a favorite centering activity of hers and also a mark of independence. Since her divorce a few years before, she had taken pride in her ability to keep her lawn looking good in all seasons. She had concealed this from Ed, instead saying that there was no need for him to shovel the driveway. It was her roundabout way of hiding her negative feelings. Ed realized that he had picked up on the concealed feeling; he had a "funny" feeling inside when Bev told him he didn't have to shovel. He had overlooked this feeling and played right into the game.

They resolved to be more sensitive to subtle cues next time, so they would not have to escalate into a battle to get permission to take space. As a joke, Bev bought Ed his own snow shovel.

Telling the Microscopic Truth

Although this point was covered in detail in the preceding chapter, we would like to give an example of how telling the truth can be used in the specific circumstances of the Upper Limits Problem. One day Marge told Tim that he had a habit she had noticed. In times of intimacy, he would sometimes make a subtle but definitely snide remark about her. He did not do it at other times, so she perceived that it was his way of defending against intimacy. Tim took in this observation and felt that it was accurate. The next time he unconsciously did it, Marge asked him to open up to what was going on inside himself and to tell the truth about it. He said that his "gut was tight" and that he felt waves of fear playing in his belly and chest. She held him while he opened up to the fear, and out came the truth: he was deeply afraid of being left by her. He felt that if he really surrendered his defenses and let himself get close to her, he would be abandoned like he was when his mother died. The pain would annihilate him. So, he made snide remarks to keep Marge distant when his Upper Limit had been exceeded. Marge gave him a great deal of appreciation for opening up to the truth and assured him that she had no plans to leave him under any circumstances. The pattern of snide remarks stopped.

Not all of your negative patterns will go away with one application of microscopic truth. It is probably better to view telling the truth as a lifestyle rather than a specific treatment. It is certainly a powerful therapeutic tool, but the commitment to the truth must be for its own sake rather than because it will bring a particular reward. If you commit yourself to telling the microscopic truth as a lifestyle, you will definitely have an easier time when you confront your blocks to intimacy. Seeing the blocks and telling the truth about them is the most potent way to dissolve these barriers.

Scattering the Ash

What else can you do when you are so full of positive energy that you are beginning to slip into negativity?

In our work we have discovered a unique phenomenon that we call "scattering the ash." The process of transformation seems to move a great deal of energy through the body. This is particularly true of rapid transformation in relationships. When you are evolving quickly by spotting and letting go of old patterns, you will tend to get a certain feeling in your body as a by-product of transformation. This feeling is a slightly gritty sensation, as if the inside of your veins are coated with grime. Along with this sensation comes tiredness and sometimes sleepiness. This is what we call "ash." We have named it this because it accompanies rapid change and follows the burning of more energy than you likely have experienced before. Although you may want to lie down and rest when you are feeling ashy, this is absolutely the worst thing to do.

The most effective way to scatter ash is through breath and movement. Sometimes even a few minutes of deep breathing or fast dancing can move the ashy sensation out of your body. We believe you will be amazed at how fast it can be alleviated. If you lie down with ash in your body, however, you can expect to wake up still feeling ashy, and sometimes worse. As you may know, 70 percent of the toxins in the body are released through breathing. The minority of toxins is discharged through sweat, urination, and defecation. This is why ash (as well as other toxins) is most effectively released through activities that stimulate your breath.

I once heard the director of one of America's largest mental health centers say that most mental illness could be eliminated by dancing by yourself an hour a day. This makes a lot of sense in light of our ash discussion. If you can keep yourself free and clear of ash on a daily basis you probably will not get stuck in any major way. One of the healthiest older people we have ever run across, the anthropologist Ashley Montagu, dances an hour a day whether or not he has a partner. We use this awareness daily in our therapy practice. When someone comes in stuck on a problem, we do not talk to them as much as other therapists might. Instead, we get them to breathe and move with the problem. How? Listen to this transcript:

> CLIENT: I've been kind of depressed this week.
> THERAPIST: Where are you feeling that in your body?
> CLIENT: (pause) Well, it's sort of a heaviness.
> THERAPIST: Where are you mainly feeling heavy?
> CLIENT: It's in my shoulders, and there's like a weight on my chest.
> THERAPIST: Breathe into your shoulders and chest so that they begin to move.
> CLIENT: (Breathes deeply and moves her chest and shoulders with the breath. Starts to sob.)
> THERAPIST: Yes, stay with it. Let the tears come. Breathe them on through.
> CLIENT: (Continues to sob for a few minutes, then stops.)
> THERAPIST: How are you feeling in your body now?
> CLIENT: Lighter, more relaxed.
> THERAPIST: Let's talk some more about what's been going on this week.

Most of this five-minute segment of a therapy session is spent physically participating with the depression and the feeling underneath it. Breath and movement are used to move the depression. The result is lightness and relaxation. It is very difficult to talk your way out of ash, but quite easy to move and breathe yourself out of it. When you are feeling an Upper Limits Problem coming on, take a few minutes for a breathing break or a short brisk walk. Turn on music and dance to it, serenely or wildly as your mood dictates. Sometimes all it takes is a few deep breaths or a few drops of sweat and you are feeling clear again. As Kathlyn's favorite T-shirt says, IF IT'S PHYSICAL, IT'S THERAPY.

Dancing, walking, and running are excellent ways of

dealing with the Upper Limits Problem. They literally get your feet back on the ground. As we mentioned earlier, part of the Upper Limits Problem is that your physical boundaries are transcended. Part of being loving to yourself is to find ways of coming back to the ground again without unpleasant side effects. Falling down is an unloving way to get yourself grounded, while taking a walk is much more kindly. Each of these activities meets the same need for reestablishing your physical boundaries, but obviously you want to do whatever is most loving to yourself.

Nonsexual Touch

Sex is an essential part of life, but too often we try to meet our touch-needs through sexual touch only. Nonsexual touch is essential to health, in our opinion, and is a superb way of dealing with the Upper Limits Problem. When you exceed your positive-energy limit, you expand your boundaries. These are a literal physical boundary as well as a psychospiritual one. For example, Kathlyn notices that one of her Upper Limits behaviors is bumping into things. She can measure whether she needs some space by the number of bruises on her legs. When she has gone beyond her Upper Limit, she loses her sense of boundary. The physical world is there to remind her. It is far more loving, however, to find conscious ways of establishing our boundaries at the new and higher level. Kathlyn's way has been to get a weekly massage. By spending an hour having the masseuse lovingly stroke the physical boundaries of her body, she has found that there is less need to have painful encounters with the physical world. Her massage therapist has a young son whom she has massaged nearly every day since his birth. He has never been sick. This is remarkable, considering all the usual illnesses that most children have.

While you may not be able to arrange a weekly or monthly massage, you can certainly create more hugs in your life. Our society is hug-phobic, and we suffer for it. Learning to give and receive nonsexual touch can transform your life in many ways. For example, Gay came from a family where touch was very rare. "I remember seeing my grandfather take my grandmother's arm as they left the funeral of her brother when I was about ten. I recall staring at this unfamiliar behavior because I had never seen them touch before, even though I had seen them nearly daily since I was little. For the first year of my relationship with Kathlyn I really got to take a close look at how uncomfortable I was with nonsexual touch. Kathlyn is wonderfully comfortable with touch and would frequently give me a hug or a touch when she would pass by me. She also likes to cuddle in the morning, whereas I was in the habit of jumping right out of bed. Sometimes I would actually find myself flinching a little bit when I would receive a hug or a pat on the back. I realized that all of this was about my fear of touch, which I had picked up growing up in a touch-less family in the macho world of the 1950s. After all, you never saw John Wayne hug anybody. He hit them, he shot them, he even went to bed with women occasionally, but a hug—never. As I overcame this old program and learned to give and receive touch more freely, I noticed several profound shifts. First, I became more in touch with my feelings. Letting myself be touched caused something to relax inside, which allowed me more access to myself. Second, my physical skin, which had always been dry and rough, became much healthier. The third change, which I know intuitively but cannot document, was that I got more healthy in general. I used to get several colds a year, often with the change of seasons. Now I rarely get even a mild case of sniffles. I can remember only one cold in the past decade, and that was when I was traveling by myself in China and Tibet for three weeks. It has been proved to my satisfaction what a lot of studies have shown—touch equals health."

Turn Your Complaints into Requests

Knowing and saying what you want is one of the most powerful skills you can learn. These skills are not learned easily, because most of us have barriers to knowing what we want, and perhaps bigger barriers to saying what we want. Few of us grew up being encouraged to deal with our wants in straight ways. We swallowed our wants, or expressed them with a whine or a tantrum, or relied on someone else to tell us what we wanted. You will be surprised, however, at how much progress you can make in life simply by phrasing what you want in your mind and out loud. In a co-committed relationship you focus on your wants and the wants of the other person(s) involved. You determine what you want, then find others who want to support you in your evolution. At the same time, you are supporting the other person in moving toward his or her goals.

Improve the Quality of Your Contract with Life

You can prevent some instances of the Upper Limits Problem by adopting a healthier belief system. Under the stress of growing up we often adopt basic beliefs about the universe that cost us later. These beliefs become our basic contracts with life. For example, due to trauma we may think: "The world is a dangerous place." There is no question that it *was* a dangerous place when you formed that belief, but later, when you are away from the real danger, you may still carry the belief in your mind. This belief causes you to see the world as a dangerous place, and to attract that quality of energy to you. It is very clear that our beliefs shape our experiences and even limit the information that gets in. In a wonderfully simple experiment, a cat's brain waves were monitored as a click was repeatedly sounded. Each time there was a click, there was a corresponding blip in the cat's brain waves. This blip indicated that the cat had registered the click. A mouse was then put outside the cat's cage, where the cat could see it but not reach it. The cat became fixated on the mouse, and now the click did not even register on the cat's brain. It was so caught up in its "gotta have that mouse" program that it did not process other present information in the real world.

Similarly, if we are caught up in programs like "the world is dangerous" or "I don't deserve love," we may not even process other information, such as people trying to be kind to us.

One of the key activities of adulthood is looking at the basic beliefs that are running our lives. We must ask: Do these beliefs work? Are they bringing us happiness? Often the answer is no; we adopted the belief under duress and it is no longer appropriate.

Killer Beliefs

One of the most destructive beliefs is: This experience is not the one I'm supposed to be having. In workshops we often call this a Killer Belief, because it can literally be fatal. Each time an event occurs, we have a choice of whether to view it as what ought to have happened or what ought not to have happened. Many people tie up enormous amounts of their energy in thinking that the events of their lives are not the ones that ought to have happened. They get into a victim position with life itself, so that they perceive that they are completely at the effect of a hostile universe. There is no positive payoff for seeing the world this way. In fact, it can kill you. If you continue to wrestle with the universe, thinking that the way it is is not the way it's supposed to be, you can burn out very quickly. In our experience as therapists, the most extreme example of this point of view was provided by a woman in a class who was the most rage-filled person we had ever seen. We never knew what had put her in the grip of her anger, but she was in constant, embittered battle with the way things were. Within a few weeks of the beginning of the class she had alienated the rest of the students by her complaints about authority figures, her family, her husband, her children, and most of the rest of the world. Nothing was the way it ought to be. And none of it had anything to do with her. Totally impervious to feedback from others, she saw herself as the lone outpost of sanity and innocence in this crazy world. She died of a massive heart attack a few months later, at age forty-five. This experience taught us to be very vigilant in noticing when we slip into not accepting what is.

A better contract with the universe is to adopt the following point of view: "The experience I am having is the one I'm supposed to be having." Accept it the way it is, and you are in a much better position to do something about it. Argue with the way it is and you squander your potential productivity. One of our clients had an experience that illustrated how powerful it can be to change this view. Her boss one day mentioned in passing that he thought she should work on improving the quality of her voice. He pointed out that she talked in a little-girl voice, and it was his view that her voice was costing her money. (She worked in a sales position that required her to speak persuasively to people.) She came in to her first therapy session outraged about this. We shocked her by agreeing with her boss. "You *do* have a little-girl voice," we said. Now she had two people to be angry at, but fortunately she let go of her "this criticism isn't the experience I'm supposed to be having" stance. She saw that she was trapped in some old patterns that had begun when her mother died when she was five. Her father could relate to her only as a little girl, so she unconsciously continued to act like one to maintain his approval. When her boss, also a father figure, criticized her voice, she felt devastated. She saw that her boss's comment was just a little hint to make her work more productive, but to her it felt as though her father was calling her whole existence into question. By letting go of her resistant stance toward the universe, she was able to clear up an old pattern that no longer served her.

Many problems can be eliminated by the following intention: I am willing to expand continuously in positive energy with totally positive consequences for myself and others. Recall our discussion of get close/have an argument, get close/get sick. These patterns are based on an unconscious intention: Every time I expand in positive energy, I need to hurt myself or someone around me. Because of our limited ability to handle positive energy, we find a way to punish ourselves after even a tiny bit of it. It is absolutely all right to learn your lessons in comfortable ways. Learning does not have to be painful, unless we believe it does. There are two ways to learn any lesson: wisdom and experience. It can often be most loving to yourself and others to learn your lessons by wisdom rather than experience. For example, the lesson "look both ways before crossing the street" can be very hurtful to learn by experience. We recommend that you make the following agreement with life: I want to learn all the lessons I can through wisdom, not experience. There are many lessons—how to make love, how to sky-dive—that one can learn only through experience. Wisdom can help to point us in the right direction. Other lessons—how we block ourselves from receiving positive energy, for example—can be learned largely through wisdom.

In a co-committed relationship you only have one big problem to solve: how to let yourself experience more and more positive energy. First you learn to spot your barriers to positive energy on a minute-by-minute basis. You gradually train yourself to find more loving ways to handle the rest periods you need between times of closeness. Rather than bring yourself and the relationship down through negative habit patterns, you find positive alternatives for getting grounded and prepared for the next expansion of closeness. Eventually, with time and loving practice, you learn how to stay balanced in a state of continuous positive energy as your relationship grows in mutual creativity.

Even the most harmonious relationships have problems to solve. To handle the inevitable twists and turns, we have devised a specific method of problem-solving that will help move you rapidly in the direction of continuous positive energy. This method is the subject of our next chapter.

SIX

A New Method of Resolving Conflict

You are almost never upset for the reasons you think you are. Often we begin working with a couple on the issue they think is the problem, only to find within a very short time that the issue and its resolution involve something they have never considered. Think of a problem as being like a series of bubbles coming up through water to the surface. The big bubbles near the surface are caused by something deeper but hard to see. The big bubbles are easy to see and therefore get our attention. Most of us get bogged down in the surface struggle; what we really need are ways to dive to the bottom of the problem, to handle it at its source.

We have devised a problem-solving strategy that allows you to get to the source of your issues quickly. It does not resemble anything people typically use to solve problems. The most popular way of resolving conflict—apologize and promise to do better next time—causes more problems than it resolves, because it doesn't touch the real root of problems. If you practice the techniques described in this chapter, you will have far fewer conflicts than you imagined

150

possible. Conflicts will be resolved more quickly, and they will not tend to recycle.

Ending Power Struggles

In entanglements, power struggles are the norm. Much conflict is generated over who is right, who is wrong, and whose problem it is. In co-committed relationships, because both people are taking 100 percent responsibility for creating the conflict, no power struggle can exist. There are no healthy ways to resolve power struggles, short of dropping them altogether. To resolve a power struggle your choices are:

1. Agree that one person is wrong and the other is right
2. Agree that both of you are wrong
3. Agree that both of you are right
4. Drop it and find a clearer way of relating

The first three strategies are unworkable in the long run, because right and wrong are within the realm of power struggles. A power struggle can be ended only when all parties agree to full responsibility for the creation of the issue. All parties agree to explore the sources of the issue in themselves. Remember, a co-committed relationship begins when both people open to being the source of what happens to them. Following is an example of a couple who wrestled with the same power struggle for months without resolution, then resolved it by *not* indulging in any of the first three strategies described above.

Lou and Cindy had been together for three years, during which time they had recycled the same power struggle "about 118 times," in their words. The issue was Cindy's son, Brian. He was reaching the peak of his rebellious-teenager phase when Lou and Cindy got together. Lou and Brian took an instant dislike to each other, and their relationship had not improved. The power struggle that developed between Lou and Cindy was that Lou would get angry about something that Brian did, then would criticize Cindy for her poor parenting skills. Cindy would defend herself, usually blaming the problem on Brian's biological father, and the struggle would escalate. The problem lay in the way they always resolved the issue. After a day or two of fighting, Cindy would capitulate and agree that Lou was right. She would blame herself for Brian's problems and would tell Lou that she wished she had never given birth to Brian in the first place. In other words, they would choose solution 1 from the list above: Agree that one person is wrong and the other is right. This satisfied Lou temporarily, but the resolution never lasted longer than it took for Brian to mess up again.

It took two radical awarenesses to clear up the problem. When we first worked with Lou and Cindy we asked them if they were willing to solve the problem. They quickly agreed, but even more quickly pointed out that the problem had nothing to do with them but was completely Brian's fault. We asked them if they would be willing to solve the problem without it being *anyone's* fault. They agreed, opening the space for their first awareness, which was that they were using Brian as an Upper Limits Problem. Whenever they had reached their Upper Limit of closeness, they destroyed it by finding fault with Brian. He could always be relied on to provide some content for them to focus on. Their second awareness was learning to take 100 percent responsibility for the problem. When Lou looked into the source of the problem in himself, he saw that Brian was very similar to the way he had been as a teenager. He was replaying with Brian the relationship that he'd had with his own father. He was shocked to find this out because he had always thought of his teen years as the worst time of his life. "Why would I be repeating it?" he asked. "To resolve it completely," we replied. This awareness led him into an entirely different relationship with Brian, and ultimately to reestablish communication with his own father. Brian responded in a new way to Lou's shift in attitude. He dropped much of his sullen defensiveness with Lou, and a closer relationship began to develop. It is for this reason that we say that people are never upset for the reasons they think they are. If we had said to Lou when he first came in that he could improve Brian's behavior by making a shift in himself, he would likely have laughed his way out of our office.

Cindy realized that making herself feel guilty for the way she had raised Brian was actually keeping her from taking effective action. She saw that she was in fact requiring Brian to be a problem in order to play out her incomplete relationship with her ex-husband. As long as Brian behaved badly, she had a place to dump her anger at his father, and a good excuse to run her "I told you so" program. The cost of all this was that she did not get to enjoy herself or her family in the present. She decided to put her energy into action rather than guilt. She contacted Brian's father and had several long discussions with him and Brian. She relieved Brian of the necessity to mess up in order to fulfill her expectations. Her actions brought about another improvement in Brian's behavior. She got Brian into counseling at school and worked out a discipline system at home. It was heartening to see how fast everything moved once Lou and Cindy shifted to co-commitment.

The Co-Committed Problem-Solving Process

The process that we have developed is organized around seven questions. Each question illuminates a specific area in which people in relationships typically get stuck. Very seldom do all of the questions have to be used to solve a problem. Each of the questions is simple but holds unlimited possibilities. You can ask any of the questions hundreds of times and get new and productive results each time.

In using the questions below to resolve relationship issues, focus more on the question than on the answer. The power of a question lies not so much in the answer but in the state of consciousness that it opens up. By asking a question, you let go of thinking you know the answer. The act of letting go is as important as the answer. So many problems in relating to each other come from getting stuck in our programs, thinking we know the way it is. If you can sincerely ask a question, you open up space in which a new solution can emerge.

We will describe the questions in detail, then give an example of a relationship problem that was solved by using all of them.

The Questions

1. How do I feel?
2. What do I want?
3. How is the past coloring my present?
4. What am I getting out of staying stuck?
5. What do I need to say?
6. What agreements have I broken?
7. How can I be of service?

Many of our clients and workshop participants have actually written down these questions and put them on the bathroom mirror or the refrigerator door. You can use these questions repeatedly in many situations without their becoming stale.

To illustrate, we will give two examples of deeply entangled couples, one of whom needed several rounds of all the questions and one of whom solved the problem after the fourth question. The first couple, Larry and Ruth, came in on the verge of splitting up. They had been fighting almost constantly for six months and were so deeply mired in their power struggle that they could see no way out. In their words, "we spend half our time fighting and half not speaking." The first challenge was to get them on record as being willing to solve the problem. As any therapist knows, the fact that a couple comes in for counseling does not necessarily mean that they are willing to solve their problems. Sometimes couples come in simply to prove that their relationship will never work, or to prove that it really is the other person's fault. Only when both people are willing to solve the problem can the productive work begin. It took one whole session to reach agreement that Larry and Ruth were open to resolving the issue. Our work with them moved fairly quickly once this basic agreement was reached.

How Do I Feel?

We asked them to stand face to face and tell each other the truth about how they felt. In our approach to therapy, we ask how people are feeling right now ("I'm mad at you"), and we try to keep our clients from conceptualizing and psychologizing. To get them to take responsibility for their feelings instead of projecting, we ask them to keep returning their awareness to their bodies. Focusing on simple statements like "I'm scared" or "I'm angry" rather than mental explanations of feelings moves people toward resolution more quickly. As Larry and Ruth communicated their truths to each other, we coached them and helped them stay focused on the process. Feelings occur in layers, and Larry and Ruth went down through their various layers rapidly. First came all the things they were angry about, then they communicated their hurts to each other. Then their fears came out. Larry was deeply afraid of Ruth's anger; his pattern was to withdraw when she got angry at him. Ruth was afraid that Larry would leave her, and he frequently manipulated her through this fear. When he really wanted to back her into a corner he would start talking divorce. Sometimes this would bring Ruth "into line," as he put it; other times it would escalate her anger. The session closed on a hopeful note, with both of them having reached a deeper level of authentic feeling in themselves. They left with the homework assignment of thinking about question 2—What do I want?

What Do I Want? (The Art of Turning Complaints into Requests)

Ruth and Larry did not get far with this question during the week; in fact, they got stuck again. When they came in the next week, we saw why. They had turned the question around, enumerating all the things they did *not* want from each other. Focusing on the negative had triggered several arguments, and they came in feeling hopeless again. We coached them on how to figure out what they wanted, assisting them in turning their complaints into requests. Most of their complaints could be turned into positive requests. Some of their complaints:

Ruth
Larry never calls if he's going to be late.
He never disciplines the children.
He never talks about anything but work.

Larry
I never get any free time.
Ruth's always telling me about some disaster as soon as I get home.
We never have any fun anymore.

We asked them to transform each of these complaints into a positive statement of what they wanted rather than what they did not have. Some of the things they wanted from each other:

Ruth
I want Larry to call if he's going to be more than a half-hour late.

I want Larry to follow through on disciplining the children. If he tells them they can't do something, make sure they don't.

I want Larry to talk about his feelings more, not just what happened at work.

I want Larry to share responsibility for handling finances.

I want Larry to help with the housework. Specifically, I want him to do the wash one day per week.

Larry
I want Ruth to be kind and supportive to me when I

get home from work instead of hitting me with a list of what's gone wrong.

I want a free night each week when I can do anything I like and not have to interact with Ruth or the kids.

I want to have more fun with Ruth.

This step produced positive movement in their relationship. Both felt better after getting clear on some of their wants. When any problem occurs, you have two choices: you can get upset about it, or you can simply figure out what needs to be done. Getting upset has a seductive quality to it; there is rich drama to be had there. The cost is that there is no happiness to be had. Happiness opens up when you drop the drama and start looking for what needs to be done. Any relationship improves when both people shift from complaints to statements of what they want.

How Is the Past Coloring My Present?

Another leap forward took place when Ruth and Larry asked themselves question 3: How is the past coloring my present? They were incredulous when they saw how their present pattern had been set in motion thirty years before. "How could two intelligent people not see something like that?" they asked. Here's what they saw. Larry, you will recall, was afraid of Ruth's anger. But he also seemed to go out of his way to trigger it. When he opened up to his past, he saw that this was precisely his relationship with his mother. She was loving but very angry, and she used her anger to manipulate the family. When Larry was around her he did not know whether she was going to give him a big hug or yell at him for something. She also had a similar relationship with Larry's father. They were either fighting, making up, or making love. There were not many calm and stable times. Ruth's fear of abandonment also had been programmed in from a past event. Her father had left the family when she was eight, throwing them into financial difficulties. Ruth was so afraid of being left that Larry could use this fear to manipulate her.

It took about five minutes for Ruth and Larry to see that their present conflict did not have much to do with

the present. It had all begun a long time ago, and their
relationship was simply a place to play out these ancient
dramas. This moment of awareness was a turning point,
because it made them allies instead of enemies. They began
to view each other as a support system for their explorations into how the past was influencing the present. They
took the pressure off each other, realizing that it was futile
to find fault with each other when they had both created
the conflict for their own purposes.

What Are You Getting out of Staying Stuck?

This question often needs explanation. People are not
used to seeing that their painful and negative behavior has
a payoff. Everything has a payoff, but often it is subtle and
not easily seen. For example, one payoff to negative behavior is that it allows you to maintain and strengthen a belief
you hold sacred. For example, you may stay in an abusive
relationship because of a belief that "life has to be painful."
You may have learned this belief from your adored but
abused mother. In your mind, it has become associated
with your mother's love; it is now literally unthinkable to
abandon the belief. Another seldom-recognized payoff is
that you stay stuck to avoid the initial anxiety of breaking
free. Getting free from an old pattern, even one that makes
you miserable, is risky because you are stepping out into
the unknown. You may get sick to get attention, because
you are afraid of asking for the attention in a straightforward way. In being straightforward there is the risk of
rejection.

Ruth and Larry realized that their main payoff was in
maintaining their belief that the other person was wrong.
When they fought they could strengthen their belief that
"No matter what I do I can't win with this person." Their
other big payoff was in limiting their positive energy. By
fighting all the time they kept themselves from acknowledging something very important and real: neither was satisfied with what they were accomplishing in the world. They
felt they were not living up to their potential as individuals
or as a couple. Fighting and blaming were ways of avoiding
looking at and doing something about this painful aware-

ness. Another way to ask question 4 is "What is the conflict preventing you from doing or seeing?" Larry and Ruth were facing crucial issues of midlife such as whether they were going to make the contribution they had always wanted to make. When they first got together they had a vision of creating a center for ecological awareness and a recycling company in their community. This dream had become obscured by their power struggles. In therapy we asked them to deal with this issue directly as allies, rather than creating conflict as a smokescreen. They generated a to-do list of steps that eventually led them toward realizing their vision.

What Do I Need to Say?

In a subsequent session we raised question 5, "What do I need to say?" They had a lot to say. For a half-hour they stood face to face and told each other everything they had been withholding for twenty years. Many of the deeper truths were ones that they both shared but had never told each other:

Sometimes I wish I had never gotten married or had children.
I have sexual fantasies about other people.
I hate our elaborate lifestyle.
I wish we lived in the country.
I hate it when the kids are rude.

There were many more, but the above give you a flavor of the level of truth-telling they were courageous enough to reach. Each time one of them would hit on a significant truth, it would cause a reaction in the other. For example, each of them got mad when the other confessed to sexual fantasies about other people. Each time this happened, the truth then had to be told about the reaction ("When you say you are sexually attracted to Gina I feel afraid you're going to leave me"). Most of us are programmed to withhold the truth for fear of the other person's reaction. Like many couples, Ruth and Larry initially punished each other for telling the truth by having blowups. With work, though, they reached the point where they could freely say how they felt without an uproar ensuing.

What Agreements Have I Broken?

In asking question 6—"What agreements have I broken?"—the proverbial hornet's nest was opened. One of the agreements Larry confessed to having broken was a "little affair that meant nothing" two years before. Ruth exploded and Larry went into shock. It was his mother all over again. The more Ruth demanded the details of the affair, the more Larry retreated into mute terror. It took three sessions to handle the fallout from Larry's telling the truth. Several times the uproar died down but burst into life again with a fresh round of accusations, justifications, and blame. But they hung in there with each other, telling the truth and listening to it from the other person. The rewards were enormous. After letting go of this old, withheld truth, Larry looked and felt like a new man. Both his color and his posture improved. The burden of carrying withheld truths cannot be overestimated. Once Ruth communicated all her feelings about having been lied to, she also looked more vital. It turned out that she had always thought something was wrong, but Larry had told her she was crazy and paranoid. Even though the truth hurt, it was preferable to living with a lie. The incident was really a test to find out if they could support each other in telling the 100 percent truth. In a co-committed relationship it is urgent to find out if you are genuinely committed to your partner's being fully alive. There is no better way to make sure than by finding out the whole truth of the person. Larry and Ruth put each other to the test, and passed.

How Can I Be of Service?

The last question—"How can I be of service?"—took Larry and Ruth into a new dimension. They began to see their relationship in a brand-new way: as producers, not consumers, of love and positive energy for each other. They began to focus on how they could support each other for being fully productive, and on how their relationship could produce positive energy for others. Other questions opened up, such as, "How can I help you reach your goals?" Rather than facing each other as adversaries, they were hand in hand, facing the future as co-creators. In the next year a number of "magical" events happened. (Such "magic" often follows the adoption of a co-committed stance toward life.) The universe has a way of supporting people who are producing, rather than consuming, positive energy. Larry got a large software contract that allowed him to set up an electronic cottage business at home. Since Larry no longer needed to be in the city, their idea of moving to the country became a real possibility. With a greatly simplified life-style, they moved upstate to a small community and at last report were adjusting well to the change. They reached a compromise on their vision of starting recycling and ecology centers by buying stock in one of the country's largest recycling firms.

Using the Process to Resolve a Sexual Problem

Rob and Jean had been married for twelve years when they came in to work on their problems, which they described as "communication" and "a dull sex life." They agreed that their communication was largely about their house and their kids; neither of them talked with the other about the deeper issues of feelings, wants, and needs. Their sexual enjoyment was marred by differences in rhythm: he reached orgasm much too quickly, in Jean's opinion, while Rob felt that Jean took "forever" to reach orgasm.

After getting them to agree that they were willing to solve the problems, we began working through the seven questions. We spent the first session entirely on the first two questions: How do you feel? and What do you want?

Jean
I'm frustrated, sick and tired of the same old thing all the time.
I'm just plain tired.
I feel numb all over, but especially in my pelvis.

I'm angry that Rob never seems to change.

I'm scared that my whole life is over; that it's just going to be like this forever.

I want a little romance.

I want to feel like I'm being made love to rather than used.

I want sex to be slower and more tender.

I want Rob to follow through on what he says he's going to do.

Rob

I'm angry that I always have to initiate sex.

I'm mad that we only have sex once every week or two, and when we do we have to be quiet so the kids won't hear.

I'm mad that we can never have sex in the morning when I like it. We always do it late at night when I'm half-asleep.

I'm scared that I'm just going to be criticized, never appreciated.

I'm afraid I'm never going to be loved the way I want to be.

I want sex to be fun, spontaneous.

I want to play more, not just go through the same old routine.

There were other feelings and wants, but these are representative of what they shared during their first session. At the end of that first hour they felt lighter but were skeptical about what difference it would make. We sent them home with the assignment of making a longer list of feelings and wants to be brought in at the next session. A week later we focused on how the past was coloring the present. As we suspected, this question revealed a treasure chest of stored patterns. Often the past comes forward to overshadow the present during the first year of a relationship. If the couple is skilled or has some good help, they move through these old patterns, sorting them out from what is going on in the present. But often the old patterns become entrenched and are still there years later, as was the case with Rob and Jean.

Rob saw that his whole life had been lived in disappointment. He was always setting up expectations that were not communicated and not fulfilled, then getting angry and sad (but of course not communicating these feelings, either). He also saw that *he* avoided sex, even though he had projected this totally onto Jean. He thought it was she who was always avoiding sex, but when we pressed him to take 100 percent responsibility he saw through his projection. He also saw how his whole pattern of disappointment and avoidance of sex had been adopted from his long-suffering martyr-mother. Jean saw that her past programming had come largely from her father. He had been so critical of her that she had spent her childhood in a constant state of fear of messing up. She had transferred this pattern onto her husband and children in her adult life. She was so vigilant about her housekeeping that she had few noncritical interactions with husband or kids. She cried when she saw how she had adopted her father's pattern and was perpetuating it with the people she loved in the present.

What were Jean and Rob getting out of staying stuck? This question intertwined with the prior one of how the past was coloring the present. It resulted in a breakthrough for them. Jean recognized her payoff. By maintaining her hypercritical stance, she did not have to bring up her old feelings of powerlessness in her relationship with Father. By holding a position of making Rob wrong and responsible for her misery, she did not have to confront the real source of her unhappiness, which lay in her still-unresolved relationship with her father. Rob's payoff was that he didn't have to get closer to Jean and thereby risk and share more. He was afraid that if he got closer to Jean it would bring up his old, unresolved feelings toward his mother, which he was doing everything to avoid facing. This moment was crucial, for we asked him to explore *all* his feelings toward his mother. Up came anger, fear, and sadness. For several sessions the focus shifted to sorting out his childhood feelings. Finally, he acknowledged long-buried sexual feelings toward his mother. He uncovered memories of her bathing him and scrubbing his genitals as a way of expressing her anger at his father. This was the turning point of therapy. Rob saw that his tendency to bury his anger toward Jean was really his way of burying his anger and sexual feelings toward his mother. Sex and anger were joined together in his mind. No wonder he achieved orgasm so quickly; he would experience just enough sex to take care of the physical need without bringing up his old feelings.

Following Rob's breakthrough, their entire relationship was reborn. So much movement came from question 4 that they did not really need to go further. Their sexual rhythms came into harmony. Once they dropped using sex as the arena for power struggles, they were free to use it as an arena for pleasure and growth. Their relationship problems had been the result of trying to keep their childhood patterns concealed. Once they began using their relationship for enhancing awareness rather than dulling it, they came into an easy synchrony with each other.

Some problems will yield to one or two of the questions, while other, more long-term problems may take many careful, loving repetitions. We use these questions as a continual process in both our personal and professional lives, and recommend that you do the same. Work with the questions until they become an automatic part of your thinking. If you go through your daily life with these seven questions in the back of your mind, you will avoid many difficult situations. When you do get stuck, as we all do from time to time, your time spent in conflict will be greatly lessened.

The magic is accessed through inquiring into the sources of the conflict in yourself rather than projecting the responsibility onto others. When you claim creativity of the issue, and open up to it through the specific tools of the questions, you align yourself with the source of magic in yourself. The dictionary tells us that one of the definitions of magic is "producing extraordinary results." Next time you have a problem, apply these seven questions and see for yourself what extraordinary results you produce.

SEVEN

Co-Committed Strategies for Communicating and Handling Difficult Emotions

In the realm of emotions, many people are functioning at a kindergarten level. There is no need for self-blame. After all, in your formal education, how many courses did you take in dealing with feelings? Personally, we cannot remember one minute spent on learning about these key issues in school, whereas hours were spent on memorizing the geography of South America. It is incredible that we have such a societal blind spot. No one ever landed in jail or a mental hospital because of a difficulty with geography, but both institutions are packed with people who have difficulty with their emotions. In this chapter we will go deeper into the subject of feelings, the basics of which we discussed in chapter 4. This is the crash course in feelings that we wish we had received in the first grade, but instead had to learn through making a lot of mistakes in our own lives and in helping others sort out their emotional errors.

Problems stem largely from those feelings that are hidden from ourselves and from others. The problems would not exist if we had a modicum of basic training in emotional awareness. What do we really need to know about emotions? The answer is simple: (1) feel them, and (2) communicate them in loving, straightforward ways to yourself and to others. If people followed these simple guidelines, most lawsuits, wars, and divorces would be unnecessary. Many problems come from hiding our feelings from ourselves; many other problems stem from hiding our feelings from others.

An example: Herb, age thirty-nine, was an accountant who supervised the work of several other accountants and a dozen assistants. He reported to the founder and senior partner of the firm. When we first saw Herb he was depressed. Depression is a secondary emotion, the result of not being able to deal with a primary feeling, usually anger. In other words, if you cannot handle anger effectively, you may eventually get a burned-out feeling inside. This feeling is what we call depression, but its true source is anger. This was the case with Herb. His boss, Henry, was an autocratic man in his sixties who had a kingly bearing and a strong need to be right. Herb frequently was angry at this man, but he did not know any effective ways to handle his anger. He did not express it to Henry because he feared getting fired. Another issue, which Herb felt was somehow related, was that he did not feel close to his young son. Herb had a close relationship with his daughter, age six, but he had never felt bonded to his four-year-old son. This issue was a source of friction between him and his wife. She sensed the distance between Herb and the boy and wanted them to be closer. A deeper problem was that Herb buried his anger so thoroughly that he did not even realize he was angry. It took us several weeks before he was able even to identify feelings of anger in his body. When he finally saw how often he experienced flares of anger at Henry, Herb's depression began to lift. Here lies a key notion: Simply acknowledging the existence of an important feeling begins the healing process.

Herb then began to search for alternative ways to deal

with the feeling. His old strategy—bury the anger and stew in it—had only led to depression. Now he needed a new strategy. We raised the question: Why not communicate the anger directly to Henry? Herb felt flurries of fear and memories of dealing with his autocratic father. He made a connection between his childhood terror of his father and his current feelings of powerlessness with Henry.

After our session Herb tried a confrontation with Henry; in his words, "I bombed." Henry flew into a rage, calling Herb an ingrate and implying that he was lazy. Herb retreated in wounded silence, but in his heart he knew something was wrong. His work had always received the highest praise from Henry, and there had never before been any mention of lack of gratitude. We suggested that just as Herb was putting his father's face on Henry, Henry was putting someone else's face on Herb. A light went on. Herb knew that Henry had a son near Herb's age who had failed to live up to his father's expectations. It was rumored that Henry had come close to disowning his son on several occasions. Herb relaxed and made another foray into the lion's den. This time the conversation went more smoothly. Henry apologized, and they had a straightforward talk about anger and fathers and sons. Shortly afterward, Herb realized that he had distanced himself from his son because he was afraid he would be like his own father. It was safer not to get close to his son than to risk projecting onto the boy his own unresolved issues with his father.

As this process unfolded over several months we saw the key points where resolutions occurred. The moment when everything shifted was when Herb quit hiding his anger from himself. Simply acknowledging his anger, as he put it, "got me up out of the mud." With the energy that was freed up by admitting his anger, he found the courage to deal with Henry straight on. At the same time, his relationship with his son became richer as he became free of his anxiety in that relationship.

We asked a very successful founder of a business: "What is the most valuable thing you've learned in the realm of emotions?" Her answer: "I've learned that all the

emotions are normal, natural, and no big deal." Two
decades of handling thousands of crisis situations boiled
down to such a simple statement! In a similar vein, an
elderly priest in one of Graham Greene's books is asked
what he has learned from a lifetime of hearing confessions.
He says that he has learned two things: People are much
more unhappy than they let on, and there is no such thing
as a grown-up.

How does it come to be this way?

Sources of Distorted Thinking About Emotions

Many problems with feelings come from childhood survival choices. Most of these choices relate not to physical
survival but to the survival of our identities. Gay gives a
personal example: "I remember learning to hide my sexual
feelings from my family, particularly my mother, because I
saw that if I got near the subject she would become acutely
uncomfortable. I chose my identity as a Good Boy over my
identity as a Real Boy, one with sexual feelings. This choice
ensured my survival as a member in good standing of the
Hendricks family, an institution of world-class sexual
repression. Later, though, I had to sort out my sexual feelings from guilt, fear, anger, and other feelings that had
become tangled up with sexuality. I got it sorted out, but
the money I spent on therapy could have bought me a
BMW. When my daughter reached puberty, I made sure to
have a conversation with her that went something like this:
'You're going to be having a lot of sexual feelings from
now on. Sometimes they'll be strong, and other times you'll
probably not think about them at all. These are normal and
natural. If you feel comfortable talking to me about it,
great. If not, that's fine, too. Just be sure to let yourself feel
them, because they're a healthy part of you. There are some
smart ways to express your feelings, and there are other

ways that will cause problems, but regardless of how you express them, the feelings themselves are healthy.' Then we went on to talk of pregnancy, contraception, homosexuality, and other things she was curious about. Now, having successfully negotiated the teen years while many of her peers were struggling with sex, she is quick to thank me for those conversations at thirteen."

Unless you grew up in an unusually healthy family you probably got little information about core feelings. The lack of information, or the misinformation, becomes a major barrier to overcome later. For example, how did your mother handle anger? Was she a martyr or a screamer? Was your father a silent sulker or a lurching hulk? How you saw the people around you handling their anger was a powerful influence in shaping how you would deal with emotions later on. Gay continues his example: "In my family, anger was hidden and never communicated, save through an occasional explosion. About once a month my mother would go into a titanic rage and release the pressure. Then the lid would be tightened down again. I learned this pattern so well that I told someone in a therapy group twenty years later that I had no anger in me. 'Oh yeah?' he said. 'Then how come you're fat and smoke heavily and have a wife you don't get along with?' Bless his heart. Although I got furious at him for saying this, I am grateful to this day. He called me on my act. I saw that I indeed had a huge reservoir of ancient rage and fear and grief. My personality was oriented around keeping those feelings covered up. And it was not working. So I got busy, and in the next year, through therapy and reading everything I could get my hands on, I changed my life. I lost a hundred pounds, quit smoking, got out of a troubled relationship, and made many other changes. One change that seemed almost magical at the time was that my vision improved. I went from 20/400 vision down to no longer needing glasses to pass my driver's test."

We have spoken of anger, but sadness and fear also have a powerful effect on us. Few of us escaped the reach of grief as we grew up. Sadness is about loss, and who among us has not lost loved ones, pets, a special house, or the innocence of childhood? As for fear, the history of our species *is* the history of fear. Not all that long ago we were huddled around fires in caves, plotting our strategies against the saber-toothed tiger and the woolly mammoth lurking outside. Less than a hundred years ago we lost half our children to terrifying diseases against which we were powerless. Now we wonder if our children and their children will escape the shadow of nuclear holocaust. Fear is here to stay; it is how we relate to it that makes or breaks us.

Defining Your Boundaries

At the very core of ourselves we have two fears that determine every aspect of our relationships. These are the fears of being alone and of being engulfed by others. On one side we fear abandonment, being left alone to be swallowed up by the universe. On the other side we fear engulfment, being swallowed up by other people. Beneath these issues is a deeper one: fear of not being. From the moment of birth, we experience the fear of not being at all. In relationship we fear the loss of self through being close (engulfment) and through being too separate. Often we flee both closeness and separateness to live in a limbo state, holding ourselves back from complete union and full autonomy.

The lifelong process of individuation is extraordinarily complicated. To make it even more so, nature has designed the beginning of our individuation process with a confusing moment: we are cut off from our mothers physically when the umbilical cord is snipped, but then are completely dependent on her for a long period of time. Boundary issues continue to provide challenges throughout life. Where do we stop and others begin? In the realm of relationships, the boundary issues are unclear. When someone tells you something and you get angry, did they *make* you angry? As we grow up we constantly encounter situations in which we cannot trust our independence. We want to but simply cannot. So we retreat into dependence again, often with feelings of anger and shame. We go forward into adult life with a confusing mixture of yearnings for autonomy and for attachment.

When our dual urges for separateness and closeness are not resolved in healthy ways, we bring neurotic distortions of those urges to our relationships. The distortion of the yearning for closeness is clinging. The distortion of the urge for separateness is withdrawing. Clingers fear abandonment; withdrawers fear closeness. Go to even a modest-sized party and you will see both extremes. Even if clinging and withdrawing are not physically visible, they still exist in subtler forms in most of us. The person who has learned not to cling physically may still find ways of doing so on the mental and emotional level. The reformed withdrawer may not isolate him- or herself at the party but may still be hiding inwardly.

People who bring unclear boundaries into relationships set themselves up for serious problems. They yearn to be made complete through merging with the other person, but when they merge they feel engulfed. They are also easily manipulated into doing things they do not want to do. They tend to overidentify with the feelings of others, so they are awash in everyone else's issues and problems. The person with healthy boundaries can empathize with the feelings of other people but does not take them on. The person with unclear boundaries is also ripe for manipulation by power-hungry authority figures such as some religious and political leaders. They may attempt to rectify their faulty boundaries through a rigid belief system of some sort, which makes them a prime target for fundamentalists of various persuasions.

Teenagers are notorious for their rebelliousness. If they cannot find a satisfying way of forging an independent self, they may resort to negative behaviors that bring their boundaries up against parents, principals, judges, and police. Many people carry their teenage strategies into their adult relationships, needing constant harassment to keep themselves in check. Many of the problematic behaviors in which people engage in relationships, from extramarital affairs to abuse of credit, can be seen as adolescent boundary-making strategies carried forward into adulthood.

It is urgent for people in close relationships to clarify their boundaries. What is required is that we forge a sense of self that remains intact whether we are standing alone or surrendering into unity with another person. Many of the activities in the Co-Commitment Program are designed to move you toward a clear and unshakable sense of self.

Recognizing Your Feelings

There are certain signs and symptoms that occur when you are having core emotions. Some of the signs are obvious—sweaty palms, clenched fists—but others are not quite so easy to recognize. It is important that you learn to listen to the subtle signals of your body, so that you will know when you are experiencing different feelings. To help in this process, we have compiled the following lists of sensations and behaviors connected with the core feelings. The lists are based on what we have learned in talking to our clients. These lists are not carved in stone; use them experimentally to find out if they fit you.

Symptoms of Fear

Nausea
Tightness in stomach and chest
Internal quivering, especially down the midline of chest and stomach
Damp or sweaty palms
Dryness in mouth
Contraction of sensitive tissue (nipples, penis)
Narrow focus in eyes; tunnel vision
Elevated heart rate
Rapid rate of thought

Symptoms of Anger

Tightness in shoulders and back of neck
Headache, especially in back of head and neck
Tight or sore jaw muscles
Clenching jaws, or nighttime grinding of teeth
Crawling or itching sensations in upper back, shoulders, arms
Outbursts at inappropriate times
Picking at fingernails

Symptoms of Sadness

Constricted sensation in chest
Dull, heavy, or numb sensation in chest
Pain along breastbone when you press it
Thoughts that dwell on the negative
Difficulty in waking up and getting out of bed in the morning
Congestion in sinus and chest that lasts longer than usual
Thinking of losses, recent and long-ago

Distinguishing Thoughts from Feelings

It is important to distinguish your feelings from cognitive processes such as thoughts and beliefs. Many of our clients confuse the cognitive and the emotional. We ask: "How do you feel right now?" and they say something like: "I feel like people don't really care about me." This statement is certainly important and meaningful, but is a thought or a belief rather than a feeling. Feelings are short and to the point. In getting to know your feelings we encourage you to focus on the physical sensations that accompany fear, anger, hurt, and other feelings. People who make the quickest progress in dealing with their feelings are those who learn to work with them as body processes.

This is not to say that cognitive processes are of less value. The real sign of health is to have thinking and feeling in harmony with each other. Many people use their thoughts to negate their feelings. They think thoughts like: "I shouldn't feel angry," or, "You should be ashamed of yourself for feeling that way." Other people are awash in their feelings and have little capacity for logic and reason. It is important to have thoughts and feelings dancing gracefully together rather than locked in mortal combat. Think of the difference it would make to our peace of mind if when we were angry we thought: "I'm angry. That's obviously the experience I ought to be having right now." Instead, we often burn up a great deal of energy running our minds counter to what our bodies are saying.

Co-Committed Communication Skills

There are several communication skills that make it much easier to maintain the flow of positive energy in co-committed relationships. There are also several communication strategies you must learn to avoid. In communicating, as in much of life, there are many more ways to do it wrong than right. Here are some of the most helpful communication suggestions we give to our clients.

Make Statements Instead of Asking Questions

Many people habitually put their statements in the form of questions. Hiding statements in this way avoids the risk of making a direct communication but creates conflict in relationships. Ask questions only when you don't know something that you need to know. Because we live in a world where lies are mixed freely with truth, we all have to develop a second type of hearing. We cannot simply listen; we must listen with an ear toward discriminating truth from potentially dangerous lies. As children we often hear the question: "Don't you think it's bedtime?" There are statements within this question, possibly ranging from "I want you to go to bed now" to "I'm absolutely exhausted and tired of being a parent and I want to go to bed." Questions of this kind are double binds: either a yes or no answer puts us in a losing situation. In our therapy practice with couples, we often hear questions like: "Don't I always tell you I love you?" and, "Haven't we had twenty good years together?" These are not really questions. The hidden statements are important to improving the relationship: "I'm angry because I've put up with you for twenty years and now you want to leave," or, "I'm hurt because you just said I never tell you I love you." When these statements are made in the form of questions, conflict inevitably follows. When people are courageous enough to make the statement they have been hiding, clarity and resolution usually follow.

It is important that you look beneath the surface of questions to find the hidden statements. In a co-committed relationship, truth always has priority, because you are committed to revealing rather than concealing. Your partner may say: "Haven't we talked about this enough for one night?" If you say "yes" or "no" you are stuck. If you say "yes," you are taking responsibility for ending the discussion; plus you are letting your partner get away with an unclear communication. If you say "no," you are still responding to the question rather than getting the other person to take full responsibility for the hidden statement. Better to say: "It sounds like you're angry and want to stop talking about this right now." Then the truth is on the table.

Listen carefully for hidden statements within your own questions as well as those of your partner. We have tried an interesting experiment in our own relationship. We put ourselves on a "questions diet," going without them for a week. It was very revealing, because we found that we often couched our statements in questions. We would ask: "Where do you want to go for dinner tonight?" when one of us actually had a desire to go to a particular place. Going on a strict no-questions diet forced us to put all our statements out on the table, risking rejection, perhaps, but also making it impossible to be ambiguous. It worked, and we have never gone back to asking questions unless there is some information we actually need to know.

Consider two famous statements: "These are the times that try men's souls" and "Ask not what your country can do for you; ask what you can do for your country." Note that John Kennedy did not use a question: "Wouldn't you rather do things for your country than have it do things for you?" This question whines and wheedles, whereas his statement became a galvanizing force for many social programs. Thomas Paine did not ask, "Don't you think these are trying times, soulwise?" If he had, we might still be a British colony.

Say "I" Instead of "You"

People weaken their communication through hiding their "I" behind a "you." For example, someone says: "What can you do when you've tried everything you know how to do?" This question conceals a powerful I-statement: "I feel despair because I've tried everything I know how to do and nothing has worked." Putting it in the form of a you-statement depersonalizes it, thereby allowing you to avoid responsibility. You-statements are also a way of avoiding pain, putting it one step removed from yourself. When hurt, you may say: "After you've been hurt a few times you don't trust anymore," rather than be direct: "I feel hurt and I don't trust anyone." The cost of hiding the direct communication is high. By staying one step removed from our emotions, we guarantee that their grip on us will not soon loosen.

Many times the healing process does not begin until an I-statement is made. A man recently divorced said: "You know, you just can't figure out what women want, can you?" Not only did he camouflage his pain in a you-statement, but he put it in the form of a question. We asked him to make an I-statement that said what he really meant. As he puzzled over how to do this, his eyes began to twitch and his chin quivered. Finally he said: "I have no idea how to please women." The tears began. We said: "It sounds like you mean some women in particular rather than women in general." He began to sob. "I never could please my mother and I never could please Barbara." This statement has healing power. It is direct and truthful and absolutely specific. When we live one step removed from our feelings, from the "I" that we are, there is little possibility of healing. When we begin to say "I," we take a real step toward freedom.

Don't Use Negatives Unless They Are True

False negatives such as "I can't" and "never" are frivolously overused, with serious consequences. They may seem trivial, but in fact they are dangerous because they allow you to avoid responsibility. "I can't" is one to be particularly avoided, unless you are physically restrained. If you are in shackles, "I can't" has relevance; otherwise, it is usually a roundabout way of saying "I don't want to," "I won't," or, "I have not learned how to." If you really mean "I don't want to," it is important to come out and say so. Saying "I can't" disowns responsibility. Suppose someone asks you to do something at three o'clock, at which time you have a dental appointment. It is best simply to tell the truth: "I have a dental appointment then." Avoid saying "I can't," because you are still shifting responsibility. In co-committed relationships you want your words to communicate the truth with power and simplicity. Similarly, the words *never* and *always* are seldom true. Statements such as: "You never, ever help me with anything," and, "Why do you always leave the kitchen door open?" are corrupt forms of important statements of feeling that need to be made clearly.

Empower Instead of Rescue

Rescuing is when you interfere with people's power by doing something for them that they ought to do for themselves. Rescuing denies the other person the opportunity to be effective. When you rescue, you actually devalue and disempower the person.

THERAPIST (to husband): How do you feel today?
HUSBAND: Well, I'm not real sure.
WIFE: He's been really angry lately.

The husband could, with time and reflection, have told his own truth. His pattern was to let his wife rescue him, then to build resentment at her for doing so. Then he would righteously blow up, and a days-long hassle would be under way. The wife actually thought she was being helpful. With exploration she came face to face with an unconscious motive that was less attractive: she was trying to prove her husband incompetent so that she could maintain her belief in the basic unworthiness of men. He, on the other hand, was playing out a drama of helplessness that had begun in his relationship with his smothering mother.

There is nothing wrong with doing things for someone as long as we are not denying that person's power. Rescuing is an unconscious pattern that interferes with the other person's ability to learn and grow. When you rush to help someone, first ask yourself if your help is in any way disempowering to the person. Then, to make sure, ask the person if your help would be disempowering. This problem is especially relevant in co-dependence. One of the hallmarks of co-dependence is doing things that look helpful on the surface but actually disempower the other person. Following are a couple of examples, culled from one day of our therapy practice. A woman thinks she is being helpful by calling in sick for her husband when in truth he has a hangover. A man thinks he is being helpful by frequently assisting his wife with her night-school assignments; the result is that she falls far behind in her class. A couple rush in several times a day to help their twin sons iron out hassles; soon they are having to do it almost hourly. All of these are examples of doing things for others that they would be better off doing themselves.

Redefining

This pattern is an insidious part of many co-dependents' communication patterns. Redefining is when a person does not respond directly to what another person has said, but instead changes the subject to fit his or her agenda. Following are several examples of redefinition from our therapy records.

HER: Do you really want to be in counseling with me?
HIM (irritated): I'm here, aren't I?

Can you hear what's wrong in this communication? She asks a question that requires a yes or no answer. He does not respond clearly with a yes or a no and instead redefines the question. His agenda is to communicate anger and to avoid responsibility. He does so by side-stepping her question.

Another example:

HIM: Did you notice that I called you this week when I was going to be late for dinner?
HER: Tuesday you totally forgot about picking Kevin up after soccer.

Again, a yes or no answer and a complete change of subject. She was so busy communicating her anger about Tuesday that she redefined the subject of conversation. Countless redefinitions occur every day, and they have similar results: distorted communication and a vague sense of incompletion. If after talking to someone you feel irritated and "off," chances are that redefining played a role in the conversation. In co-committed relationships the partners avoid redefining; instead, they are careful to respond to what each other has said, without interjecting their own points of view.

Devaluing

This pattern comes in several forms. Interrupting people while they are speaking is probably the most common type of devaluation in communication. When you are interrupted, the other person is saying: "I'm more important than you are. My point of view has priority." Interruptions always cause problems in communication, although often neither party realizes why their interaction has become obstructed.

Another form of devaluing is self-denigration. Putting yourself down draws negative attention to you and lowers your positive energy. We once attended a lecture by a well-known author and psychologist. He began his talk with the following statement: "We only have forty-five minutes so of course we won't be able to get into anything very meaningful. . . ." The energy in the room deflated like a punctured balloon. He could easily have said: "We have forty-five minutes, and I commit myself to telling you everything that's essential about the subject in that time." This statement would have charged the room with energy and power.

The alternative to devaluing ourselves and others is simple: consider us all as equal and absolutely worthwhile. Prepare, however, to spend a lifetime mastering this view. The world is full of inequality, but this need not affect our sense of equality within ourselves and with those around us.

The Co-Committed Alternative

In the co-committed relationship you absolutely must support each other for opening up to deep feeling. The more

you feel, the more alive you are. Feelings are our spontaneous reactions to things, and of course you must learn appropriate ways to express your feelings. It is not wise to stop
your car on the freeway, as one of our clients did, to get
out and throw a temper tantrum about something your
partner has said. However, assuming you are mindful of
the proper time and place for their expression, your emotions are sacred in the co-committed relationship. The Following is an example of how one couple learned a better
way to be with and to express their emotions.

Mary initially withheld her fears from Dan because she
thought he would get angry at her. She had a number of
fears that emerged as she and Dan grew closer. She was
afraid of her sexuality and her anger. She had sealed off
these feelings as a result of the trauma of sexual abuse in
her childhood. Her sexual relationship with Dan was the
best she had ever experienced, but the more her sexual feelings emerged, the more her anger came to the surface. Her
experience in her family was that she had to withhold her
feelings at all costs, lest the sexual abuse by her father
would get back to her mother. But when she withheld her
feelings from Dan, he sensed that something was wrong.
"You're acting funny," he would say. "You make me wonder what you've been up to." Then Mary would deny that
anything was going on. Dan would poke more; Mary would
withdraw further. Dan would get mad; Mary would break
into tears and say: "I can't ever share my feelings with him
because he gets mad."

In counseling, we invited Dan to *be with* Mary and her
feelings as much as he could. Immediately he noticed that
he was holding his breath and tensing his muscles. We
pointed out that he looked frightened by Mary's feelings.
He agreed, and this awareness produced a shift in the relationship. Mary saw that he was just as scared as she was.
She shifted from seeing him as an angry person to seeing
him as afraid. They were equals. Dan released the tension
in his posture and took a deep breath. As Mary began talking about her fear he leaned forward, still breathing deeply,
and put his hand on her shoulder. This supportive gesture
helped Mary open up more to her fear, and she talked more

animatedly. Mary's posture relaxed too, and she became aware of a lifelong pattern: "I've never been able to share my feelings since I was a little kid, for fear of being punished." She realized that she was projecting this pattern onto Dan. With this insight her tears spilled over and she began to sob deeply. Dan started to hold his breath, pulling back from this deeper release of feeling. He quickly saw what he was doing, though, and leaned forward again to support Mary.

Mary's crying deepened as Dan held her and rocked her gently. "I love everything about you," he murmured to her. "Even this?" she sobbed. "Even that," he said, stroking her hair. It was a deep, intimate, life-changing moment for both of them. She found out that it was all right to go into her deepest feelings, and he found that he could support her no matter how she was hurting. "You really want to know all of me?" Mary asked. Dan looked at her for a long time, then said: "I feel closer to you when you share all of yourself. I want that for me, too. You help show me what's possible for myself."

Mary and Dan learned to feel and speak the truth and to support each other while opening up to the truth. In a co-committed relationship, you encourage each other in opening to the depths and heights of yourselves. You support each other in furthering the commitment to being fully alive and fully creative. This commitment is powerful, and you will be challenged on it daily. Are you willing to be fully alive and open to the complete range of human experience? Are you willing to be with your deepest feelings and those of your partner? If so, you are well on your way to true intimacy and co-commitment.

EIGHT

How to Keep the Past from Intruding on the Present

In this chapter we will discuss some of the major factors that limit people on their way to co-commitment. You may find your core pattern in some of the ones we describe. To make this inquiry successful, you will have to do something quite courageous: drop all your notions about how other people and the world itself are influencing your life, and look into how you are influencing other people and the world by your attitudes. We ask that you begin with assuming that you are 100 percent the creator of everything that happens to you. You may have a dozen or more excellent arguments of why you are not responsible—your unhappy childhood, unfair coaches, dull parents, a bad neighborhood—but we want you to drop all those arguments for a while. If you will accept those rules, let's play.

You are the absolute creator of what happens to you. This means *now*. We don't mean that you chose to have a birth defect or chose to move to Cleveland at age two. We mean that *now* you are the creator of what happens to you. There is awesome power in knowing this fact. As long as there is even one tiny part of you that thinks the world is doing it to you, the world is going to do it to you. When you know 100 percent that you create it, you will start influencing the world around you in a much bigger and more positive way.

The problem is that there is usually some old belief or program inscribed in your mind that causes you to create a less powerful version of yourself. To illustrate, Gay shares the following.

"I mentioned earlier that I turned my life around in 1969, losing a hundred pounds and clearing up my eyesight. In the following year I changed careers and got out of a bad marriage. This period of rapid change was facilitated by my sudden understanding of one of my major glitch-points. I recall asking myself, during one of my sleepless nights in the peak period of misery prior to changing my path, how I could have set up my life in such a destructive way. I made a count of all the destructive things I was doing: smoking, being grossly overweight, living without a loving relationship, hiding all my true feelings. Why? Suddenly I was confronted with a stunning realization: I was replaying my father's life down to the last detail. He was fat, smoked, and was by all accounts heavily defended against love and positive energy. He had died of all these things at age thirty-two. And I was in my midtwenties, well on the same path. How could I have been so blind not to see what I was doing? Well, the sad truth is that I did not see it because I was so busy doing it. It is the very nature of these deep-seated programs to look like they are not programs at all: they look like the way it is. One of the major wake-up moments in life is when we discover that something is not the way it is, but simply the way we see it.

"Fortunately for me, I got the message. I realized I was a dead man if I did not make some radical changes quickly. So I moved like a dervish for a year until I had gotten off the track of my programming and had some control over my life again. The wisdom of these changes became apparent two years later when a colleague of mine, similar to me in many ways, dropped dead at age twenty-six. He was very overweight and had some of the same psychological issues that I've described, but he chose to go in a different direction. He scoffed at my weight loss program and, always the practical joker, bought me a five-pound box of chocolates after I had lost fifty pounds, in an attempt to sabotage me. He was quick to put down counseling, exercise, and self-improvement in general. I felt angry and deeply saddened when he died of a massive heart attack before taking even the first breath of his potential."

Sometimes you may find that your central limiting pattern is simply a replay of a script you learned from a parent or someone else in the past. We all are products of our conditioning. Don't bother asking yourself if the past is influencing your present. Assume it is. Simply ask how. The answers you get will not always be pleasant to entertain, but the payoff is enormous. As we said earlier, asking the questions is more important than the answers you receive. In any case, we don't have much of a choice. If we do not inquire into our barriers, we are shortchanging ourselves so radically that we are effectively out of the game. In truth, the process can be fun, not painful. It all depends on whether you greet what you learn with an "aa-ha" or an "oh-no."

Roles are a subtle and pervasive form of programming. By fulfilling the requirements of a role, you tend to create things that are appropriate to that role. If you are drawn toward a role as a lawyer, for example, you will tend to manifest more money than if you are drawn to the role of homemaker. Much of the manifestation we experience comes simply from assuming a role that has established agreements and expectations associated with it. There are general agreements that govern various roles in life, and by stepping into a certain role you take on those agreements for better or worse. Lawyers make more money than homemakers; they also work such long hours they have little time for families. So, if a lawyer seems adept at creating money, we do not need to look beyond the general principle to understand that ability.

On the negative side, roles cause us much trouble in goal creation. Forgetting that we have unconsciously made agreements by stepping into a particular role, we can become very confused. For example, the lawyer may want to consider his or her family's complaints about being overly intellectual and manipulative. A lawyer's daughter told us recently: "Mom, when I tell you how I feel, you assume I'm the opposing lawyer and start lecturing me about not making sense. My feelings make sense to me; I just want you to hear them."

Another problem with creating through roles is that often our roles are not freely chosen. We have worked with many successful people who have distinguished themselves at fulfilling a role only to grow miserable in it. When they explore the reasons, it often emerges that they were led into the role against their deeper wishes. For example, a friend who is a dentist recently realized that he had never wanted to be a dentist. He went into the profession because his father had challenged him to take the aptitude test and he had scored very high on it. Everyone said, "Oh, great, dentists make lots of money, it's a secure profession—do it!" Twenty-five years later he saw, with some grief, that he really had wanted to be a writer.

We often play out roles the way we saw them played out in childhood. We may play out the role of a suffering parent because that is the way our parents behaved. For example, a client came to us asking how she could stay in her marriage and be healthy. She had been sick almost since the day of her marriage. She stayed in the relationship "because of the children," as her parents had for twenty-five years before divorcing. It took many months of work to disentangle her relationship from patterns she had learned as a child. She and her husband are now creating a new relationship based on seeing each other more clearly and currently.

It is now well known that children of abusive parents are more likely to abuse their children. It is less understood that everyone has the choice, even at a young age, to take charge of their lives and make their own rules. We have worked with many clients who see themselves as victims. When we examine closely the origin of that helpless role, we see over and over a choice point in childhood: "Either they're crazy or I am." The child moving toward autonomy decides, "They're crazy; I'm going to make my own rules."

The victim decides, "I'm crazy; they're bigger and must know better."

Roles also carry the cultural weight of generations of gender expectations. For example, women are expected to maintain the extended family and social bonds through letters, calls, and plans. Men are expected to be good team players and handymen, valuing the bottom line over feelings. By age five we have all received and integrated thousands of nonverbal cues about masculine and feminine behavior. Most adults still move through the world with unexamined styles that filter and color every interaction.

Projection Is Often the Culprit

In projection, we see the movie on the opposite wall, and we forget that we are the source of it. We see a problem around us, and it looks so "out there" that it doesn't even occur to us that we have created it through the way we look at the world. To illustrate how powerfully projection can color our world, consider the example of Gloria, a loan officer at a bank.

She was rapidly growing disenchanted with her job because she felt excluded by her fellow loan officers. She also complained that they were untrustworthy. She could cite many examples of their exclusions and untrustworthiness. It seemed that the problem had never occurred when she was a teller or even head teller. We asked her what else was going on in her life when she got promoted to loan officer. She told us that at about that time she had discovered her husband was having an affair and the marriage had begun to crumble. She asked him to leave, and he took refuge with one of his brothers. His brothers and their wives rallied around him, telling her that she should give him another chance. Her husband, in retaliation for her kicking him out, took all the money from their savings account. No wonder she felt excluded and could not trust. As it happened, most of the other loan officers were men.

When they went out to lunch together and didn't invite her, it looked like exclusion to her. That was her mind making meaning, based on how she felt. When one of the men forgot something or failed to return a call, her mind manufactured meaning around the event. To her it looked like untrustworthiness, not just a forgotten phone call.

With a bit of work, Gloria came to see how she was projecting the problems with her family onto her work life. Her feelings were coloring her perceptions, and she was making the world fit how she felt. She was putting out the signals "I can't trust" and "I feel excluded," and the world was cooperating with her. When she discovered how all of this worked, she experienced a quick shift. Suddenly she started getting lunch invitations from the other loan officers. She made an interior correction, and suddenly the world seemed to treat her differently. As the result of clearing up a major glitch inside herself, she straightened out a problem that looked very much "out there." Her inquiry also had a more tangible payoff: she was soon promoted to a vice presidency.

Our perspective may sound radical: Problems with people "out there" rarely have anything to do with them. People are simply screens onto which we cast our projections. Is this hard to accept? Wait, it gets worse. They are busily casting their projections onto you at the same time! This means that people are not really relating to one another most of the time, but to their own projections. When you begin to see that virtually everyone is projecting, you may feel like resigning from the human race. However, as you move through the despair, you may begin to see it as an opportunity to find out who you, and those around you, really are.

Gay shares a personal example from the realm of work relationships: "I once worked for a man whom I first liked, then came to dislike. I had to interact with him on a regular basis, and soon my mind began to be cluttered with arguments with him that I would replay over and over. I would mentally edit the arguments so that I came out the winner, although in our real-life arguments I generally lost. Pretty soon I found myself complaining about him and gathering allies against him among my co-workers. This strategy met with only limited success—most just shrugged and said, 'That's the way he is; don't let it bug you.' I managed to find one ally, though. He and I agreed that we were the most unjustly treated of all. Daily we discussed some aspect of our boss's shortcomings as a human being. I continued this pattern for several months until one day I had a revelation. I was driving home from work, busily rehashing an argument in my mind, when suddenly I thought, 'That's enough!' I decided then and there to seek another solution. I took a deep breath and asked myself what the whole issue was about.

"Within moments several profound realizations came to me. I saw that I was trying to get from this man what I had never gotten from my father. I was seeking his approval and becoming angry when he would not give it. In short, I was replaying an old family script with my boss. No wonder I was making myself miserable. Even if my boss had been able to give me meaningful approval, it wouldn't have mattered anyway. If I am trying to get Father's approval through my interactions with father substitutes, no amount of approval will help.

"In discussing my realizations with a friend I got even more information. My mother had never really recovered emotionally from the shock of my father's early death. Her way of dealing with her complex feelings about my father's death was to idolize him. He became the family saint. Later in life I came to expect saintly behavior from male authority figures. When they let me down, as they always did, I would be angry at them and dismiss them entirely. As you can no doubt see, this 'saint or nothing' approach to men influenced my relationship with my boss.

"My relationship with my boss changed after that day. When I stopped using my old programs in our interactions, our relationship quickly shifted. I saw him as just another person, one with good points and bad points. The reason why my peers' original advice—'don't let it bug you'—didn't work was that I had to learn why it did bug me in order to sort it out."

Projecting Past Authority Issues onto the Present

Our problems with authority usually begin with our parents, then we extend them out into our growing world of teachers, coaches, and bosses. Developmental psychologists tell us that the toilet-training period is the traditional time for working out our issues with authority. It is the first time the world of big people says: "Do it here. Don't do it there." There are only three ways to go in dealing with authority. We can accept it calmly, obeying it when it is good for us and rejecting it when it is not. We follow authority when it tells us to cross with the green light but not when it tells us to take the stranger's candy. That is the healthy way, and, as you know, it is not easily learned. The two other ways are not so healthy. The first is rebellion, in which we squirm against the strictures of authority. The second is overadaptation, where we go along with even unhealthy authority while secretly rebelling inside. Neither path is rewarding. The first can lead to jail; the second to ulcers.

We once asked an authority on authority to estimate how many people have a healthy relationship to authority.

"One out of twenty," he replied without a pause.

"Our species is in trouble, then," we said.

"Yep."

The next day, as he was driving us to where he would give his lecture on authority, he was apprehended for doing 43 miles per hour in a 30 zone. To make matters worse, it was a school zone. Even the experts have trouble with authority.

The Authority Process

Many people have found the following process to be useful in revealing their problems with authority. We invite you to take fifteen minutes to experience this simple but powerful activity.

1. Close your eyes and relax quietly for one minute, or until you feel calm and clear.

2. Think of all those who have or have had authority over you. Think of them as one aggregate unit: Authority. Notice the body feelings that go along with this thought. Notice sensations of tension in your body. Now dismiss these feelings and thoughts, and go back to relaxing until you feel clear and calm.

3. Think of all those over whom you have authority. Think of them as one aggregate unit. Notice the body feelings that go along with this thought. Notice sensations of tension in your body. Relax for about a minute, or until you feel calm and clear.

4. Now think of how you would like to feel with authority figures. Let a feeling develop in your body that is your ideal way of feeling in regard to authority figures. When you have the feeling, think of Authority again as one aggregate unit. Associate the thought of Authority with the positive feeling in your body. When you have done this, think of how you would like to feel with those over whom you have authority. When you have the feeling, think of those over whom you have authority as one aggregate unit. Associate the thought with the positive feeling in your body. When you have developed a clear, positive feeling about authority, open your eyes.

Traumas

Out of painful life events, often sudden and beyond our control, come deep emotions such as grief, rage, and terror. Out of these emotions come decisions that will affect our lives long after the traumas occurred. For example, a girl is sexually abused at a tender age. Out of the rage and terror of this experience comes a decision: Don't trust men. This decision shows up later in life in her relationships with men. A boy sees his father work himself into an early grave. Out of this observation comes a decision not to try very hard in life. Later his boss tells him that he seems not to try very hard.

Perhaps you have not experienced much trauma. Or perhaps you have had a substantial amount but have not let it bother you. If you are like most of us, however, you have had trauma and it has bothered you. At one seminar in which we were discussing traumas, there was a woman who had been born in a Nazi concentration camp and had walked all the way across Europe when she was five years old to get to the boat to take her to the United States. Next to her was a Southern California surfer type who complained that his mother had sometimes been late picking him up from his guitar lessons when he was a kid. Both of them had about the same amount of emotion in their voices as they discussed their traumas. Clearly, it is not what happens to you that matters, it is how you feel about what happens.

Frozen Feelings, Frozen Words

In traumatic situations there are always strong emotions and powerful communications. However, in the midst of trauma it is not easy to feel what we need to feel and say what we need to say. Often we simply want to blot out everything: we are overwhelmed by the pain. For example, we have worked with many people who have gone through the untimely death of a spouse, close friend, or parent. In each situation there were major unfelt feelings and unspoken communications. Society promotes keeping up a good front and burying the authentic feelings and communications.

Our client Shirley had been married to Sam for twenty years. Their relationship had been a struggle but they had worked on it and eventually things had smoothed out. On the day after a big snowstorm Shirley asked Sam several times to shovel the walk. He said he wanted to watch a football game and would do the walk later. An argument ensued. Sam stomped out to shovel the walk. Five minutes later he was dead of a massive coronary. Naturally, Shirley was left with a great deal of grief and guilt. Over the next weeks she obsessed over her last conversation with Sam, staying up night after sleepless night. Her friends tried to reassure her, but to no avail. When she came for counseling she was about to quit the job she had held for years. Her unresolved issues regarding Sam's death were interfering with her work, which was highly people oriented. As we worked together we saw immediately that anger was the one feeling she had not let herself experience. When we brought up the subject of her anger at Sam, she accused us of rudeness, insensitivity, and disrespect for the dead. She denied any anger, insisting that Sam was an angel and a saint. But, interestingly, after this conversation she slept through the night for the first time since his death. Shirley was smart enough to see the connection, and in our next meeting she let the anger pour out. She was furious at herself for pushing Sam, and furious at him for not standing up to her. Her nagging and his sullen acquiescence had been a pattern throughout their marriage. And it had likely proved fatal.

Sometimes the one barrier that holds us back is an unexplored emotion. When Shirley let out the anger, she could move on with her life. How many of us, though, go through deep traumas and do not get the lesson? By not inquiring into our blind spots, we continue to stumble along toward the next trauma. As we have said, there are only a handful of core emotions that we need to be in touch with. The communications we hide inside are more varied but often fall into three categories: regrets, resentments, and love/compassion. In the latter category are statements like: "I forgive you," and, "I love you." Saying "I love you" seems such a simple thing, and it is, if you can do it. But many people go to their graves without having said it to someone who desperately wanted to hear it from them.

Most of us have to help ourselves as best we can in difficult times. If only we had a guardian angel standing by in times of trauma, we would hear advice like: "Keep breathing. Feel your feelings. Communicate clearly to someone who'll listen. Love yourself anyway. Don't take it personally." Instead, the traumas of our lives have tremendous impacts. Under stress, we freeze ourselves into patterns of feeling and belief that later affect everything. Out of our traumas come limiting beliefs such as:

> I can't trust.
> I can't feel.
> I can't feel good.
> I can't be creative.
> Nothing I do seems to help.

It is imperative that you study key junction points of your life and take stock of any mental, physical, and emotional locks you have created during those times. To assist you in this inquiry, we have developed a process that many people have found useful.

The Trauma Process

1. Take out a sheet of paper and draw a line across it horizontally. Make a vertical mark for each year of your life. Now start at your conception and make a note of each trauma and positive experience you recall. Draw a line up for each positive experience, and a line down for each negative experience. Extend the line higher and lower, depending on the intensity of the experience and its impact on you.

2. When you have finished the life-experience chart, take out another sheet of paper. List your traumas down the left side of the paper, then make three more columns: Emotions, Decisions, and How It Affects My Life Now. For each trauma, list the emotions you felt at the time in the Emotions column, then list any decisions you made at the time, and how all of this affects your life now. Use the following example for reference.

Trauma	Emotions	Decisions	How It Affects My Life Now
My father died	Grief, anger fear	I'm powerless I don't believe in God Don't trust men	Have difficulty relating to men in my life Have few male friends

3. *Discuss this process with a partner or friend, then look over it again. Many people find that they leave out important items the first time through.*

Habit Patterns

Along with traumas and authority issues, most of us have a stack of old habit patterns we have learned in the past. These can become the barriers that keep us from reaching our full potentials. Habits are learned in two main ways: by watching what goes on around us, and by doing what works. Dad takes a certain tone of voice when discussing finances with Mom, and you find yourself using the same tone with your spouse thirty years later. Or, you find that what works in your family is to be funny, or to be sick, or to be a "good kid." Most of these patterns are unconscious and remain so until we do some creative work on ourselves.

Certain unconscious patterns never bring satisfaction. If you see yourself in any of the following descriptions, you will have to clear it out of your relationship in order to reach co-commitment.

The victim. This pattern casts you as the helpless victim in a hostile universe. You are forever being "unfaired against," in the memorable words of one of our clients. One of the unfortunate tendencies of the victim is to seek the alliance of fellow victims. They form little victim clubs, united in their helplessness against the world. When you offer them a suggestion, they say: "I already tried that but it didn't work."

We frequently ask people to study carefully their thoughts about responsibility. Do you have thoughts like: "It's not my job," or "What could I do?" or, "Some people get all the breaks"? In your interactions with others, do you find yourself claiming blamelessness or seeking the alliance of others in proving your lack of responsibility? Through careful observation of their victim thoughts, we have seen many people dislodge these tenacious patterns.

Mr./Ms. Righteous. In this pattern you elevate your feeling of self-worth by putting down others. The perpetrator of this program is saying to the world: "I'm good and you're not. Everyone is incompetent but me. I sacrifice and serve and what do I get out of it?"

In the early stages of couples' counseling, the therapist often must mediate attempts by each spouse to prove how bad the other one has been. This pattern makes a specialty of making the other person wrong: others are devalued and placed in a one-down position relative to you. If you are feeling particularly bad deep inside, it can sometimes ease the pain to think of others as wrong. Of course this habit never pays off in any long-term positive sense, but it can give short-term pain relief.

The hero. Closely related to Mr./Ms. Righteous is the hero. In this pattern your thoughts and conversations are aimed at proving that you are a good person. The basic message is "I'm all right." The underlying question is "Aren't I?" Listen carefully to your interactions with others. Do you find yourself describing yourself as good, strong, self-sacrificing, and so on? Do you spend time justifying yourself, either in your thoughts or your spoken words? If so, you may be running the hero program. It is very popular.

Why do people do it? Because at the core they don't

feel worthwhile. The false front is a way of bolstering their fragile sense of self. The problem is that, by not facing their inner sense of smallness, they never get to be as big as they really are. As long as their false front is held high, there can be no honest confrontation with their authentic inner feelings. It is through this confrontation that real heroes are made.

One-down. In this program you put yourself down, either in your thoughts or in your interactions with people. You operate from a one-down position relative to others. You may think: "If only I were more like . . ." This feeling of lesser value may lead you to flatter others, claim incompetence, or shrink from competitive situations. Sometimes this program is used to fish for compliments, while at other times it is used to get others not to expect too much from you. The pain of failure is lessened if you are already girded with expectation of it.

Not my fault. This is the pattern of avoiding responsibility. Many people have a formula engraved in their minds that goes: failure plus good excuse = success. It is often very hard for us to stand up and say: "Yep. I did it and it didn't work." It takes real growth to be willing to catch the flak without shifting it to someone else.

Healing the Past

To get free of these and other troublesome programs, we must begin by taking a dispassionate look at where we are stuck. We need to find out what patterns our programs are maintaining. Following this discovery we can look at what wants and needs our programs are helping us meet in sneaky ways. Then the question becomes: How can I meet these needs in straightforward ways? For example, let's say you notice one day that you are running the hero program. You notice that you are bragging to a friend over some achievement that you are exaggerating. You look beneath the surface and see that you are doing so because you are secretly scared that you are not fulfilling your potential. At that moment you have a choice. You can cover yourself and brag some more, or you can take a huge risk: tell the truth. Suppose you came out and said: "I realize I am boasting because I'm really afraid that I'm not doing as well in my life as I ought to be." This is the stuff of which personal breakthroughs are made. Truly, your life will never be the same again. The next time it will be a little easier to dive beneath your patterns and be authentic. Success hastens to reward those who are engaged in this kind of heroism.

Completions

It takes a special kind of courage to face and deal with our past incompletions. Often these incompletions are the most significant barrier to expressing our full creativity in the present. Go on a hunt for any areas of incompletion, large or small, and you will not be disappointed. A burst of creativity will often follow the completion of some long-left issue. Clearing up an incompletion gives you a feeling of aliveness that you can get nowhere else.

There is a strong drive in us toward completion. If you say you are going to do something and do not do it, a part of your mind is tied up with that incompletion until you clear it. One of the most important areas in which we all need completion is in the realm of repressed feelings. A monk may repress his sexuality in order to form a "good monk" ego, only to be obsessed with sexual thoughts in his meditations. This happens because nature keeps presenting to us whatever we have left unfinished. If we hold tightly to our positions in the face of repeated opportunites to reach completion, we lock ourselves into cycles of inner conflict. An even costlier result: to get away from incompletions we may withdraw awareness, so that we are numb to information from our own deeper selves as well as from the universe.

If you need to complete something from your past relationship with your parents, you may find yourself in repeated conflict situations with them or with people who remind you of them. Many people have not communicated to their parents their deepest feelings of anger, fear, or sadness. These incomplete communications detract from their ability to communicate freely in the present. If you are having trouble moving forward in some area in the present, look back at similar incompletions in your past.

For example, a man in therapy with us expressed a desire to make more money in his profession. Even after expressing this goal, he did not take any steps toward manifesting it. We asked him to inquire into incompletions around money. It quickly became clear that he had an abundance of incompletions; there were many people to whom he owed small sums of money. Worse, he had "good reasons" for not having repaid them: one creditor had moved to another state; a second one had not been paid because our client was angry at him. With some prodding he came to see that these incompletions and "good reasons" were costing him his aliveness and the possibility of success in the present. He carefully and scrupulously began to repay everyone he owed. In some cases he had to go to great lengths to track down the person, but eventually he located and cleared all his debts. As if by magic, he began earning more money. An unexpected contract came his way, an old debtor came through on an outstanding loan, and he was under way to a better future. That the past can be obstructing the future is hard for many of us to see. Once you train yourself to look for incompletions if things are not moving in the present, you are in a much stronger position.

In another situation, a couple, married less than a year, came to us for counseling with regard to sexual, financial, and communication problems. Even in the first session it became clear that the husband, Mel, had not completed his relationship with his former wife, whom he had divorced three years before. He had a lot of anger at her, which he

projected onto Alison, his present wife. He also had financial entanglements with his ex-wife, which were at the root
of some of his and Alison's financial problems. Because of
the financial drain of these incompletions he and Alison
could not afford to buy a house.

We asked both of them to make a list of all the incompletions they each had, including emotional and financial
issues, as well as anything else they could think of. On Mel's
list were such things as: "I am still angry at my ex-wife
but I'm still sexually attracted to her, too." On Alison's list
were items like: "I have been putting off paying back student loans, even though I can now afford it." While some
issues on their lists were relevant to their current problems,
many others were simply random incompletions from their
earlier lives. We told them that the process of completing
incompletions was more important than the content. In
other words, we have found that it does not matter which
of your incompletions you tackle first, as long as you get
going on at least one of them. So we had them develop a
plan for turning all their incompletions into completions.
Mel made arrangements to meet with his ex-wife in the
presence of a mediator to begin to handle the financial
issues. Alison started her list by making the first payment
on her student loans. It was heartening to see how taking
care of old incompletions had an immediate positive effect
on their relationship. Sex improved, as did communication.
They became allies in the process of cleaning up their lives,
whereas before they were well on their way to becoming
enemies.

Where in your life are incompletions robbing you of
positive energy? To help you see, please answer the following life-changing questions.

What feelings have I separated myself from?

What relationships have I left incomplete?

What do I need to do to complete them?

What agreements have I broken and not cleaned up?

What have I said I would do that I have not done?

What have I agreed not to do that I have done?

What communications have I left unsaid?

What have I started and not finished?

To whom do I owe money?

Whom do I need to forgive?

To whom do I owe appreciation?

The last two questions are particularly powerful. In order to complete your relationship with the past you need to express forgiveness and appreciation to those who have given you a boost, *even if they also wounded you.* In therapy we have seen hundreds of people's lives change right after they forgave and appreciated someone from the past. When you hold tightly to old anger and withhold your expressions of appreciation, you have no breathing space, no room for positive energy to flow through you. The moment you forgive and say "thank you" a relief flows through you, bringing fresh energy that propels you forward. Incompletions have a stronger grip on us than most people realize. They make us drive through life looking at the road only through the rearview mirror. A real transformation occurs when you shift your vision to look through the windshield. Co-committed relationships can exist only between people who see each other for who they are, not distorted through the filters of past incompletions.

NINE

What to Do When You Feel Stuck

In close relationships our patterns sometimes become so interlocked with the other person's that we get stuck. You can get stuck even when you're not in a close relationship—*everyone* gets stuck now and then. If you try to avoid being stuck, you become more stuck. So, let's simply acknowledge that stuckness sometimes occurs and see what we can do about it. Some people think that if their lives were working well they would not get stuck. This is both wildly optimistic and erroneous. A workable measure of your progress is how fast you can get free when you are stuck and how many ways you know to get free. If you are growing and changing a lot, you will likely get stuck and then free yourself many times in the course of a week.

When you are stuck, it is usually because you need to learn or experience something for your growth. For example, you may get stuck because you need to learn about anger, which you've been avoiding dealing with all your life. As you get older, life has a way of giving you one opportunity after another to embrace things you've been trying to avoid. What is actually happening is that the creative part of your mind is devising one situation after another for you to learn about anger. But there is another part of the mind that is full of resistance; it wants to avoid situations where you might learn something new. So, one part of you tugs you toward situations where you could learn something important to your growth, while another part tries to keep you the way you are. This resistant part of the mind is deeply conservative; it thinks: "We have survived until now acting this way, so let's not change." And it's right. You *have* survived. But perhaps you are now interested in more than just survival. You may be interested in prospering, having fun, becoming enlightened. As long as you settle for just survival, you cannot reach any of these higher goals.

The first thing to do when you feel stuck is to pause and let yourself fully experience it. You need to learn from the feeling of stuckness before you go beyond. Following is the way we teach people how to use the feeling of stuckness as an opportunity for growth.

The Stuckness Process

Begin by acknowledging to yourself: "I'm stuck." Say it over a few times in your mind. Listen to the tone of voice you are using. Whose voice is it? Yours? Your parent's? Someone else's? Where is the voice coming from? The front of your mind? Side? Back? Just notice—there are no right or wrong answers.

Now, notice how you experience the feeling of stuckness in your body. Is it a pressure in your chest? A tight neck? Knot in the stomach? Queasiness? Exactly what are the sensations associated with being stuck?

What do these sensations remind you of? How is this familiar? With whom are these feelings associated? At what time in your life did they first begin?

What do you need to learn from being stuck? What is the message here that you need to pay most attention to?

What do you need to do about these feelings of stuckness? Is there someone to whom you need to talk? Are there actions that need to be taken?

Who can best support you in attaining real freedom right now in your life? Who can be unflinchingly honest with you, and you with them? How can you get the support you want in becoming free?

As you can see, the purpose of this process is to assist you in being with your stuckness, in learning from it rather than resisting it or judging it. There is tremendous power in treating any feeling this way, but particularly stuckness. If you can catch yourself at the bottom of a negative spiral and be with the unpleasant feelings in a loving, attentive way, you will learn something very transformative. Use the Stuckness Process as often as you wish until you experience a shift in your stuck feelings.

Often you will notice that getting stuck follows a power struggle with yourself or someone else. In a power struggle the goal is to be right, not to be happy. We get trapped in a game that has no satisfying conclusion for either party: even if you get to be right, it does not feel satisfying for very long at all. Only authenticity is ultimately satisfying. Being right is a cheap substitute that lasts, in one of our client's words, "for about twenty minutes, just like cotton candy." Indulged in often enough, it can make you sick, just like cotton candy.

The following are two examples of the Stuckness Process in action.

Bernie and Martha came in for a recent session looking like cartoon versions of the shrew and the mouse. Martha's eyebrows were frozen in a formidable frown. She sat with her arms and legs crossed, lips pursed, an implicit "Well!" in her frequent, deep sighs. Bernie's forehead was frozen in deep horizontal lines. He wedged himself into the other end of the couch so that he was half-facing his wife. He held his breath and sneaked glances at her regularly. Neither one spoke for quite a while. After some initial probing, Bernie verbalized his stuck feeling:

"I feel like an emotional yo-yo. I can't seem to stick to my own stuff. If Martha is up, I feel great. But if she's upset, I start to feel anxious and agitated. I think I have to do something to fix it."

Martha then talked about how angry she got whenever she tried to express something she was feeling or working with, and Bernie would rush in and try to make it better. "I just want you to listen to me! I don't need to have you fix anything." Bernie had heard this request before and had tried to comply, but it seemed he just couldn't help himself.

We suggested that Bernie use the Stuckness Process at this point.

Begin by acknowledging to yourself: "I'm stuck." Say it over a few times in your mind.

"I just get paralyzed. I can't seem to focus on anything else until she feels better."

Listen to the tone of voice you are using. Whose voice is it? Yours? Your parent's? Someone else's?

"It's my mother's, a kind of sighing and moaning sound. She had arthritis pretty bad and had to rest in bed a lot when she got these spells. I would wait on her when I got home from school." (Bernie paused for a few minutes here and closed his eyes.)

Where is the voice coming from? The front of your mind? Side? Back? Just notice—there are no right or wrong answers.

"The voice seems to come from the side and back. Oh yeah, like when Mom would sigh if I left her room."

Now notice how you experience the feeling of stuckness in your body. Is it a pressure in your chest? A tight neck? Knot in the stomach? Queasiness? Exactly what are the sensations associated with being stuck?

"I have a kind of fluttering sensation right under my ribs. I'm holding my breath. My eyes feel buggy, like they're popping out. My whole body feels pressed in, squeezed."

What do these sensations remind you of? How is this familiar? With whom are these feelings associated? At what time in your life did they first begin?

"Sometimes I could do things for Mom or around the house that seemed to help. She'd feel better, and I remember feeling happy and needed. But a lot of times she'd really be hurting and I couldn't do anything to help. I felt really helpless."

What do you need to learn from being stuck? What is the message here that you most need to pay attention to?

"Well, I think I need to learn which are my feelings and experiences and which belong to someone else. Like I couldn't make my Mom's pain go away, and I can't make Martha's problems disappear. I also feel like I need to find some new ways to feel useful, instead of hovering around and waiting."

What do you need to do about these feelings of stuckness? Is there someone to whom you need to talk? Are there actions that need to be taken?

"I can see I need to talk more about what it was like to not have my father at home—he worked all the time—and to feel so responsible for my mother. Maybe I need to talk to my dad about that. With Martha I can see that I need to speak up and not always wait for her to set the pace. I could also ask if she wants some help instead of playing the 'white knight' all the time."

Who can best support you in attaining real freedom right now in your life? Who can be unflinchingly honest with you, and you with them? How can you get the support you want in becoming free?

"I have this friend at work who always seems to know what's going on with me—drives me crazy when he gets right up in my face. But I guess he really sees me. We have lunch together sometimes. I know he would like to get tighter. Yeah, I can ask for his support."

Martha virtually melted while Bernie was going through the Stuckness Process, and afterward they spent several minutes talking quietly about changes they wanted in their communication. We also explored the word *wait* with Bernie, since it was so pivotal in his process. Bernie discovered three levels of meaning in the word: *waiting on,* as in the waiter in a restaurant; *waiting for,* as in being passive and reactive; and *weighting,* as in the heaviness of responsibility. Once he really saw the ripple effect of those early experiences with his mother, he began to separate those pictures from his current life and possibilities for growth.

Len and Carrie felt stuck in a pattern that had occurred many times in their short marriage. Carrie had what they both called "spells," where "out of the blue" she just became furious, felt like "nothing's working," and wanted to leave. In fact she often walked out and disappeared for hours, leaving their young daughter with Len or a neighbor. Len's response was to become immobilized after trying to make light of these spells and trying to reason Carrie out of her blackness. He said he felt confused and didn't know what to do. After determining that they were committed to each other and willing to solve the problem, we suggested that each explore the Stuckness Process while the other witnessed.

Len's Process

Acknowledge to yourself: "I'm stuck." Say it over a few times in your mind. Listen to the tone of voice you are using.
"The voice is disapproving, shrill, insistent, almost like a hiss."
Whose voice is it? Yours? Your parent's? Someone else's?
"It sounds like a combination of my mother's and grandfather's."
Where is the voice coming from? The front of your mind? Side? Back?
"I hear it and feel it on the top back part of my head."
Just notice—there are no right or wrong answers.
"My head started to pound when you said that."
Now, notice how you experience the feeling of stuckness in your body. Is it a pressure in your chest? A tight neck? Knot in the stomach? Queasiness? Exactly what are the sensations associated with being stuck?
"My back between my shoulder blades feels stiff and achy. My head isn't pounding so much but I feel dizzy. I have these pings in my chest, sharp zigzag pains."
What do these sensations remind you of? How is this famil-

iar? With whom are these feelings associated? At what time in your life did they first occur?

"When I think back to the earliest times I remember feeling this way, I was seven. My grandfather—my mother's father—moved in with us for several years before he died. It seemed like he took over, running the house like his old army base. My mother and father each retreated. My mother got really busy and tidy, and was always yelling at us to do something, or do it over better, stay out of Grandpa's way, things like that. My father got stony and stoic. He retreated to the garage and made gadgets. I realize that I felt abandoned and really angry, but I didn't learn how to express that."

What do you need to learn from being stuck? What is the message here that you need to pay most attention to?

"I need to really feel my anger and know it better, so I don't use it to beat up on myself. I think I've responded to Carrie like she's my grandfather. Seems like I've gotten caught between taking on my mother's storming around and my father's stoicism."

What do you need to do about these feelings of stuckness? Is there someone to whom you need to talk? Are there actions that need to be taken?

"I've always loved to chop wood. Now I see why. I can do that to help release tension. I need to say when I'm angry and take a stand when Carrie starts slipping into a 'spell.' I don't know what it's about yet, but I need to keep telling the truth for me."

Who can best support you in attaining real freedom right now in your life? Who can be unflinchingly honest with you, and you with them? How can you get the support you want in becoming free?

"My older brother Tom lives in town, and we've always been close. I know he'd be there for me, and I've always been able to tell him anything. He'd probably think this was like a detective story where you put together all the clues and solve the mystery."

Len had experienced sadness, anger, fear, and finally some lightness and happiness during the process. We encouraged him to stay with his feelings as we turned to Carrie.

Carrie's Process

Acknowledge to yourself: "I'm stuck." Say it over a few times in your mind. Listen to the tone of voice you are using. Whose voice is it? Yours? Your parent's? Someone else's?

"I hear my own voice saying, 'No! I won't!' over and over. Kind of angry, but scared too. I sound really little, three or four years old. The voice comes from behind me." *Just notice—there are no right or wrong answers.*

"I feel really sad." (She began to cry and sob for several minutes.)

Now, notice how you experience the feeling of stuckness in your body. Is it a pressure in your chest? A tight neck? Knot in the stomach? Queasiness? Exactly what are the sensations associated with being stuck?

"My throat feels really tight, like there's a cord around it. Both temples ache. My hands are very itchy and my feet and ankles hurt."

What do these sensations remind you of? How is this familiar? With whom are these feelings associated? At what time in your life did they first occur?

"I remember having these huge temper tantrums from when I was really little—they were famous in the family. I really wanted my father to pay attention to *me*." (Carrie was the youngest of five, the "surprise baby.") "But I've known about those for a long time. It feels older than that. . . ." (She was quiet for several minutes.) "I really knew somehow that they didn't want me, and I was *not* going to be born. I was two weeks late and the doctor used forceps after my mother got exhausted. I've never wanted to be anywhere where I suspected I wasn't welcome."

What do you need to learn from being stuck? What is the message here that you need to pay most attention to?

"I think that I've never really decided to **be here**, not just in my marriage but in the world. I need to choose to be here."

What do you need to do about these feelings of stuckness? Is there someone to whom you need to talk? Are there actions that need to be taken?

"I need to do some bodywork to release this old pattern. I feel that massage would really help. I need to speak these feelings when they arise, rather than walking out. I also feel I need to move, anyway, rather than dig my heels in stubbornly."

Who can best support you in attaining real freedom right now in your life? Who can be unflinchingly honest with you, and you with them? How can you get the support you want in becoming free?

"Len, I'd like to make that commitment with you. I know you're there for me and that I've shut you out. Would you be willing to be my partner in becoming free?"

Len responded by moving over to hold Carrie. As they talked, we left the room to give them some time alone.

Elise's Process

Elise is an attractive, young professional who came in for counseling specifically to clear up whatever was preventing her from having an intimate relationship with a man since her divorce five years before. She had, as she put it, "tried everything from singles' bars to the Sierra Club," but the men she met were always unavailable. They were married, confirmed bachelors, or commitment phobic. One man had been secretly dating another woman while seeing Elise. One weekend when he didn't arrive for their date, Elise called his home and learned that he had just gotten married and was off on his honeymoon. Needless to say, Elise felt stuck in a pattern she didn't understand. She was quite willing to discover its source, so we suggested the Stuckness Process.

Acknowledge to yourself: "I'm stuck." Say it over a few times in your mind. Listen to the tone of voice you are using. Whose voice is it? Yours? Your parent's? Someone else's?

"I'm surprised how hard it is to say I'm stuck. I can

feel myself not wanting to admit that. . . . The voice has a droning quality, very tired and flat. It sounds like my father's voice the morning after he'd been drinking a lot." *Where is the voice coming from? The front of your mind? Side? Back? Just notice—there are no right or wrong answers.*

"I feel the voice in my throat just under my chin. As I pay attention to it, I feel really sad."
Now, notice how you experience the feeling of stuckness in your body. Is it a pressure in your chest? A tight neck? Knot in the stomach? Queasiness? Exactly what are the sensations associated with being stuck?

"My mind feels blank, like right after you turn off a light in a dark room. I feel a huge lump in my throat. My belly is all roily and churning. I have some sharp pains in my right hip and leg. My toes feel tingly. And between my shoulder blades is achy and sore."
What do these sensations remind you of? How is this familiar? With whom are these feelings associated? At what time in your life did they first begin?

"I can feel my mind not wanting to look at this. Saying, 'What's the matter with you! You couldn't keep your husband, what makes you think some other man wants you!' What a battle! No wonder I get so tired. . . ." (She paused for a few minutes, crying softly.) "What all this reminds me of are the fights my parents had when Dad drank. I used to go and sit in my closet and turn the light on and off, on and off. I wanted to do something else but I couldn't think. She finally left him when I was nine. She went back to work, and we all had chores and after-school jobs. I would see Dad occasionally when he'd roll into town, whisk us off for a day doing some wild thing, then disappear for months."
What do you need to learn from being stuck? What is the message here that you need to pay most attention to?

"I feel like I've been waiting for someone to come and fill this terribly lonely feeling that is stuck in my throat." (She began to cry again for several minutes.) "You know, I've been lonely all my life. It didn't matter whether Don (her ex) was there or not. I really think I need to learn to be alone, to be my friend."

What do you need to do about these feelings of stuckness? Is there someone to whom you need to talk? Are there actions that need to be taken?

"I need to talk to my father, but he's dead. . . . I can talk to him in my mind. There are lots of things I wanted and didn't get. Oh, I see the pains in my leg were about wanting to kick him. I still feel really angry at him, but sad, too. . . . I can see I need to court myself, to spend time doing loving and kind things for myself, like taking myself out to dinner. Or to Europe; I've always wanted to go to Europe, but I was waiting for a man to take me. Oh, just like waiting for Dad to show up and take me somewhere exciting."

Who can best support you in attaining real freedom right now in your life? Who can be unflinchingly honest with you, and you with them? How can you get the support you want in becoming free?

"I have a friend I've known since high school. We know each other really well, having gone through the hills and valleys over the years. We can talk about anything. I know she'd be thrilled to help me get through this one."

Elise had begun to realize the source of her inability to have what she wanted. She took several months in the process of befriending herself, and had a great time in Europe, by herself. She met a man in England and has now gone back for a long visit.

CONCLUSION

Envisioning a New World of Intimacy

We have a deep need for closeness and unity with others. This need has evolved through millions of years, and will likely be with us to the end of time. Until recently all we required of our relationships was that they provide survival, security, and the continuation of the species. Now we have added a stiff new requirement: Our relationships must bring happiness, fulfillment, creativity, and even enlightenment. From the perspective of our work and experience together, this new requirement is perfectly natural and offers immense possibilities. But it calls for a rare kind of courage and a new set of skills. Brand-new territory is being explored, as wide open and full of possibility as the frontier of outer space. Courage is required because practically every step you take will be a venture into the unknown. After all, how many times in your life have you actually seen the kind of relationship you want? When we began our own journey to co-commitment we had absolutely no models for what we wanted to create. We had high intentions and intense faith; the rest had to be invented as we went along. Now our relationship feels like magic, but it took years of practice to make it so. Even magic takes practice, particularly in an area where the stakes are so high and the forces of old conditioning are so strong. We encourage you to view your journey to co-commitment as a lifetime project. That way you may have greater patience with yourself when you have slip-ups.

In times past, cloth was made colorfast through the dip-and-fade technique. Each day the cloth was dipped in the dye, then hung up to fade in the sun. The next day it was dipped again, and again hung up to fade. The fading was as important to the process as the application of the dye. Only by fading the cloth could it be made to withstand the rigors of further wash and wear. The same is true for practicing the skills of conscious loving. Dip the cloth every day by reading the ideas and practicing the activities. But then take the skills out into life, into all your close relationships. Expose, risk, experiment: Fade the cloth. With loving practice, you may find that these new skills integrate themselves effortlessly into your life.

Many of our clients have found that what seem like tiny experiments in conscious loving often yield powerful breakthroughs. For example, a woman told us of an amazing incident that happened right after she began applying the skill of telling the microscopic truth to her life. She found it very hard to tell the truth around her husband, but one morning she took what she thought was a tiny risk. As she was talking to her husband, she noticed a tightness in her stomach. She said, "My stomach feels really tight right now. I'm not sure why." He blinked, and blurted out, "It's probably because I've been lying to you." Then he poured out a litany of things, large and small, that he had been withholding from her. In five minutes of intense communication their relationship emerged from the half-world of hidden secrets into the light of conscious loving. Over the next six months they continued to practice more skills, but she dates the transformation of their relationship to that one moment of seemingly innocuous truth-telling on her part.

We devised the activities in the next section for people who want to speed up their learning of the material in this book. Each of the activities crystallizes a skill that we have found to create positive relationship change in our workshops and therapy sessions. The activities will give you concrete ways to put the concepts to work for you. We have lived these concepts and skills day and night for many years now, and as a result we have experienced more joy than we ever imagined. If you are choosing to embrace conscious loving in your life, you have our blessings and everything we know about how to do it. We want to live in a world of people who are aware, honest, and open to love. Our species has demonstrated that we can walk on the moon if we put our minds to it. Now let's turn to an even more crucial task, the creation of an earth full of people who are celebrating each other in conscious love.

PART
TWO

The Co-Commitment Program:Activities for Transforming Your Relationship

Introduction

Now that you have heard the words, let's play the music. The activities in the program are designed to give you the experiences that accompany the concepts in part 1 of this book. The activities are grouped to follow the seven steps in chapter 4. There are two additional sections designed specifically to develop communication skills and solve problems. We recommend that you do the activities in the order given. We have designed the sequence of activities in each section to allow you to stay balanced and grounded as you make your journey to conscious loving. You may want to skip around from section to section as you become interested in certain areas. Be sure, however, to include *all* the sections as you work through the program.

Some of the activities are short and focus on only one

219

skill. Others are longer and contain several steps. You may want to take a few days to learn and integrate the lengthier activities. Remember that by choosing conscious loving you are setting in motion a powerful transformation in yourself. Respect its power, and be loving to yourself as your clearing process unfolds.

Along the way you will occasionally hit a snag. This is natural and you should expect it. Remember when you learned to ride a bike? Tipping over gave you important feedback about learning to ride smoothly.

When you hit snags you may not always be aware of it. You may find yourself thinking: "I give up," or, "This is ridiculous," or, "I think I'd rather just go back to sleep." All these are signs that you are on the verge of a breakthrough. Just before the transition to a higher level of consciousness, expect to get stuck; your ego has a vested interest in maintaining the status quo. Your ego is used to a certain way of being, and when you threaten it by moving to a higher level, you shift its foundation. "Uh-oh," your ego says. "You're moving into unfamiliar territory. Let's do something to get back to where you've been comfortable." Your ego has many ways of tipping over your bike. Expect this, and get back on again after a fall. Be loving and respectful to yourself, and do not settle for less. Similarly, people often get stuck right after a big breakthrough. They are not used to experiencing all that new, positive energy, so they create a way to bring themselves down. Just notice these processes as they pass through you, and keep on working with the program. The activities in chapter 9 may be especially useful at these times.

It is not necessary to work continuously through the activities. Feel free to take a few days off now and then to integrate what you have learned. We recommend, however, that you pick up where you left off. **We do not recommend that you pick your favorite activities and focus on them to the exclusion of others.** Invariably, when people do that, they skip over the very activities they most need to do. For the best experience, commit yourself to *all* the activities in the program. Conscious loving is certainly worth fifteen or twenty minutes a day. Going through all the activities will likely change your life, but you may find equal value in continued use of the program. Many of our clients repeat the program once a year as a tune-up. No matter how many times you do the program, your experiences will be different, reflecting the current state of your development.

Because people learn in different ways, we have constructed the activities to fit various learning styles. Some activities involve writing, others involve verbal communication. Many of the activities involve physical movement, which is extremely important. To learn the skills of co-commitment, you absolutely must go beyond ideas and into the world of bodily experience. In addition, the physical activities help keep you grounded. Ideas take you out into space; body-oriented activities bring you back down to earth. Both space and grounding are essential, and the activities are designed to enhance both dimensions in you.

We offer you these activities because they work: *they move people*. They can also be fun, and we urge you to play as well as work through them. Some of the activities are designed for you to experience by yourself. For others you may need a partner with whom to work and play. If you are not in a close love relationship right now, try to find a friend who wants to move toward co-commitment. No matter whether you do the activities alone or with a lover or friend, many crucial lessons await you.

What to Do If You Cannot Find a Partner

It is not essential to have a partner to clear up your co-dependency issues. Eventually you will have to go out into the real world and apply what you've learned, but you can handle all the groundwork on your own. In fact, sometimes it is easier to work out these issues by yourself than to do so while in a relationship.

Approximately half of the activities in the program can be done on your own. Of course, all of them can be done with a friend or a close love partner. If you are working through the program unassisted, you will find the following activities easy to do by yourself:

- Creating Commitment
- Getting Present
- The Healing Dialogue
- The Choice Map
- The Feeling Map
- Breath and Feeling
- Core Beliefs
- Goalswork
- Keeping Agreements
- Completing Feelings
- Completions List

There are several activities, the Healing Dialogue, for example, that can be taped so you can listen to them later, without having to reread each instruction. In addition, we advise you to keep a journal to record your explorations in the program.

If you or your partner is a novice explorer, we suggest you begin with the following activities to get more comfortably acclimated before diving further into the program:

- The Harmonizing Process
- The Healing Dialogue
- Understanding the Energy of Relationship
- Bare Bones Communication
- The Choice Map
- Learning to Tell the Microscopic Truth

Now, one last word of advice. Enjoy!

Co-Commitment Activities

Co-Commitment:
The Harmonizing Process
Creating Commitment
Supporting Each Other
Goalswork

Learning to Love Yourself:
The Healing Dialogue
Getting Present
Reclaiming Feelings
Reclaiming Your Body
Exponential Loving

Learning to Feel Your Feelings:
The Feeling Map
Being Present for Feelings
Completing Feelings

Claiming Creativity:
The Choice Map
Expressing Yourself Fully
Dropping Projection
Core Beliefs
How to Get What You Want Without Compromising
What Step Are We Doing?

Learning to Tell the Microscopic Truth:
Parts One to Four

Keeping Your Agreements:
Keeping Agreements
What Role Are You Playing?
The Completions List

Learning to Live in a State of Continuous Positive Energy:
Breath and Feeling
Enlivening Love
Consciously Taking Space
Microscopic Love

Communications Skills:
Understanding the Energy of Relationship
Creating a Safe Space
Bare Bones Communication
Whole Body Listening
Deepening Communication

Problem-Solving:
In the Heat of the Moment
Out of the Rut
Finding Where You Are Stuck

Co-Commitment

The Harmonizing Process

The purpose of the Harmonizing Process is to help people in relationships establish a feeling of unity between them. The process is an easy-to-learn technique that couples (or any two people) can use in two ways. First, it is very useful when an argument is actively in progress. You can move from stuckness to unity, often very quickly, when you use the Harmonizing Process. Second, the process can be used to prevent much conflict by doing it as an everyday practice to build unity and a sense of shared purpose. All it takes is willingness. Are you willing?

Instructions
1. Sit comfortably, face to face. First, pick who will be partner A and who will be partner B. Partner A, close your

eyes and breathe slowly in and out to a 4-count. Breathe primarily in your abdomen. Breathe in, 1 ... 2 ... 3 ... 4 ... out, 1 ... 2 ... 3 ... 4, at a slow tempo. Continue to breathe in this way and relax your abdomen. Partner B, watch partner A's breathing and match it as closely as you can. Continue for two to three minutes.

Now, switch roles. Partner B, close your eyes, and breathe in and out to a 4-count, as described above. Partner A, watch partner B's breathing and match it as closely as you can. Continue for two to three minutes.

2. Partner A, slowly breathe in and out to a 4-count. Partner B, close your eyes and listen to the sound of partner A's breath. Match it by listening to it. Continue for two to three minutes.

Now, switch roles. Partner B, slowly breathe in and out to a 4-count. Partner A, close your eyes and match partner B's breath by listening to it. Continue for two to three minutes.

3. Now, each of you match the other's breathing by watching and listening to it. Slowly breathe in and out to a 4-count, and match each other's breathing by watching it and listening to it. Continue for two to three minutes.

4. Continuing to match breathing, move your chairs side by side. When you are comfortable, each of you place your hand somewhere on the other's back. Close your eyes and match each other's breathing by feeling with your hand the rise and fall of the breath. Continue for two to three minutes.

Now gently separate contact and relax for a little while, still sitting side by side. When you are ready, open your eyes and spend a few minutes discussing your experience.

Discussion

People who have used this process report exquisite experiences of coming to know each other more deeply. Barriers and misunderstandings seem to melt away. One woman told us: "I really could understand Evan's viewpoint in a whole new way. I almost felt for a moment that

I *was* him." This process is well worth the time invested to make it a part of your daily life.

Creating Commitment

This activity will teach you how to form a blueprint for the transformation of your relationship. Once you have created the blueprint together, it will be the foundation for all your further exploration. A mutually envisioned foundation assures that both of you are in deep agreement about what you want to build. For example, if one of you really has a castle in mind, while the other dreams of a cottage by a lake, this activity will give you the opportunity to bring your visions into alignment.

This process is also designed to give you practice in participating fully in your communications. One of the main purposes of commitment is to bring all of your being and resources to focus on a goal. In this activity you will speak with your whole self, which will bring up the support of inner resources you may not realize you possess.

Step One

Each of you write down the full list of your core commitments. Write each of the following commitments at the top of a blank page of your notebook or journal.

• I am committed to being close, and I am committed to clearing up anything in the way of my ability to do so.
• I am committed to my own complete development as an individual.
• In my relationships, I am committed to revealing myself, not to concealing myself.
• I am committed to the full empowerment of people around me.
• I am committed to acting out of the awareness that I am 100 percent the source of my reality.
• I am committed to having a good time in my close relationships.

Take one commitment at a time and say it to yourself. Then pause for ten to fifteen seconds and notice what thoughts, images, or feelings come to your awareness. Write or sketch your responses in your journal on the page below each listed commitment.

Example: I am committed to the full empowerment of people around me.
   —Afraid I'll be leaned on
   —I won't get enough
   —Head itches
   —Exciting
   —How do I do that?
   —You won't need me anymore
   —Hot feeling in my cheeks
   —Picture of Dad in his new car

When both of you are finished, take some time to share what you wrote.

Step Two

Stand facing each other at a comfortable distance. Decide which of you will be the first communicator and who will be the responder. Communicator, say each commitment out loud to your partner, then pause for ten to fifteen seconds to notice your responses. Responder, your task is to watch the communicator's body language and to encourage full, straightforward, direct communication.

Some things that are *not* full, straightforward, and direct are: shrinking, tucking your chin, looking at the floor, coughing or clearing your throat, holding your hands behind your back, whispering, forgetting half the words, yelling, finger-pointing, and inserting new words. These are all messages from your unconscious. When these or similar events occur, it simply means your unconscious is speaking. If you notice that you are doing any of these things, tell the microscopic truth about it, then repeat the commitment.

Responder, assist the communicator to speak with his or her head up, eyes level, and body open. Be the cheerleader and coach for full participation.

Example:
COMMUNICATOR: I am committed to having a good (cough, cough) time in my relationships.
RESPONDER: I notice that you coughed. What's that about?
COMMUNICATOR: My throat feels scratchy. I feel tears behind my eyes. I'm afraid I'm too somber and can't learn to have fun. I'm afraid you'll think you picked a dud and leave me.
RESPONDER: Yes, I hear you. Take a breath and say the commitment again.

Switch roles after each of you has communicated a commitment. Take turns communicating and responding to each commitment until both of you feel clear, energized, and fully present.

Supporting Each Other

When we give our emotional weight to something or someone, we are giving an essential part of ourselves. Giving and receiving weight in relationships can take the form of support, dependence, demand, or threat, depending on your intention and the way you use your weight. If you are making a decision together and one of you goes limp, your partner can feel deserted. If you use your weight to push your partner around, you are communicating an unyielding stance, to which your partner might respond: "What's the use, it's like talking to a brick wall."

Our language is heavily laden with references to weight. Weight has to do with impact and the many ways we use it to influence our relationships. We can "throw our weight around," give up and become a "dead weight," behave in interactions like a "heavyweight," and have "weighty" arguments. Our language connects weight with power.

Our deep beliefs about support, strength, and weakness are connected to our emotional experience of our physical size and weight. Some beliefs we've often heard from our clients:

- If I ask for support it means I'm weak.
- I've always done everything by myself.
- This family takes care of its own.
- Nobody knows how to support me the right way.
- Support just means leaning on somebody else.

This activity, "Supporting Each Other," is designed for you to explore your ability to give and receive support and to bring to awareness any obstacles you've put in the way. If you give and receive weight easily in your relationship, you are more likely to feel supportive and supporting. Before you can make more-conscious choices about your support needs, you must see what you are doing. In a co-committed relationship, support is like the fulcrum of a seesaw, where half the fun is riding the waves of energy as you exchange support for each other. Some questions for discussion follow the activities.

Instructions

1. Stand facing each other and put your hands together with your partner's, palm to palm. Lean in toward each other several inches. One step at a time, move your feet away from your partner, keeping your back straight, until your bodies form a capital A. Stay there for a moment, noticing your body sensations, thoughts, and feelings. Then come back to standing on your own, and notice the differences in the way you experience your weight.

2. Stand side by side, leaning against each other. How do you have to shift your body in order to lean into each other but not fall over? Notice if your position feels comfortable or uncomfortable. After a minute or two straighten up and stand back to back, leaning into each other's back. Experiment with positions that allow both of you to feel you are sharing weight. After a few minutes, return to supporting your own weight.

Discussion Questions

• How do these patterns show up in our daily interactions?

• What do I want to change about my response either in giving or receiving support?

• Is there anything about which I need to ask for support, and how might I do that? (*Example:* "I realize I want your support in the presentation I have to make at work tomorrow. Would you be willing to listen to it and tell me if I am coming across clearly?")

Goalswork

It is possible to create and realize goals by consciously using your mind's power to design its own reality. Manifestation depends on how you consciously go about creating what you want in your life.

This four-part activity is the most effective form of conscious manifestation that we know. In the first part you'll brainstorm goals alone and with your partner. (You may want to skip ahead now to "The Choice Map," p. 250; the notes you make there may be particularly helpful as you go through this process.) Thinking positive thoughts about what you *want* rather than what you don't want begins to set the stage to realize your goals. For example, when you think and work with what you want, you tend to see more opportunities to accomplish those goals than you do when you focus on what to avoid.

In this section you'll manifest goals in three ways. Because each of us processes information differently, our three methods work best in combination. With all forms of manifestation it is your willingness and sincerity that gives them power. Use this activity to create goals to which you can commit, ones that have "heart" for you. The discussion section will address some common questions and experiences.

Instructions
Part One

In your notebooks, each of you make two lists: Things I Want for Myself, and Things I Want for My Relationship. Consider the material, emotional, and spiritual realms when you make your lists.

Example:
Things I Want for Myself:
• I want a new red sports car.
• I want to love my body and nurture it in a healthy way.
• I want to know my purpose in being here on this planet.

Things I Want for My Relationship:
• I want to share equally in child care and creating family activities.
• I want to have a great sexual relationship.
• I want each of us to be so happy in our work that we bring that excitement to our time together.

Make your lists as long as you want. When both of you are finished (for now), share your lists with each other. If your lists are radically different from your partner's, schedule some discussion time to discover the actual source of the disparity. It may be a withholding, a projection, or a reluctance to open to unexplored possibilities.

Part Two

1. There are two roles in this activity, the coach and the player. Decide which of you will be the first player and which the first coach. Player, choose a goal that you want to realize. Focus on what you want rather than on what you're not getting. For example, change, "I want to stop getting into hassles with my mother," to something like, "I want to have a close and clear relationship with my mother." When you have decided on a goal, the coach will ask you three questions: How is it now?, What is the result you want to produce?, and Declare your goal.

Example:
COACH: How is it now?
PLAYER: My mother and I seem to fight every time we see each other, and I get really upset about it.
COACH: What is the result you want to produce?
PLAYER: I want to have a close and clear relationship with my mother.
COACH: Declare your goal.
PLAYER: I consciously choose to have a close and clear relationship with my mother.

Coach, your task is to assist the player to state his or her goal in a positive, clear, and current manner. Have the player declare the goal until his or her whole body communicates clearly and fully.

When the player has answered the three questions, switch roles. When both of you are finished, write down your declarations in your notebooks.

Part Three

This activity also has two roles, the lover and the player. Decide who will take which role. The lover will direct the player by asking: How is it now?, then instructs the player to take a moment to love him- or herself for the way it is.

Example:
LOVER: How is it now?
PLAYER: I weigh 150 pounds and I hate the way I look.
LOVER: Take a moment to love yourself for the way it is.
PLAYER: As I do that, I feel some sadness, but also some relief. I can begin to see why I've kept myself heavy. Then I won't have to deal with men's attention, which is scary.

Each of you take a turn at being the lover and the player. Then rest for a moment before going on to part four.

Part Four

You will both do this activity individually as you sit comfortably. Take turns reading the following instructions to each other verbatim:

"Relax and close your eyes. Picture, feel, or hear your goal as vividly as you can. (Pause for ten to fifteen seconds.) Now breathe slowly and fully for two minutes. Imagine that your breath forms a fluffy cloud that holds and supports your goal. Now rest for a moment or so before coming back."

Discussion

One of the barriers to conscious creation of goals is our fear of figuring out what we really want. We worry that we will create something that will turn out to be detrimental to our overall growth. In these activities, we simply have to go by trial and error. Do your best at figuring out what you want, create it, and then be willing to make corrections if it is not quite right. "The Choice Map" (p. 250) will give you practice in discovering what you most deeply want.

We can learn as much from the misses as the hits. We have collected many humorous stories of people's misses. For example, one woman made a long list of the qualities she wanted her ideal man to have, forgetting to include that he be available. So she met exactly the right man, except he was deeply committed to bachelorhood. The film *Bedazzled* is one of our favorites because it vividly illustrates how careful you must be in spelling out your goals. The hero in the movie makes a deal with the devil, bartering his soul for seven wishes. He keeps attempting to create a relationship with a woman he knows but always leaves some unclarity for the devil to trip him up. For example, he says that he wants to be surrounded by worshipful, adoring women. "Is that what you really want?" the devil asks. "Yes!" he says. Instantly he is transported to a convent, where he is surrounded by worshipful women, none of whom worships him.

People sometimes fear that their goalswork will mess up in a big way, like Dr. Frankenstein's, or that a huge black hole in the universe will open and swallow their best intentions. To address this issue we suggest the Cosmic Clause, to begin or to end any creation experiment: "May all my manifestations have totally beneficial consequences for me, others, and the world in general."

If the results of your goalswork don't match your intentions, consider the following actions.

1. Clear up any unfelt feelings about the situation. Feelings begin to clear at the moment you become willing to feel them. For example, a single woman client of ours has been working to create a lifetime mate. The man who appeared in her life recently, whom she thought she wanted, turned out to be authoritative and controlling. After her initial feelings of indignation, she began to explore the relationship as a mirror of her unexperienced feelings regarding control and authority. She discovered a well of anger and sadness about her previous live-in relationship. She said, "If I didn't control our lives, nothing would happen! And when I stopped controlling, he left." She realized that she needed some time to fully experience and love these feelings before she was ready to consider another intimate relationship.

2. Pay attention to any body trauma associated with the situation. For example, if you create a goal of getting a promotion, and find that your shoulders are becoming tense and sore, you may want to consider the tension as a body-mind message. You can use massage, acupressure, or other physical treatments to assist you in exploring the connection between more success and physical discomfort.

3. Clear up any unconscious motives dragged along with your clear motive. People often have conflicting intentions in goalswork. For example, you may consciously want a new sports car because you like its power and efficiency. You may also want it to prove to your father that you are a success, and to compete with your older brother who has a Mercedes. When you create with two motives, it is the unconscious one that tends to manifest. These unconscious motives need to be acknowledged and experienced to clear the way for the conscious motive.

We recommend that you reserve a section of your notebook to record your goals and your results.

Learning to Love Yourself

A close relationship stirs things up, and often what floats to the top are the unloved parts of ourselves: our bodies, our feelings, our histories, our thoughts. These activities are designed for several purposes: to help you reclaim parts of yourself that you have disowned, and to help you learn the art of embracing and opening up to these parts rather than working to improve or to get rid of them.

These activities outline the steps you'll need to unwind your *Yuck!* reflex. For example, a client recently said, "Yuck! I don't want to love my thighs, I want to get rid of them." Turning with love to face what we have hated or repressed takes some practice. You'll have the opportunity to increase your loving response to yourself and to your partner.

The Healing Dialogue

The Healing Dialogue can be practiced together or individually. It is designed to give you direct access to your Inner Self, the part of you that contains all your original, creative reactions to things. Most of us have assembled an Outer Self, which is based on what is socially acceptable in our environment.

The Inner Selves of all human beings are remarkably similar; the Outer Selves are remarkably varied. This is because what works in one family may be utterly different from what works in the family next door. For example, one child may learn that quiet sulking is the way to express anger in his or her family. In the family next door, another child may learn to bottle up anger and turn it into a headache.

If you are fortunate, you grew up with a friendly relationship between your Inner and Outer Selves. In other words, you will not have a large gap between how you feel on the inside and how you act on the outside. For example, if you feel tension in your neck, you look inside, and you realize, "Oh, I'm tensing my neck because I feel pushed and annoyed by this job deadline."

Unfortunately, many of us have been living in the Outer Self for so long that we have lost touch with the Inner Self. We have been so busy protecting the Inner Self and assembling more complex layers of the Outer Self, that we have lost touch with the Inner. So, when the Inner Self becomes buried under a pile of decisions to ignore it, it must speak to us sharply, through the language of the body: pain, tension, conflicting impulses, or illness.

The Healing Dialogue works because it sets up a new relationship between your Inner and Outer Selves. When the Selves are in disharmony, you are more likely to project disharmony onto your partner by withholding, going numb, blaming, confusing, and so on. Using the Healing Dialogue will increase your direct contact with your Inner Self. That contact itself seems to create change, no matter what content you discover. Harmony between your Inner and Outer Selves will also allow you to solve relationship issues in a new way, by allowing information to emerge directly from the deepest part of you.

At first, you will do the Healing Dialogue seated, with your eyes closed. Later, as your skills increase, you will learn how to do it in movement and in daily life. You begin by going through several steps to relax your body and get in touch with your Inner Self. Then you select an issue or problem to work on. You ask questions of your Inner Self, then you listen for answers. The answers may be words, pictures, or even physical sensations. The answers may seem not to correspond directly to the issue you're asking about. We've found that the process creates the space for answers to emerge in the right time and place. For example, you may do the Healing Dialogue to inquire about the source of your irritability and not get any definite answers during the process. Later, while brushing your teeth or doing some other mundane task, an old memory likely will surface that makes sense.

The Healing Dialogue works because it creates a shift in the relationship between your Inner Self and your Outer Self. Of course, the increased harmony you experience extends to your relationship.

Instructions

When you are ready to begin, one of you will find a comfortable place to sit for fifteen to thirty minutes. Your partner will read the Healing Dialogue while you fully relax into the experience. It will take approximately fifteen minutes for each of you to complete this activity. You can then exchange roles, or you may want to arrange separate times for each of you to experience the process.

If you are doing this alone, simply ask yourself the questions and answer them. It may make it easier if you tape-record the instructions and questions, then play it back to yourself, thereby allowing you the time needed to respond.

The following instructions are to be read aloud, verbatim, except for the material in parentheses (unless you are tape-recording the exercise). The words in parentheses are instructions to the person who is reading the Healing Dialogue to you.

Sit comfortably. Close your eyes or leave them open, whichever is most comfortable to you.

1. Tune in to your whole self. . . . (Pause for five to ten seconds. From here on, whenever you see (or hear yourself saying) three dots, it means you should pause for five to ten seconds.) . . . Let your awareness go into your whole body. . . . See, feel, and listen to your whole body. . . . Be aware of your fingers and toes. . . . Be aware of your hands and feet. . . . Be aware of your arms and legs. . . . Be aware of your shoulders and hips. . . . Be aware of the front of

your body. . . . Be aware of the back of your body. . . . Now notice your whole-body feeling. . . .

2. As a whole, do you feel warm, cool, or a combination? Tell me aloud what you feel.

3. As a whole, do you feel tired, refreshed, or some of each? Tell me aloud what you feel.

4. As a whole, do you feel relaxed or tense, or a combination? Tell me aloud what you feel.

5. Notice a part of your body, and let your awareness go to that part. . . . See, feel, and listen to it. . . . Notice whether it changes or stays the same. . . . Now notice another part of your body, and let your awareness go to that part. . . . See, feel, and listen to it. . . . Notice if it changes or stays the same. . . .

6. Now think of a relationship issue or problem you'd like to solve. Just let any problem into your mind (pause ten to twenty seconds). Now think of another relationship issue you'd like to solve (pause ten to twenty seconds). Now think of one or several more (pause thirty seconds).

7. Now choose one issue and think about it. . . . Notice what you feel in your body as you think of it (pause ten to twenty seconds). Now tune in to that feeling in your body. . . . Notice any thoughts that arise as you keep tuning in to your body feeling. Keep returning your awareness to your body, and let any thoughts come (pause thirty seconds).

8. Now ask your body questions, and let your body answer. Always let the sensation itself answer. Do not make up the answers in your mind. Asking the questions is the important part. Don't worry about whether the answers come right away. . . .

• Is this issue familiar? Let your body answer.
(pause ten to twenty seconds)

• Where am I experiencing this in my body?
(pause ten to twenty seconds)

• Do I want to solve this problem? Let the feeling itself be your answer.
(pause ten to twenty seconds)

• What are my intentions here? . . . Am I trying to get approval? . . . Am I trying to get control of myself or someone else?

(pause twenty to thirty seconds)
  • Does it feel as if my survival is at stake?
(pause ten to twenty seconds)
  • Is being right more important than solving this problem?
(pause ten to twenty seconds)
  • What do I need to learn from this situation? Open to your body's knowing.
(pause ten to twenty seconds)
  • Am I embracing this or withdrawing from it?
(pause ten to twenty seconds)
  • What do I need to feel to be completely free of this?
(pause ten to twenty seconds)
  • What needs to be loved here? . . . Let yourself be with that now.
(pause thirty seconds)

9. Now, let your attention go to a place in your body that feels connected to this issue you've been exploring. . . . Be aware of that place. . . . Keep returning your awareness to that place until you feel some kind of shift in the sensations in that place. . . . Raise a finger when you have felt a shift. (This step may be repeated several times. After the person has raised a finger, say, "Let your attention go to another place in your body that feels connected to this issue. . . . Keep returning your awareness to that place until you feel a shift.")

10. Would you like to explore more issues, or are you ready to finish? Tell me out loud which you prefer.
(If the answer is "explore more," go back to number 7 and repeat through 10. If the answer is "finish," go on to number 11.)

11. If you are ready to finish, ask yourself: Am I willing to have this issue clear up? Tell me out loud what your answer is.
(Accept either yes or no.)

12. Take a few moments to love and appreciate yourself inside (pause twenty to thirty seconds).

13. Now take a minute or two to relax inside before returning your attention to the outside.

14. (Wait until attention has returned to the outside.)

Can you think of anything you need to say or do that would help facilitate the material you were exploring just now?

(Discuss, and let your partner take a few minutes to jot down discoveries in his or her notebook.)

Discussion

People generally have a few questions when they first explore this activity. One that comes up frequently is: "I don't think I did it right. Is something really dramatic supposed to happen?" This process is both profound and subtle. Sometimes change occurs gradually without the *"aha!"* that we may expect. Sometimes the change is cumulative over several repetitions of the process. We suggest that you look at overall changes in the quality of your relationship with yourself and with your partner to evaluate the effectiveness of the Healing Dialogue.

Another common question is: "What is a shift? What am I supposed to feel?" A shift is a physical, experiential sensation of something changing. Sensations can become bigger, smaller, or move to another part of the body. A shift can also be a thought or an image. If you notice it, a shift has occurred.

The Healing Dialogue will improve the quality of your daily life. You'll notice that issues get resolved more quickly, that new solutions occur as if by magic, and that the big swings of feel good/feel bad smooth out over time. Most people begin to experience noticeable changes after practicing the Healing Dialogue regularly for two to three weeks.

Getting Present

Instructions
Step One

In your notebook, make a list on the left half of a sheet of paper. Finish the sentence:
- I'll love myself when . . .

Examples: I'll love myself when I lose ten pounds.

I'll love myself when I get a good job.

I'll love myself when everybody else is happy.

Make the list as long as you can, bringing up all your considerations. Then, on the right half of the paper, next to each sentence write:

• I love _____ completely now.

Examples: I love my body completely now.

I love my work completely now.

I love myself with my kids completely now.

Discussion

People have asked us what possible use it could be to say you love something that you *know* you can't stand. The act of saying you love something that seems unlovable brings its negative aspects to the surface. Then you need to love those feelings and thoughts. As you continue actively to love each negative trait, a shift begins to occur. One woman commented: "I find it really possible to look deeply into myself now because I don't have to make anything wrong. I don't quite understand how it happens, but when I love myself for being mad at myself, I feel more at home inside instead of fighting myself all the time."

Step Two

Take your list and look at the right-hand column, where you've written: "I love ——— completely now." Read each one aloud, then pause for ten to fifteen seconds. Notice any negative thoughts or feelings. You may go through several sentences without finding a negative response, or you might be inundated on the first one. Underline each sentence that brought up uncomfortable or negative thoughts and feelings. For each of your underlined sentences complete the following outline.

"I love _____ completely now."

List your responses.

Take each response and use it in the following sentence:

"I love myself for _____."

Example:
"I love my body completely now."
Responses: Yuck! My thighs are disgusting!
It's hopeless, nothing will ever change.
I should appreciate that my body is healthy.
I feel tension at the back of my neck.
I love everything but my ankles.

Sentences: I love myself for feeling disgusted with my thighs.
I love myself for feeling hopeless and thinking nothing will ever change.
I love myself for "shoulding" myself.
I love myself for feeling tension at the back of my neck.
I love myself for excluding my ankles.

Discussion

People have found that they can continue to work with these lists over time. You can add to your responses as more areas surface to be loved. You may notice shifts in your experience toward more openness and more acceptance.

Reclaiming Feelings

This activity has two purposes: to give you the experience of befriending more of your feelings, and to provide the experience of welcoming and witnessing your partner's feelings, as discussed in chapter 4.

Instructions

One partner, the speaker, will say this sentence out loud to the responder, and the responder will reply as follows:

Speaker: "I am willing to feel all my sadness." (Pause and notice yourself for ten to fifteen seconds.)

Responder: "I can love you for that feeling." (Pause and notice yourself for ten to fifteen seconds.)

Speaker, read aloud each of the following sentences. Pause for ten to fifteen seconds after each sentence.
- I am willing to feel all my anger.
- I am willing to feel all my fear.
- I am willing to feel all my joy.
- I am willing to feel all my sexual feelings.

The responder will reply each time: "I can love you for that feeling." Let one partner go through the whole list before you switch roles.

Discussion

Several of our clients and students have remarked that feeling their joy and sexual feelings was more difficult and brought up more troublesome reactions than fear, anger, and sadness. This activity will show you which experiences you allow for yourself as well as which experiences you try to control in your partner. For example, one woman realized that it was all right for her partner to feel sad, but it definitely was not all right for her to feel sad. Her family protocol involved a lot of caretaking and stoicism. She could give comfort, both in her family and through her church, but she had learned that her sadness was self-pity and "weak." She used this activity to begin to allow herself to claim all her feelings, including her sadness.

Reclaiming Your Body

We experience life in our bodies and we communicate through them. Most of us learned, in many ways, to disown this fundamental source of our experience. The purpose of this activity is to bring you back into friendly contact with your body.

Instructions

1. The speaker will complete the sentence, "I am willing to fully claim my _____," naming a body part that

has seemed unlovable. Your partner, the reflector, will notice what your body does when you say this phrase.

Example:

Speaker: "I am willing to fully claim my upper arms."

Reflector: "You made a face as if you smelled something bad, and you pulled your shoulders back."

Speaker, repeat the phrase until you can say it directly, clearly, and without distortions. Then switch roles. Complete several sentences, naming different parts of your body.

2. Choose who will be the receiver first and who will be the lover. Receiver, identify some part of your body that you feel is unlovable. Lover, touch that part and let your love flow out into the receiver's body. Receiver, let your breath and awareness move around the edges of that place. Notice its shape, texture, color, and any other qualities. Describe to the lover what you notice. Mention any body shifts you experience. For example, you may notice a part getting warm, changing color, or feeling tingly. After five to ten minutes, switch roles.

Discussion

We've never met anyone who initially loved everything about his or her body. We want the flow of positive energy within you and between you to be fully grounded. As you learn to communicate and explore life with more of your body, you'll be able to participate more fully in the dance you both are creating.

Exponential Loving

When we are stuck, the last thing we think of is to love the issue or the experience. This activity is designed to give you a break from figuring out what to do. You'll simply love the situation and your experience of it. In other words, you'll practice *being with*, rather than *doing to*.

Instructions

One of you, the receiver, will lie down on the carpet or bed. Your partner, the catalyst, will sit behind your head. Receiver, choose a problem or issue in which you feel stuck. You can also choose something in answer to the question: What needs love right now?

Receiver, describe the problem or issue briefly to the catalyst. Catalyst, place your fingertips on the receiver's forehead gently. Receiver, describe your body sensations and your thoughts as the catalyst touches your forehead. Then rest quietly while both of you focus as much love as you can on your experience. Love it just as it is, until the receiver feels something shift in thoughts, images, or sensations. Then pause and rest a moment or two, and switch roles.

Discussion

We find it most useful to avoid analyzing this experience. When you have each had a turn, rest for a few minutes and continue with your day. The shifts from this activity may show up when you're taking a walk or doing the dishes a few days later.

Learning to Feel Your Feelings

These communication and writing activities will open the doors to feelings you've hidden or frozen. Bringing your feelings into the light will promote discoveries and growth within yourself and in your close relationships.

The Feeling Map

Introduction

The purpose of this activity is to help you notice how you experience your basic feelings. You will have a number of opportunities to notice the specific sensations associated with your basic emotions as you sense them in your body. These experiences will add information to your Choice Map (p. 250) and will assist you to tell the microscopic truth.

Instructions

This activity has two roles, the speaker and the listener. Listener, get comfortable and close your eyes. Speaker, read the following aloud, verbatim, to the listener.

1. Think of something you feel sad about. Perhaps a loved one you have lost, or a painful time in your life. Picture it in your mind, think of it any way you can, and feel it in your body. (Pause for fifteen to twenty seconds.) Now notice how you are experiencing the sadness in your body. Where do you feel it the most? What are the specific sensations you are experiencing? What happens to your breathing? Be aware of the minor sensations as well as the major ones. (Pause for one minute.)

2. Think of something you feel angry about. Imagine a recent angry event or a long-ago one. Perhaps think of the person in your life you have felt most angry with. Think of it, and feel it in your body. (Pause for fifteen to twenty seconds.) Where do you feel anger in your body? What are the specific sensations of the anger? Notice any changes in your breathing as you feel anger. What draws your attention first? Is the sensation big; does it take up a lot of space inside? Notice the smaller sensations. Tune in to how you feel anger in your body. (Pause for one to two minutes.)

3. Think of something you feel fear about. Think of a time in your life when you were most afraid, or of a recent time you were scared. Think of it and feel it in your body. (Pause for fifteen to twenty seconds.) Where is the center of fear in your body? What sensations do you experience when you tune in to your fear? Notice the large sensations and the small ones. Tune in to fear as you notice your body. (Continue for one to two minutes.)

4. Describe to me anything you've noticed or learned. Then take a few minutes to add discoveries to your journal.

5. Switch roles and repeat the process.

Discussion

As you are exploring this activity, take the attitude that you are a Martian and know absolutely nothing about human feelings. Let yourself notice details, qualities, and tones that will allow you to describe your experience. Avoid assuming anything. For example, if you notice tension when you tune in to fear, be aware of the pull of the tension, where it seems to start, how strong it is, and what it seems connected to in the rest of your body. Focus on description, not evaluation or judgment. Remember, a Martian wouldn't treat anger any differently from fear. The more we can learn the language of the body, the richer our communications will be.

For example, a client in a recent session said he felt "anxious all the time." When we pressed him to describe his experience more specifically, he discovered that he had lumped a whole group of experiences into "anxiety": stomach knots, shivering, pulling sensations in his neck, dry throat, clenched jaw, worry thoughts, tears, and so on. As a lump, anxiety had seemed insurmountable. As discrete sensations, his experience began to shift and lead him to the source, which was buried in his early experience.

Being Present for Feelings

This activity will allow you to practice being with your partner while deep feeling is emerging. Instead of rushing in to fix it or trying to talk your partner out of feeling, you'll be practicing a kind of nondoing that allows tremendous opening and closeness to occur. Most of us try to stop our partners from feeling those emotions that are troublesome for us. In this activity we encourage you to be aware of what can happen through the power of presence.

Instructions

Begin sitting with each other. Choose who will communicate first. Communicator, answer the question: *Where do you feel your fear in your body?* Partner, do your best to *be with* that feeling as the communicator tells the microscopic truth about it. When the communicator is through, share your responses as you intended to be present.

Example:

Communicator: "I feel my fear mostly in my stomach area, but also in the back of my neck. In my stomach I feel these sharp ribbons waving and jiggling against my stomach walls. The back of my neck feels crawly like someone's pulling my skin up over my head."

Partner: "It was so hard to stay here. I found myself thinking about dinner and what I need to do at work tomorrow. I pulled back and noticed that I felt little shivers in the back of my neck when you were describing your fear. I think maybe I keep busy so I don't have to feel my fear."

Go through each of the following feelings using the same format:

* Where do you feel your anger in your body?
* Where do you feel your sadness in your body?
* Where do you feel your sexual feelings in your body?
* Where do you feel your joy in your body?

Let one person communicate all these feelings before you switch roles.

Discussion

Many couples discover that their feelings overlap, and that they are much more sensitive to each other's feelings than they realized. Through this activity, feeling "deals" often become visible, such as the unconscious agreement for one partner to interrupt the other's sadness with cheer-up messages and the other partner to change the subject whenever fear arises. Learning to be with feelings is a very powerful tool that will enhance your ability to tell the microscopic truth in every area.

Completing Feelings

Communication in relationships is enhanced by expressing feelings fully and completely. This activity has two purposes: to recognize which feelings you allow completely and which you edit in some way, and to recognize patterns of communication of feelings.

Instructions

In your notebook, each of you complete the following sentence:
- When I feel sad, I want to . . .

Example: When I feel sad, I want to run away.

Complete each of the following sentences:
- When I feel angry, I want to . . .
- When I feel scared, I want to . . .
- When I feel sexy, I want to . . .
- When I feel happy, I want to . . .

Discussion

You may want to complete each sentence several times if you notice you have more than one impulse. Sometimes these impulses can even be in conflict with each other. For example, "When I feel happy I want to jump up and down, and I also want to hide so nobody notices me."

When we begin to see our feeling patterns we have more choice in their expression. One woman saw that she only slammed the door and walked out of the room during arguments with her husband when she felt scared. She had always thought that that was how she responded to her anger. She saw that door slamming was a generic response she had learned in her family, and began to understand her husband's frustration with her behavior when they were trying to work something out.

When we can be aware of and experience all of our feelings as they occur, it allows us to be present in the creative moment. For a while you may find that you notice your patterns after the fact. This delayed reaction is natural at first. With continued practice, your awareness and expression will come closer and closer together. One couple noticed that when they first started this activity, it took about a week for the core feeling pattern of an argument to surface. During the delay time, they experienced their interactions as being a little "off" in ways they couldn't quite pinpoint. Now they're down to several minutes' delay time and lots of liberated free energy to share.

Claiming Creativity

The Choice Map

The ability to know and to state clearly what we want is a central skill in conscious loving. Many of our conditioned roles have taught us to be very aware of what others want. In fact, many of our clients have said that they had learned it was selfish to consider their own wants at all. When asked, "What do you want?" the co-dependent says, "I just want what you want, dear." Hundreds of times we have heard our clients say, "I have no idea what I want." Others do not even know *how* to know what they want.

The purpose of this activity is twofold. The first is to give you tools to construct your internal map of responses— how to know what you want. People make choices based on a unique set of internal experiences. For example, when considering where to go for dinner, one person may remember the taste of their favorite dish, another may picture the decor in a particular restaurant, and another may recall the level of noise and smokiness. Our responses to these internal maps are generally unconscious.

The second purpose is to give you experiences in making choices and noticing your responses. So many of us have had negative experiences around making choices that we give up, suppress our wants, develop secret strategies for getting our needs met, or develop a sense of scarcity about resources. Kathlyn overheard a family's conversation in a restaurant recently. The mother asked the young daughter, "What do you want to eat?" The little girl said, "I want the lobster." Her father immediately said, "No you don't. That's too much for you." Her mother said, "Oh, that's so rich, you'll be sick! Wouldn't you like something else?" The girl was firm in her decision, and an argument ensued that left the girl in tears and both parents on edge. Imagine the difference if one of them had asked, "What is it about the lobster that you like? Its shape, or the fun of finding the meat and dipping each piece in the butter?" Or, "What would you like that's under ten dollars?"

Choosing a meal is far simpler than choosing what we want in a relationship. Most of us lack experience in going beyond the boundaries of what we have learned. As children we were usually provided with a set of choices and have continued to look for the visible, externally obvious alternatives: to pick this or that. Our insides are much more imaginative and can put new things together that our conditioned selves couldn't generate. This experiment is designed to help you discover the *process* of choosing.

Instructions

Take turns reading the directions to your partner, and leave time for discussion at the end. There are two roles in this activity: choice-maker and instruction-reader. Decide who is going to go first. Choice-maker, get comfortable in a chair and leave your eyes closed during the directions.

Instruction-reader, read aloud the following instructions verbatim.

1. Begin saying "I want" out loud, pausing for fifteen to twenty seconds between each repetition. Notice what thoughts, images, and sensations arise during the pauses. Say "I want" four to five times, with the pause in between.

2. Now tell me out loud what you notice during the pauses. Repeat "I want" and pause, noticing and saying out loud what you are aware of and where you notice your experience in your body. For example, you might say, "I want," and feel a twitch in your left eye. Just tell me out loud what you notice: "I felt a twitch in my left eye." Notice if more than one internal response occurs. For example, you may notice a twitch in your left eye followed by the brief image of your grandmother playing the piano followed by the memory of her clearing her throat. Let yourself say your process out loud just as you experience it.

3. Now experiment with different vocal tones and intensities. For example, say "I want!" righteously and emphatically, or in a whining whisper. Again, pause and notice your internal responses, saying them out loud. You may notice that you have a judgmental or critical voice that comes in and says, "This is silly, I haven't got time for this nonsense!" or, "You're bad and selfish and always get everything!" Just report these voices as they occur.

4. Say "I want" as you reach out to grasp something imaginary. Pause fifteen to twenty seconds and notice what arises in your thoughts, images, sensations, and emotions. Tell your experience out loud.

5. Think of something you know you like and want and imagine it in front of you. Say "I want" as you reach out for it. Pause for several seconds and notice what arises. Now think of something you know you really dislike and imagine it in front of you. Say "I want" as you reach out for it. Pause and notice your internal experience. Tell me the differences you noticed between the two experiences.

6. Now ask yourself, "Do I want a drink of water right now?" and watch your internal experience very closely. If you decide you do want a drink, go and get one, noticing your reaction to satisfying your wish. If you did not want a drink, notice how you knew that you did not.

7. Now focus on your relationship. Close your eyes and ask, "What do I want in my relationship?" Pause for twenty to thirty seconds to notice what you come up with. Repeat this question out loud two or three times. Sometimes you won't get an answer but rather an opening or a shift in body sensation, such as your shoulder tension. An answer may come later.

Discuss what emerged, then switch roles.

Expressing Yourself Fully

In some ways the key to ongoing transformation is very simple. Each moment you have the choice to participate in your experience or to stop it. We've given many examples of withdrawal and other ways people stop their experience.

Our purpose in this activity is to give you experience with your total response to participating or withholding. Use your journal to note your questions, discoveries, and ideas for further exploration.

Instructions

1. Stand facing each other. Choose who will be the communicator first and who will be the receiver. Communicator, locate a sensation in your body, such as tingling, pressure, itchiness, and so on, then deny your experience. Tell yourself you're not experiencing that sensation. Notice your response as closely as possible. Now locate that sensation or another one and communicate what you experience as specifically as you can. Let your whole body communicate. Notice the difference between withholding and going all the way with your expression. Switch roles and repeat.

2. Communicator, find an emotion that is cycling through you right now, experience it for a moment, then stop it. Notice how you stop your feelings (your breath and tense places in your body are good places to start looking). Now locate the emotion again and use your whole body to communicate the microscopic truth of this emotion. Notice the difference in your sense of aliveness between hiding and revealing. Switch roles and repeat.

3. Communicator, notice an impulse to move, start to move, then stop. The movement can be a gesture, head tilt, or whole-body impulse. The size of the movement doesn't matter. Study the way you stop movement; that's one way you stop spontaneity. Now notice an impulse and act it out, moving even more than you would normally. Share with your partner the differences you notice. Switch roles and repeat.

4. Communicator, start to share verbally something about yourself, then say, "Never mind." Be aware of that statement's effect on your aliveness and presence. Then share something about yourself, perhaps something you've never shared, as fully and comprehensively as possible. Notice how alive you feel. Switch roles and repeat.

Discussion

The content of particular experiences isn't as important as your willingness to participate fully with the experience. Discuss your experiences with your partner. Ask what differences he or she saw in you when you were withholding and when you were participating.

If you find yourselves getting into right-wrong battles, as the majority of couples do, this activity is particularly helpful. By focusing on what is true—your own sensations—you get beneath the level of what's right and what's wrong.

For example, a couple invested in who's right could get embroiled in an argument as follows:

> CLAIRE: I asked you to walk the dog an hour ago, and now she's messed the carpet.
> DON: I didn't hear you. I was busy balancing the checkbook you overdrew last month.
> CLAIRE: One of the *only* things I ask you to do around the house is walk the dog, and I always end up doing it or cleaning up!
> DON: I never wanted the damn dog anyway!

If Claire and Don were committed to telling the microscopic truth, the conversation might unfold in a different direction:

> CLAIRE: Don, I just noticed that the dog messed on the carpet. Did you forget to walk her?
> DON: Oh, jeez, I did! You know, I was doing the checking account and started having resentful thoughts about your overdraws last month. I didn't really talk to you about it at the time. Seems like my anger spilled over into "forgetting."
> CLAIRE: When I came in earlier to ask you to walk the dog, I realize now that I was nervous and jittery. I was afraid you'd be mad about the checkbook, and I think I brought up the dog to distract

you. I really want to look at why I'm not being responsible with money.

Dropping Projection

Dropping projection is perhaps the single most powerful action you can take to transform your relationship toward conscious loving. Part 1 of this book has given you many verbal and interactional examples of projection. Here we want to provide opportunities for you to explore your whole-body patterns of projection and to make new choices that will support you in dropping projection.

Instructions

In all of these activities you will mold your partner's body into different shapes, as if he or she were clay. Molder, you'll want to notice your response to creating actual representations of your projections. Clay figure, be cooperative with the molder's purpose.

1. Molder, shape your partner's body into the shape that physically represents **who you think your partner is.** When the molder is satisfied, clay figure, share what you experience being in this shape. Don't get involved with the figure's accuracy; stay with your experience. Particularly notice if you experience yourself as a character or an image.

Example: "In this shape I feel kind of awkward, almost like a bird with spindly legs. I feel rather weak, as if I would wobble if I tried to walk." After the clay figure has shared, switch roles and repeat.

2. Molder, shape your partner's body into a physical representation of **who he or she *ought* to be.** Mold until you feel satisfied. Then listen to the clay figure's experiences and images. Switch roles and repeat.

3. This time you'll take turns shaping your partner's body **as if it were your own,** into the following variations:
   • how your father or mother wanted you to be
   • how a successful male/female looks
   • how you think your partner thinks you ought to be

Take time after each molding to hear the clay figure's experience.

Discussion

Write your discoveries in your journal. For example, after a woman molded her husband's body into a tyranni- cal, big-chested shape, he said: "I feel older and stiffer than I experience myself, and more bent, as if I were carrying a burden." His wife suddenly realized that she had created an image of her father. They excitedly began to explore other ways in which they were not seeing each other clearly. People have created whole galleries of projected characters, including an octopus, a mouse, a sports jock, a simpering princess, a wolf, a thundering giant, a nerd, and a sleuth.

After you have written in your journal, tell your part- ner: "I am willing to see and experience you as you are, and I am willing to be fully myself with you." A friend was recently uncovering a positive projection she had carried for her family. She was the caretaker, the "nice one." As she began to claim her needs and wants, she uncovered her fear of dropping the nice persona and her fear of people's response to a more assertive and possibly more abrasive woman. "They might not like it," she said. True. There definitely are ripples or waves to be ridden when we drop projections. The payoff is vitality, spontaneity, freshness, and renewed deepening with yourself and your partner.

Core Beliefs

This journal activity is designed to increase your awareness of your deep beliefs about yourself in relation- ship. They are the underlying assumptions that control our responses and interactions.

Instructions

1. Choose a relationship issue that comes up repeatedly and write it in your notebook. Write the following three questions under the issue, leaving blank space under each one.
   • What is my belief about this situation?
   • Where did I first learn this?

• Am I willing to learn something new here?

2. Take time to let your mind and body be with this issue. First write down all the beliefs you can think of. Some examples of core beliefs:

• No matter what I do it doesn't make any difference.

• Assume the worst.

• I have to keep everything under control or something awful will happen.

• I'm helpless.

• I'm stupid; I never do anything right.

• Men are no good; they only want one thing.

• Women are out to trap you.

Now scan back over your life and jot down times when you learned these beliefs: incidents between your parents, times at school or with your friends, scenes from television, and so on.

3. Finally, ask yourself if you are willing to learn something new. Take each negative core belief and make a positive sentence out of it. For example, change "Men are no good" to "Men are great."

Discussion

This activity is especially useful in uncovering the source of projections. For example, a man recently discovered that he believed that if he got close to his wife, she would leave him. Frequently he would start to get suspicious and sad in the middle of a close time with his wife. Using this activity, he found that the source of his belief was that twice his mother had left to go into the hospital with miscarriages, once when he was still nursing, and once after a vacation where he had spent a lot of time with her. He had gotten closeness and loss merged in his mind and had come to see the world that way. Knowing the source of his belief and being willing to learn something new enabled him to stay present longer in times of closeness and to tell the truth about his experience without fear of abandonment.

How to Get What You Want
Without Compromising

Most of us grew up thinking that to be in a relationship meant settling for less than you wanted. In a recent class Gay's students posed this relationship question: "Suppose the husband's brother and sister-in-law are visiting the area for Christmas. The wife doesn't like his relatives and doesn't want to spend time with them. What should they do?" When Gay responded: "How about telling the truth about it?" the class exploded. "What! How can you do that, it's Christmas, it's *family*!" Most of us have learned that in certain situations, you have to swallow the truth and compromise.

A friend of ours recently provided another, more complex example. He and his wife were enjoying the later part of a close evening together. His wife, Debby, said: "What would you like to hear?" Joe considered briefly and replied: "I'd like to listen to the Julian Bream album." "Oh, Julian Bream," Debby replied. "Did you know we have a new Herbie Hancock? It's really nice. Do you think you might like to hear that?" Joe then felt confused, but he agreed to listen to the new album. After Debby put it on, Joe realized that he was beginning to feel irritated and sad. He shared these feelings: "This seems familiar. I say what I want and somehow it doesn't happen." Debby inquired into her process and saw that in adolescence she had developed a habit of avoiding direct requests because her brothers had often teased her about her "weirdness." She had also learned that it was "better" to think of others first, so she suppressed her true desires and became proficient at manipulating to get what she wanted. She wanted Herbie Hancock, but she wanted Joe to want it too, so that she would not have to risk wanting it and being rejected. No wonder we get so confused!

Instructions

In this activity we want you to consider the possibility that everyone concerned can have what they want. First, try on that idea and notice what old thought programs roll out.

Examples:

• Marriage is based on compromise.

• If everyone got what they wanted, things would just fall apart.

• There isn't enough to go around.

• I feel uncomfortable just thinking about it.

Note these beliefs and body responses in your notebook for future reference.

1. Stand and face each other. This activity has two roles: talker and listener. Decide who will be the talker first. Talker, say aloud: "I am willing to have what I want." Pause for ten seconds, then repeat this sentence. The listener just listens. After four or five repetitions, switch roles and repeat.

2. The talker now repeats every ten seconds: "I am willing for you to have what you want." Both talker and listener tune in during the pauses to fully experience their responses. After four to five repetitions, switch roles and repeat.

We suggest that you apply your willingness first to small decisions, such as where to have dinner, what TV program to watch, or which side of the bed to sleep on. Practice telling the microscopic truth until you feel some ease with describing your body sensations, feelings, and experiences. If each of you continues to open up to and share the microscopic truth, new alternatives emerge.

Discussion

Another example illustrates getting what you want in an emotionally important decision. Emily came into her therapy session just before Thanksgiving feeling tearful and irritated. The holidays are famous for bringing up old feelings about our families. In Emily's case, her favorite grandmother had died just before Thanksgiving ten years ago. Over the years, Emily had grown increasingly unwilling to celebrate with turkey, trimmings, and relatives. "It's just not the same, it's so phony. I *hate* Thanksgiving!" That time of year reminded her of her grandmother pulling her legendary cherry pie from the oven. The family had always gathered at Grandmother's house, and the smells, decorations, and her grandmother's stories *were* Thanksgiving for Emily. We explored Emily's unfinished grief and then asked: "What do you want to do?" At that moment she was still embroiled in her feelings, but she agreed to think about it.

The night before Thanksgiving she woke up at about three o'clock feeling restless. She began practicing some relaxation activities we had given her, and while doing them she became aware that she really wanted to be active; she didn't want to sit around and eat all day. She told her plan to her husband, who was awake by then. "Let's put the turkey in the oven on a timer, get the kids up, and go skiing." Her husband agreed, and the children were thrilled to get up before light and have a big adventure. They packed up and headed to a nearby ski resort, had a wonderful day on the slopes, then headed home for the turkey. Everyone had so much fun that they decided to make it an annual ritual.

What Step Are We Doing?

An important aspect of problem-solving is pacing. We are born with different rhythmic preferences, sometimes much to our parents' frustration. Can you remember being told to "hurry up, now!" or to "just sit still for a minute!"? In our adult relationships we carry those rhythmic preferences into our decision-making processes. Some people like to approach an issue from many different angles, lingering over the possibilities before finally selecting their path. Others see it, get it, do it, and move on. If you are paired with someone whose rhythm is different from yours, you may find that many of your arguments revolve around who's too fast and who's too slow. This activity will bring your preferences to light and suggest some ways to satisfy both of you. You may want to do this activity outside where you'll have plenty of space.

Instructions

Decide who will be the leader and who will be the follower. Follower, walk beside the leader and match the leader's pace throughout this activity. Leader, think about current issue you're exploring as you walk. Notice what walking speed allows you to be most in touch with yourself. Move at that pace for a couple of minutes. Follower, notice your response, whether this pace feels too fast, too slow, or just right. Leader, speed up now and notice the effect on your thought process and your ability to concentrate on the issue. Follower, switch pace when the leader does. Leader, now walk much more slowly and notice the shifts in your thoughts and feelings. Continue at this slow pace for a few minutes. Leader, now return to your in-touch pace and notice if you feel more able to be with the issue. Then switch roles and repeat.

Spend some time now applying this information to your daily decision-making process. What can you do to allow the most effective process for each of you? Write your responses in your notebooks.

Discussion

Using this activity, a man discovered that he opened up many creative possibilities by listening to African music when trying to solve a problem. A woman realized that she needed to slow down and found the Healing Dialogue most useful.

Your natural rhythm may not match your partner's. We usually interpret this to mean: (1) There's something wrong with me (or them); or (2) He or she doesn't love me. Neither is true. When you simply acknowledge your need, you can shift your timing to make room for your partner. One couple made up of a lingerer and a speeder came up with this solution: The lingerer engages in his speculations and musings until he feels satisfied, then brings this information to his speedy wife, who takes it in one gulp and adds her speedy response, and they use the composite picture to make the decision.

Learning to Tell the
Microscopic Truth
(Parts One to Four)

In every relationship there is a unique rhythm to times of needing closeness and times of needing space. One couple's pulsation might have long periods of intimacy and only minutes or hours for alone time. Another pair may live in different cities because of job situations and get together for intense weekends. This activity will give you a sense of what pulsation works best for you.

One of the things you may discover first is how enmeshed you are with your partner's pulsation. You may be surprised to find that you experience a wave of fear or that you withdraw when your partner moves away. Most of our problems in this area have been unconscious. This activity is designed to bring your patterns to awareness.

The steps outlined will allow you to communicate your intimacy and independence needs clearly and easily by practicing telling the microscopic truth. There are four parts to this activity, each of which focuses on one basic principle and practice. We recommend that you practice each part until you become comfortable with it before moving on to the next part. Feel free to go back and practice this activity over a period of weeks. Our friends and clients who have practiced telling the microscopic truth testify to its immense possibilities. Give yourselves time to discover these in your own lives.

You will need a room large enough for you to stride ten or twelve steps without colliding with walls or furniture.

Part One

Instructions

This activity has two roles, the mover and the witness. Decide who will be the first mover. Your partner will be your sounding board and witness. Witness, stand in one place. Mover, start by facing your partner, about three feet away. Move backward step by step until you notice a shift in your body experience. For example, you may notice a twinge in your right shoulder or a fluttering sensation in your belly. *Describe* that shift as minutely as you can to your witness. Witness, simply listen and notice your own experience. Save verbal responses for later.

Mover, when you have described your body experience, begin stepping closer to your partner. When you feel a shift in your body experience, describe it aloud to your partner. Your body experience may include a specific thought, such as, "I must look silly." It may arise as an image, even a surprising one, such as a boat with wings. It may also arise as an emotion, such as sadness, fear, joy, or anger. Do your best to describe *just what you experience* without judgments or interpretations.

Move away from and toward your partner ten to fifteen times. Each time you move, stop when you feel a shift and describe your experience. Then switch roles and repeat.

Discussion

Take as long as you need to talk about what you learned. Notice whether moving away or coming closer felt more comfortable. Ask yourselves if any responses were familiar. We do this activity with couples more often than any other, and a typical reaction is, "Why, that's just what we do!" Did any patterns in your relationship emerge?

Give your partner feedback about *your* experience without interpreting theirs. For example, one participant recently exclaimed: "I really see now that each time Sally comes close to me I kind of flinch and look away. I feel afraid, but it feels so familiar that I know I'm not afraid of Sally. It's someone else. I got yelled at a lot as a kid, and I can feel my anticipation that Sally will yell at me too."

It may take some time to see what you are actually doing. For instance, one member of a couple backed up about twelve feet from her partner and then said: "I feel sad when you move away!" Her boyfriend looked stunned, because he hadn't moved at all.

You may find that you feel awkward or can't find the right words to describe your experience. Just keep practicing; use sign language or mime if that's your style. Take time to let yourselves get familiar with this activity.

Part Two

Instructions

This activity also has a mover and a witness. Mover, begin to back away from the witness. Stop and describe your experience when you feel a shift. Witness, describe any body experience you had when the mover stopped (tensions, pains, worry thoughts, pleasant sensations, and so on). Mover, take steps toward the witness, then away, ten times. Then switch roles and repeat, making sure to save time to share your discoveries.

Part Three

Instructions

Both of you are now going to move *at the same time*, closer to and farther away from each other. Start moving slowly. Stop when you feel a body shift and describe your experience aloud. Don't try to take turns; you may both be talking at the same time, both backing up, getting nose to nose, and so on. After a few minutes begin varying your speed. Go faster and with a more uneven pace. Then change the direction of your path. For example, you can back toward your partner, circle, crouch and sneak in, or dash away. Play with the possibilities.

Part Four

We pass each other probably several dozen times in a week. Each time, we give each other signals about whether we want closeness or separateness. In this activity you have the opportunity to highlight those signals. Uncovering the truth will bring you to greater depth and discovery with each other.

Instructions

Choose a day that is agreeable to both of you, and practice telling the microscopic truth each time you come into the same room or leave the same room. Describe your body sensations as closely as you can. Claim creativity by monitoring when you go into explanations, justifications, or projections. Each time, gently bring yourself back to your body experience.

Keeping Your Agreements

Keeping Agreements

This activity is based on the skills you have learned in the previous activities. Knowing and telling the microscopic truth is essential for you to commit to what you want. Knowing your feelings is prerequisite to making your Choice Map and getting feedback from your Inner Self. The power of keeping agreements lies simply in keeping them. It's not complicated. If you don't keep your agreements, your relationship won't work quite as well as it might. We include agreements with yourself as well as those with others because they are just as powerful a base for your integrity.

Instructions

1. In your journal, each of you make a list of recent agreements you broke or didn't fully complete. Remember the last month and jot down even the "little" agreements you didn't keep. Next to each one, write the microscopic truth about not keeping that agreement.

Example:
• I bounced a check and didn't tell you. I was afraid you'd be angry.
• I ate all the cookies I brought home "for the family." I felt discouraged and was comforting myself. I didn't even notice I'd eaten the whole box.
• I talked to your ex and said I wouldn't tell you, even though we agreed to let each other know when we had contact. I was afraid to bring her to your attention because I think you still care for her.

Share your lists with each other.

2. Make three columns on a blank sheet in your notebook, and head them as follows: What, When, and Check-in.

Start by listing three agreements that you are willing to make with your partner (What), the time involved (When), and the date when you'll communicate your experiences (Check-in).

Example:

What	When	Check-in
1/2 hour walking together	daily	Sunday night

Use a calendar or appointment book if necessary to keep track of your agreements. Some couples use refrigerator notes or erasable marking boards. When you check in, focus on contacting your feelings and telling the microscopic truth about your experience. Avoid apologizing if you break your agreements. Concentrate on discovering the source of broken agreements and what behavior you need to change. Acknowledge completed agreements. Each time you check in, make another agreement.

Discussion

After you have some experience making and keeping agreements, you'll find that your personal lives run more smoothly. You might want to ask your partner's support for an agreement you want to make with yourself, or another person. Kathlyn gave the following experience from her personal life: "I have experienced a tremendous personal transformation by asking Gay's support in losing weight. For years I would make agreements with him about our eating style, then eat secretly in the car or when he wasn't home. It looked like I was keeping agreements because I only ate when I was alone. In order to maintain the secret I had to lie to myself about what I was doing, not see how heavy I was, and withhold my full energy from Gay so that I could protect the secret. One night Gay basically said, 'You're fat, and I want you to look at what that is about.' After my initial defensive reaction (best pictured as a combination of sulking, indignation, and resignation), I took the opportunity to examine the source of this decades-long pattern. I began telling the minute truth to Gay about every aspect of my weight: body image, history, embarrassment, dreams, everything I could think of. Telling the truth gave me real support for keeping my agreement with myself to transform my body. Over the several months that the transformation took, I noticed that other aspects of my life smoothed out and became lighter. My work deepened, money flowed more easily, and my relationship with my son became even more fun."

Under the Check-in section of your notebook, keep track of the benefits you experience from keeping your agreements. You'll find that honoring agreements builds a powerful web of light that will surprise and delight you.

What Role Are You Playing?

This activity and the Completions List (p. 269) address different aspects of incompletions. When you complete old feelings, things from your past—broken agreements, and so on—a tremendous amount of energy is freed to create what you want in the present. As you explore these activities, notice the difference in your experience and level of joy.

This activity will help bring unconscious roles to your awareness. You can then discard what no longer works, adapt the effective parts of your roles to your current life, and make new decisions about the roles you want.

Instructions

Take turns reading the following instructions out loud to your partner:

1. Sit comfortably, eyes closed if you wish.

2. Rest for thirty to sixty seconds.

3. Listen to each question that follows, then pause for ten to fifteen seconds to allow your mind and body to respond. The information may come in an unusual form. You may hear the question, for example, and the answer may come in the form of an energy fluctuation in your body, such as tingling or buzzing.

What roles have I taken on in my life? (Pause for ten to fifteen seconds.)

To what extent are my roles freely chosen? (Pause for ten to fifteen seconds.)

How much of what I create (positive and negative) is due to my roles? (Pause for ten to fifteen seconds.)

Now rest for a moment or two, then bring your attention back to the room.

When each of you has heard the questions, take some time to share what you discovered.

Discussion

As discussed in chapter 8, roles form much of the background on which we project our current relationships. In your exploration focus especially on aspects of your roles that you don't generally question. Those things that we assume are "real" can be roles we've assumed without really choosing. This activity can assist you in making conscious choices in your roles. For example, a client recently realized that she had been assigned the "stupid" role in her family, for many complicated reasons. For two decades she lived her life stupidly, sabotaging two marriages and chances for business success before she began to question her real intelligence. She was willing to do the work to uncover her essential nature, which involved recognizing her mother's inability to share any attention with another female and all her feelings in response to that truth. When she experienced the source of that role, she said: "I feel alive for the first time in my life. I know I could go back to school now and enjoy it. I feel I have myself now. I even think I could have a relationship now without giving my power away because I don't have to be stupid anymore."

The Completions List

The Completions List is designed to organize and facilitate ongoing completions. The act of eliciting, expressing, and completing unfinished business will free you for more conscious loving with your partner. You will need a separate section in your notebook for this activity.

Instructions

1. At the top of a blank page, each of you make three columns titled as follows: Incompletions, Feelings and Truth, and Action Date.

Under Incompletions, record unfinished business you discover. Under Feelings and Truth, note communications that haven't been acknowledged and communicated. Under Action Date, write the time frame and the specific action you will take to complete that unfinished business.

2. Now decide who will take the role of explorer first and who will be the guide. Explorer, sit in a comfortable chair with your notebook and pen open on your lap. Guide, read aloud the following instructions verbatim: Close your eyes and shift in whatever way will allow you to be even more comfortable. Take several deep, slow breaths into your relaxed belly as you sink into the chair. (Pause for fifteen to twenty seconds.) I am going to read you a list of questions. As you hear each one, let yourself picture, sense, and listen to whatever responses arise. Notice whatever comes.

• What feelings have I separated myself from? (Pause for fifteen to twenty seconds.)

• What relationships have I left incomplete? (Pause for fifteen to twenty seconds.)

• What agreements have I broken and not cleaned up? (Pause for fifteen to twenty seconds.)

• What have I said I would do that I have not done? (Pause for fifteen to twenty seconds.)

• What have I agreed not to do that I have done? (Pause for fifteen to twenty seconds.)

• What communications have I left unsaid? (Pause for fifteen to twenty seconds.)

• What have I started and not finished? (Pause for fifteen to twenty seconds.)

• To whom do I owe money? (Pause for fifteen to twenty seconds.)

• Whom do I need to forgive? (Pause for fifteen to twenty seconds.)

• To whom do I owe appreciations? (Pause for fifteen to twenty seconds.)

Now rest for just a moment, then open your eyes to list in your notebook any incompletions you discovered.

When the explorer is finished, switch roles and repeat.

Discussion

You may find that some incompletions come to your awareness at a later time. When you start the Completions List you are opening the space for incompletions to bubble to the surface. You can trust that your intention will continue to flush unfinished business until you are current. You can use your list on an ongoing basis to chart your completions. Charting them frees your mind from carrying that information. It also empowers your intention to complete. Be sure to note a specific date by which you will have completed that item. This will support your action and prevent slippage.

Remember that the action needed to complete something may be internal as well as in relationship. For example, if you haven't forgiven your ex-husband for leaving the marriage at the hospital door where you were having your first child (which actually happened to one of our clients), you may need to feel your anger as you relive the experience before you can call him to express your microscopic truth. Forgiveness usually follows the release of anger.

You may be surprised to find an old storehouse of incomplete acknowledgments. Our incompletions are not always negative. Appreciating someone for teaching you something valuable or modeling a magnificent way of being is just as enlivening as completing past feelings and agreements.

Cross out the line when the incompletion is complete. Invest the time to make your list both work and play. You'll be amazed at your increased joy and creativity.

Learning to Live in a State of Continuous Positive Energy

After you have become accustomed to telling the microscopic truth to each other, saying what you want directly, and experiencing and expressing your true feelings, you may begin to see that all your issues are really one issue: How much positive energy can I handle? The purpose of these activities is to expand your ability to experience and to have more fun and happiness in your life.

Breath and Feeling

Breathing and feeling are intimately entwined. As a child, did you hold your breath when you were scared or hurt? We still do it as adults. Restricting the breath is a quick way of stopping an unpleasant, unwelcome feeling. The trouble is that it also stops your life energy in general. Many people think there are two faucets, marked GOOD FEELINGS and BAD FEELINGS. They think you can turn on the good one and leave the bad shut off. There is only one faucet, however, and it is marked FEELINGS. You turn it on, take what you get, and after a while it becomes mostly positive. It is similar to when we go to our mountain cabin after an absence: we turn on the faucet and are greeted by spurts and pops and brown-tinged water. Then, after running for a few minutes, there is clear mountain stream water. Our feelings work much the same way. If the faucet's been off for a while, expect some initial debris.

This activity will assist you in developing a new relationship with your feelings, which will allow you to have more freedom in your close relationships.

Instructions (to be read aloud to your partner)

1. Think of a situation that triggered sadness in you. Reexperience your sadness now. Notice the sensations of the sadness and where you feel them in your body. (Pause for ten to fifteen seconds.) Now gently breathe into and around those feelings of sadness. Go to meet them in your body with your breath. Surround the sensations of sadness with your breath. Let each breath permeate the feeling of sadness. Notice what happens to the sadness when you breathe into and around it. Continue doing this for two minutes.

2. Think of a situation in which you felt angry. Reexperience your anger now. Notice the sensations of the anger and where you feel it in your body. (Pause for ten to fifteen seconds.) Gently breathe into the anger. Breathe into and around the sensations of anger. Let the breath permeate the anger. Notice what happens to the anger as you breathe into it. Continue for two minutes.

3. Think of a situation in which you felt fear. Feel the fear now in your body. Notice the sensations of the fear and where you feel it in your body. (Pause for ten to fifteen seconds.) Breathe gently into the sensations of fear. Feel the sensations in your body and let your breath surround them. Notice what happens to the fear when you breathe into it and around it. Continue for two minutes.

Let yourself rest inside for a moment, then jot down what you learned in your notebook.

When you are finished, switch roles and repeat.

Following is an example of what one person wrote about fear in her notebook:

"I remember vividly being afraid to fly. When I tuned in to those sensations in my body I felt a little faint and dizzy, and my hands were sweaty. I tensed all my muscles just a little anticipating any jiggling of the airplane. My breath was shallow, my throat dry, and I was slightly nauseated. When I began breathing into the sensations, they got worse at first, and then began to fade gradually, almost like when fog clears in the sun."

Discussion

Much of the unconscious behavior in relationships revolves around holding on to a certain feeling or attitude or trying to avoid one. For example, our client Susan recently described a series of power struggles she had had with male authority figures, teachers and doctors. When we explored the commonalities of these situations, she realized that she was furious with them for not acknowledging her. When we asked if she might be angry at someone else, she realized she was enraged at her father. We asked if she had ever shared her anger with her father directly. She blanched as she said that even thinking about it was frightening. When she was growing up, everyone else in the family, especially her father, played elaborate versions of "Uproar!" complete with thrown furniture, drug overdoses, verbal tantrums, and general chaos. Susan had retreated into an outwardly compliant role, but inwardly she held on to her anger and periodically exploded toward other older men. She is now beginning to own her anger and express it directly to her father, so she doesn't have to create difficulty in her life.

Enlivening Love

Instructions

1. Each of you make a list of the three best things you can say about each other.

Example: You are very kind. Your voice is beautiful and inspiring. You give so much love to me and others.

Then take turns saying aloud to your partner each phrase you've written. Speaker, do your best to let your whole body communicate. Responder, try to allow your body to get big enough to contain those good feelings. Let yourself breathe fully, take it in, and move to circulate the good feelings.

2. Both of you make a list of three daily things your partner does that make your life sweeter.

Example: You take time to pick the food I like most. You wake up in a good mood. You really listen to me.

Take turns reading your statements to each other.

Discussion

Use your discoveries to notice your deflection patterns and other ways you stop yourself from fully receiving positive energy in your daily life. When you notice a pattern, take a moment to love it and be with it. Then take a big breath and release it. You may want to rest a moment or take a little space from time to time to integrate a new positive energy.

Consciously Taking Space

This activity will be of special significance if you are working through the program with your love partner. As we stated in chapter 5, taking space is one of the most effective ways to integrate Upper Limits phenomena. This activity gives you the opportunity to practice this skill. We've found that the best time to take space is when things have been going well for a while. You can also take space, or plan for a convenient future time, at the first sign of the downward slide.

Instructions

Today your assignment is consciously to take space from your partner. You will separate from each other for an agreed-upon length of time. We suggest that it be at least two to three hours. Your purpose is not to do anything productive. Simply take space. Go somewhere and do something by yourself. Avoid doing anything that has to be done. In other words, do not use your alone time to fix the dishwasher or make a run to the mall. Take a walk, read a book, or go to a movie by yourself. Or perhaps surprise yourself by not even thinking about how you will spend the time. After you have finished taking space, rejoin your partner and discuss the experience. How did you feel? What did you find yourself thinking about? Did you have any urges during the time alone (for example, wanting to over-eat, or to be with your partner)?

Discussion

People have had a wide range of responses to this activity. Most often we've heard: "I didn't realize I had such strong reactions to being by myself." We've talked with many couples who have *never* spent any time apart. Often their first reactions to this new experience reflect ways they bring themselves down. One woman became obsessed with worrying about her college-age daughter. She finally called from a pay phone to find that her daughter was at a football game. Another woman became physically ill after a half-hour at the park. She sat down under a tree and went over some of the questions she remembered from the Healing Dialogue. She discovered how afraid she was to have open time and space with nothing to do. After another half-hour of being with these questions she began to relax and enjoy her space. A man found himself making lists of things that had to be done. Another man began fantasizing about what his wife might be doing. He almost got to the point of storming a neighbor's house, where he was sure she was entertaining one of their friends, before he realized that his mind had run amok without its usual programs.

Not everyone discovers that taking space is like opening Pandora's box. Many people have mentioned that taking space is like a minivacation; things look different when they come back. One man said: "I really *saw* the shapes of the pine trees and where the new growth was. There were smells that reminded me of lying out in the meadows as a kid watching the clouds. I felt so deeply refreshed when I came home. And without even planning it, I saw my wife Dorothy in a new way. I really saw her beauty and her strength." A woman reported: "I got some perspective on my irritations. I realized I was just overloaded, and my nerves had gotten fried. Taking a ridiculously long bath really soothed them."

We recommend incorporating these minivacations into your relationship. Use your discussions of your experience to generate a list of Upper Limits cues, signals that your nervous system needs some integration time.

Microscopic Love

In this activity you'll explore the experience of loving your partner at a more fine-grained level. A long-term relationship can get bogged down in shorthand communications that may be disconnected from the moment. For example, Husband runs out the door as Wife pecks him on the cheek. "I love you," he throws over his shoulder. "I love you too," she mumbles as she shuts the door. We're interested in the actual body experience of loving and appreciating your partner. This activity is an invitation to participate in the unfolding growth of your love.

Instructions

All day today, when you have the thought, "I love you," tell the microscopic truth about your experience instead of saying the phrase, "I love you."

Example: When you came into the room just now, I felt a rush of heat in my chest and cheeks and had the thought, "I can't believe my good fortune."

Communications Skills

Understanding the Energy of Relationship

The combined energy of two people is much more than 1 + 1. When we come into a close relationship, our energy is deeply stirred by the catalyzing effect of the beloved. What we do with this increased energy determines the path of the relationship. This activity is designed to illuminate your response to the very thing that draws you together.

Instructions

This activity is done with a partner. Choose who will be partner A and who will be partner B. With your partner, stand facing the same direction, about three to four feet apart. Take a moment to scan your mind and body to notice your thoughts, images, and sensations. Then slowly turn to face each other, and stand without speaking, maintaining eye contact for one minute. Now scan your mind and body and notice any differences you sense.

Now turn to face away from each other. Notice what sensations and feelings come into your awareness. Reconnect with your experience again and notice the fluctuation in your energy.

Now you will make several turns toward and away from your partner. Remain facing your partner each time for one minute before you turn away.

1. Turn toward your partner, noticing any impulses to say something or to laugh. Remain there for one minute. Now turn away. Notice what you are feeling and thinking.

2. Turn toward each other again. Partner A, make yourself smaller. Contract, shrink, tuck in. Partner B, stand naturally each time you face your partner. Remain there for one minute. Then turn away and notice yourself for a moment.

3. This time when you turn toward each other, partner A, make yourself as big as you can. Puff yourself up. Stay there for one minute, then turn away and be aware of any differences you notice in your experience.

4. Turn toward each other again. Partner A, be totally stonefaced, give no response at all. Be impassive for one minute, then turn away.

5. Face each other once more. Partner A, notice your impulse to do something. Let yourself do it. Notice another impulse and do it. Follow a third impulse, then turn away.

When partner A is finished, switch roles and repeat. Afterward, share your experiences with your partner.

Discussion

The energy of close contact is profound, and most of us initially respond unconsciously to the increased energy of intimacy. During this activity we've seen people get bright red in the face, burst out chattering, get dizzy, get nauseated, develop instant muscle spasms, start blinking uncontrollably, get the hiccups, start squirming and shifting, jingle pocket change, shred tissue, clench fists into pockets, pull hair, scratch furiously, and so on. These are eruptions of the unconscious when faced with the increased energy of intimacy. We want you to be aware of the tremendous force that is available for growth or encumbrance.

Creating a Safe Space

Instructions
Step One

One person will be the speaker and one the amplifier in this communication activity.

1. Speaker, say aloud: "It is safe for me to feel all my anger."

Amplifier, assist the speaker to enlarge any gestures he or she made with the statement as it is repeated. For example, if the speaker starts to make fists, have the person use his whole upper body to brace and strike out with fists. You'll have the most fun with this if you really take it all the way, making a caricature of your expression.

2. The speaker will then say each of the following sentences. The amplifier will assist the speaker to enlarge each one in turn.

- It is safe for me to feel all my sadness.
- It is safe for me to feel all my sexual feelings.
- It is safe for me to feel all my fear.
- It is safe for me to feel all my joy.

Step Two

1. One partner, the feeler, identify a recent experience of fear and remember it as vividly as possible. When you have described your experience, your partner, the reflector, will say:

- "It is safe for you to feel all your fear," or
- "I can love you for that feeling."

Pause for a few minutes while each of you notices the feelings and thoughts that arise from this experience.

2. Then, feeler, let yourself recall in turn an experience of anger, sadness, joy, or sexuality, and feel it as completely as you can. Reflector, give verbal permission for each feeling. Feeler, receive your partner's permission to go fully into each feeling. Feeler, share any memories or connections you make as you explore. Then take time for the reflector to share any responses from the experience of giving permission. When the feeler has completed each feeling, switch roles and repeat.

Discussion

When giving feedback in this activity, practice telling the microscopic truth. Sometimes you'll have very positive, pleasant responses, and sometimes the activity will stimulate more difficult reactions. For example, if the feeler is amplifying fear and his or her partner begins to feel nauseated or angry, use the discussion time to describe the experience. The reflector might say, "When I said, 'It is safe for you to feel all your fear,' I began to feel impatient. I wanted to move away, go faster. My skin felt, and still feels, kind of crawly, and I'm breathing more heavily. As I stay with these sensations, they feel familiar. I remember when my mother got scared, she would kind of wind up and spin out, get hysterical and start yelling. I guess maybe I'm afraid you'll flip out like she did." You may want to write these reactions in your notebooks for later reference. We've found that the more you can stay with describing the microscopic truth, the more a foundation forms that leads to deeper awareness and more intimacy.

Bare Bones Communication

The elegant simplicity of direct communication is like Zen meditation practice, and the goal is similar: just so, just as it is, nothing extra. Tremendous transformation occurs when we speak directly from our deep experience. In this activity you'll have the chance to experience the power of getting down to the bone.

You'll need a tape-recorder with microphone for this activity.

Instructions

1. During this part of the activity, one person will be speaking and the other listening. With the cassette deck recording, the speaker will have two minutes to voice a concern and a request—something that you have feelings about, and something you want. Listener, carefully notice your internal responses. Then you'll switch roles, and your partner will have two minutes to communicate a concern and a request.

2. Now rewind the tape and listen to your communications. Listen for the voice qualities that you respond to most directly. These will be the tones that seem to match the content. Also notice what seems extra, the overtones that don't match the content. Studying these tones will give you access to your intentions in communicating. Most often we don't mean what we say; we mean what is underneath. Some of the intentions that we often add to our communications are: justifying our position, blaming the other, sliding into the victim position, staying in control, or asking for approval. Take responsibility for noticing your extras and sharing your discoveries with your partner.

3. Now go back and communicate the original concern or request again. This time focus on saying just the thing itself. You may find that you take less time, feel lighter, and get a clearer response. *This skill is essential and takes time to refine.* If you intend to communicate just the thing itself, that intention will set the stage for clarity.

Whole Body Listening

This activity is designed to help you uncover the relationship between verbal communication and body experience, and to increase your ability to tune in to your partner more deeply and develop more channels of communication.

Instructions

Speaker, describe where your body becomes tense when you feel upset. Then lean back in your chair or lie down comfortably. Listener, put your hand on the tense or sore spot and be with your partner through your hand contact. Speaker, breath into, around, and through the tense spot. Say aloud whatever you notice and experience. Continue for five to ten minutes. Then pause for a moment to be with each other in silence. Switch roles and repeat.

Discussion

It is possible to continue deepening your communication and knowing of your loved ones. You may find that transparency continues to grow and to connect you more richly to each other as you practice this skill.

Deepening Communication

Real communication and transformation occur when we feel heard and seen as we are. The experience of being understood is often what we're really after when we make contact. This activity clears the path so that the flow of communication is unimpeded.

Instructions

Each person will have two five-minute segments to communicate about anything he or she is exploring, without interruption.

1. During the first five-minute segment, the listener will focus on not interrupting *verbally*. Do your best, listener, to open yourself to simply hear what your partner is saying. You may notice powerful temptations to interrupt for "good

reasons": to explain your side, to correct, to give an opinion
or reference ("Oh, I read something about that ..."). Be
aware of what occurs inside when you don't interrupt.
Notice what other kinds of information open up. Then
switch roles and repeat.

2. During the second five-minute segment, the listener
will focus on not interrupting verbally *and* nonverbally.
Our bodies can be very sneaky at sabotaging. Here are just
a few of the many ways we've seen couples interrupt each
other: tapping fingers, looking around, fidgeting, reaching
out to groom the speaker, humming, clipping fingernails,
clearing the throat repeatedly, lighting a cigarette. As you
are listening, focus on opening your body to receive the
communication. Then switch roles and repeat.

Discussion

If we receive our partner's communication clearly, the
basis for conflict becomes less powerful. Much conflict
arises from our conviction that we already know what our
partner is thinking and feeling. It is as if most of our awareness is looking back over our shoulder at past interactions
and only a small part of us is present for what is actually
occurring. An English professor described it as "finishing
the song." "I developed a relationship song based on some
early, bittersweet, romantic experiences. Then I wandered
along humming the tune in my mind. If I met someone who
began singing just one line of my song, I filled in the rest."

Discuss your listening style. See if you can discover
what gets in the way of hearing clearly. See if you notice
recurrent themes, such as finishing the other person's song,
anticipating the punch line, or distracting your partner.

Problem-Solving

When problems emerge in your relationship, you need
a technique for shifting to a new state of mind. A relationship issue is very difficult to solve if you remain in the same

state of mind that created the problem. In trying to solve the problem, your mind will do more of what it's already doing: trying harder, justifying more, blaming more loudly, figuring out why, and so on. The following activities will help you to expand your state of awareness to allow possibilities and solutions to emerge from your Inner Self.

In the Heat of the Moment

This activity is designed to be used when your unconscious catches you. For that reason, we recommend that you memorize the simple steps so that you can remember to use them in the thick of a sticky problem.

Instructions

1. Think of a problem and discuss it briefly to make sure you are both thinking of the same issue. Declare aloud to each other: "I am willing to solve this problem." Keep saying it until your whole body feels willing.

Discussion

Go beyond your rationales and excuses until you can clearly say: "Yes, I am willing." Don't stop with halfway statements, such as, "I'm doing this stupid activity with you, aren't I?" Those responses may come first, though, and need to be acknowledged. Keep declaring your willingness until you feel it and your partner sees it. One couple spent most of a day working with us unraveling all their responses to, "Yes, I am willing to solve this problem." They progressed through, "It's all your fault," "I should have listened to my mother," "I won't do anything until you apologize," and many other attitudes before they were actually willing to solve the problem. A combination of feelings is normal, such as, "I am willing to solve this problem, and I'm afraid," or, "I don't know how."

2. When each of you has clearly communicated your willingness to solve the problem, continue discussing it, but *drop out your words.* Communicate using sound, sign language, and movement. Have a nonverbal conversation. You

might jump up and down, make unusual sounds, or "paint" the issue with your hands. Continue communicating until the problem shifts or a solution occurs.

Example: Beth and Charles were using this activity to sort out a habitual power struggle around using the kitchen. When they dropped out the words ("Don't put yogurt in the sauce!" "All right, I'm leaving. You make dinner!"), Charles made sweeping hand gestures as if he were clearing space in front of him, and Beth put her hands out stiffly in front like a policeman directing traffic. They circled each other for a few minutes, clearly doing a territorial dance. Charles suddenly realized that his suggestions and demands were really about wanting his presence to be recognized. Beth began to see that her self-importance was also tied up in defending her culinary skill.

Discussion

This activity is designed to pull you out of habitual responses and patterns. Often the heart of the issue emerges quickly when it isn't covered with our reflexive responses. It can also remind you that nothing is more important than making your relationship your top priority.

Out of the Rut

This activity is designed to help you break out of old, deadening habits. It deals with the deadly "always" syndrome. There may be things you repeatedly do in an argument, but if your partner says, "You always . . ." the gloves come off. In this activity you'll take responsibility for the things you *always* do, and learn two effective tools for opening to conscious loving.

Instructions

1. Each of you make a list in your notebook of the things you always end up doing in a discussion or problem-solving situation.

Examples:

I always:
- Drop into a whispered voice
- Point my finger
- Walk out in a huff
- Cry
- Forget my point
- Feel stupid

2. First, decide on an issue to discuss. Then, each of you choose one thing you always do and exaggerate it as you talk with each other. Take it much farther in the direction it's going. For example, let your whispered voice become just mouthed words. Or take your pointed finger into whole-body jumping up and down as you thrust your arm forward. Continue for a minute or two.

3. Now continue your verbal and nonverbal dialogue, but take what you always do and change it into its opposite. For example, change your stupid feeling into a smug and satisfied look as you strut around. Or, instead of walking out in a huff, stay in one place, look your partner in the eye, and breathe into your belly slowly. Continue for a minute or two.

Discussion

Problem-solving works best when all feelings and expressions can be conscious. Since upwards of 80 percent of our communication is nonverbal, communication is much clearer when our expressions match our feelings. "Always" expressions are out of touch with the immediate present. When we can drop ineffective communications we get to have more fun and eliminate circular processing.

Finding Where You Are Stuck

Problems often form around some attitude that we cling to as if it were a life raft. As we've seen, we often have good survival reasons for adopting these attitudes. When we carry them over into adult relationships, however, they frequently become heavy and cumbersome and drag us out of a flexible responsiveness to what is actually occurring. This activity will help you develop the art of letting go. A problem often feels dense and pressured. This activity will assist you to make space in your breath and movement, so that your creative self can step in and easily form solutions.

Instructions

Decide who will be the holder first, and who will be the player.

1. Holder, take a physical position that represents some part of the problem that you're holding on to right now, for whatever reason.

Examples:

- Crossing your arms on your chest ("Prove that I'm wrong")
- Curling into a tight ball ("I just want to go away")
- Turning your body away ("It's no use")
- Holding your back stiffly ("I won't bend on this")

Player, try on the holder's position; mirror him or her so you look exactly alike. Try on the holder's perspective from this position and share aloud what you experience as you mirror this holding pattern. You may both be surprised at what you discover.

2. Holder, keep returning to your original position between each of the next three steps.

Player, first try to make the holder feel better. Help your partner out of that stuck place, sympathize with his or her plight. Make your rescue attempts both verbal and nonverbal. Continue for two to three minutes. Both of you notice your reactions to these roles.

3. Holder, return to the original position. Player, put on your most disapproving face. Think disapproving thoughts about the holder's position. Continue for several minutes. Both of you notice your experience.

4. With the holder in the original position, player, put your hand where the holder's body looks most tight, and just be with him or her. Love that place and everything that might have created the need for it. Love that place until the holder reports an experiential shift.

Pause, discuss for a few minutes, then switch roles and repeat.

Discussion

In this activity you get a chance to walk in your partner's shoes. One woman, when trying on her husband's arms-crossed position, said: "Wow! I feel strong and steady, not angry at all. I always thought you were angry when you did that, but I can see that you're really supporting yourself."

When our positions become conscious they often melt away. For example, Janice began to notice that when men she dated started to ask her about herself, she would invariably freeze her face in a polite but cold smile, no matter how attractive they were. Using this activity, she discovered that she had adopted a "nice at any cost" mask to protect herself from her family's dinnertime brawls. The dinner would progress from inquiries about school, to hostile remarks, to accusations, and finally to dishes being slammed down. Janice had found that she could disappear behind a nonthreatening smile and avoid most of the chaos. When she reexperienced and understood this pattern, her face changed dramatically, and her inner liveliness and maturity became visible.

ABOUT THE AUTHORS

GAY HENDRICKS is a professor at the University of Colorado, a psychologist and educator, and the author of fourteen books in his field. He has presented lectures and workshops to mental health professionals and educators in North America, Europe, and Asia. His doctorate in Counseling Psychology is from Stanford University. Dr. Hendricks was one of the early leaders in mind-body integration, which has emerged as the unifying point of view of several fields, including medicine, psychotherapy, and education. Among his books on this subject are *The Centering Book, Learning to Love Yourself, The Second Centering Book,* and *Centering and the Art of Intimacy.* His textbook, *Transpersonal Approaches to Counseling and Psychotherapy,* is widely used in graduate programs in this country and abroad.

KATHLYN HENDRICKS has been a practicing psychotherapist and educator since 1971. She is a leading theorist in the movement therapy field and trains graduate students at NAROPA Institute and other universities. Her doctorate in Transpersonal Psychology is from the Institute of Transpersonal Psychology. She is the author of numerous articles in her field, and the co-author of several books, including *The Moving Center* and *Centering and the Art of Intimacy.*

Kathlyn and Gay live in Colorado Springs. They are the directors of The Hendricks Institute for Bodymind Integration, which trains professionals in the Hendricks Method.